CANON LAW

CANON LAW

A COMPARATIVE STUDY WITH ANGLO-AMERICAN LEGAL THEORY

JOHN J. COUGHLIN, O.F.M.

OXFORD
UNIVERSITY PRESS

OXFORD
UNIVERSITY PRESS

Oxford University Press, Inc., publishes works that further Oxford University's objective of excellence in research, scholarship, and education.

Oxford New York
Auckland Cape Town Dar es Salaam Hong Kong Karachi Kuala Lumpur Madrid Melbourne Mexico City Nairobi New Delhi Shanghai Taipei Toronto

With offices in
Argentina Austria Brazil Chile Czech Republic France Greece Guatemala Hungary Italy Japan Poland Portugal Singapore South Korea Switzerland Thailand Turkey Ukraine Vietnam

Published by Oxford University Press, Inc.
198 Madison Avenue, New York, New York 10016

Library of Congress Cataloging-in-Publication Data

Coughlin, John J., O.F.M.
Canon law : a comparative study with Anglo-American legal theory / John J. Coughlin.
p. cm.
Includes bibliographical references and index.
ISBN 978-0-19-537297-7 ((hardback) : alk. paper)
1. Canon law. 2. Common law. 3. Catholics—Legal status, laws, etc.—United States. I. Title.
KB243.C68A33 2010
262.9—dc22 2010019792

Note to Readers
This publication is designed to provide accurate and authoritative information in regard to the subject matter covered. It is based upon sources believed to be accurate and reliable and is intended to be current as of the time it was written. It is sold with the understanding that the publisher is not engaged in rendering legal, accounting, or other professional services. If legal advice or other expert assistance is required, the services of a competent professional person should be sought. Also, to confirm that the information has not been affected or changed by recent developments, traditional legal research techniques should be used, including checking primary sources where appropriate.

(Based on the Declaration of Principles jointly adopted by a Committee of the American Bar Association and a Committee of Publishers and Associations.)

In Piam Memoriam
Honorable Frank X. Altimari
Judge of the United States Court of Appeals for the Second Circuit

CONTENTS

PREFACE AND ACKNOWLEDGMENTS

It risks a violation of humility to write about one's self, but sometimes the risk is necessary in order to offer understanding of one's work. Ever since I studied civil law at Harvard Law School and canon law at the Pontifical Gregorian University in Rome, I have been interested in *utroque iuris* and the possibility of comparative law. Civil law and canon law each represent vast fields, and the problem of writing a comparative study of them is one of focus. In this book, I focus principally on three specific topics in contemporary canon law: the clergy sexual abuse crisis; the ownership of church property; and the denial of Holy Communion to Catholic political officials. I recognize that these topics are timely and not without controversy. However, my selection of these contemporary topics serves as a means of exploring deeper long-standing theoretical issues in canon law. Specifically, this book examines antinomian and legalistic approaches to canon law. The study, teaching, and practice of civil and canon law have instilled in me an appreciation of the rule of law. This appreciation leads me to examine antinomianism and legalism in terms of their impact on the rule of law in the Roman Catholic Church. My hope is that the book's comparison of canon law with what I shall describe as Anglo-American legal theory will bear insight about the function of canon law in protecting individual persons and the common good.

When I entered the Franciscan Order in 1977, it never occurred to me that I would one day be a law school professor. Shortly after my ordination as a priest in 1983, Father Alban Maguire, O.F.M., then the Provincial Minister of Holy Name Province, asked me if I would be interested in studying moral theology and ethics. A somewhat vague notion of mine that the practical implications of ethics were expressed in law led to the idea of a joint Ph.D./J.D. program. During my time as a law student, Father Alban proposed the alternative that upon completion law school, I would obtain my doctorate in canon law at the Gregorian. Although I was initially skeptical about this alternative proposal, discussions with several of my professors at Harvard including John Mansfield, Mary Ann Glendon, Alan Stone, M.D., and Andrew Kaufman convinced me that the combination of civil and canon law was a worthwhile endeavor. These conversations proved fortuitous as a letter of obedience from Father Alban soon sealed the deal.

In addition to assigning me to study canon law, Father Alban also thought that my knowledge of civil law would be enhanced by a clerkship with a federal judge. Again, this was for me a heretofore uncontemplated possibility. The Honorable Frank X. Altimari, Judge of the U.S. Court of Appeals for the Second Circuit, kindly selected me to serve as one of his law clerks. The experience of clerking was one of great learning about the law and about life for which I remain profoundly grateful. I dedicate this book to the memory of my teacher and friend, the late Judge Altimari. As a doctoral student at the Gregorian, I was blessed to encounter then Monsignor Raymond L. Burke and Father Urbano Navarette, S.J., both of whom personified the holy priest and dedicated scholar. The doctoral dissertation that I wrote at the Gregorian, under Burke's direction, with Navarette as chair of my defense board, was my initial attempt at comparative legal study. In the *mysterium vitae*, it was not my own great designs but rather the knowledge, wisdom, and goodness of others that cultivated my interest in canon and civil law.

The project of writing this comparative study formally started in 2003 after I joined the Notre Dame law faculty. A series of summer stipends from the law school assisted me in carrying out the work. During the time that I have been working on this project, I have also tried my best to fulfill an array of responsibilities as a teacher, canonist, attorney, and above all, as a priest. My life at the University of Notre Dame has proved enormously rich in this regard. In particular, the past seven years at Notre Dame have afforded me an intense pastoral experience. Given my various responsibilities at Notre Dame, a good portion of the writing of this book occurred during the holidays and summer months while I lived with my Franciscan brothers at Saint Stephen's Friary on East 82nd Street in New York City. Father Angelo Gambatese, O.F.M., and the community at 82nd Street have consistently welcomed me with Franciscan warmth. During the final months of this project, I taught simultaneously at the Notre Dame law program in London and the Gregorian in Rome. In Rome, I lived with the Franciscan community at San Isidoro. With my addition, there were fifteen of us in this international house of the Order, and the friars were patient with me as I struggled to be more fluent in Italian. In fact, Father Primo Piscatelli, O.F.M., and the other Franciscans of the community, could not have provided a more serene and contemplative environment in which to bring such a project to conclusion.

As I bring this book to completion, I wish to express my gratitude to a number of persons who directly assisted me with the work. My colleagues at the Notre Dame Law School, Robert E. Rodes, Jr., and John Robinson, patiently read and commented on the vast majority of this book in various drafts. In rendering this service, they not only improved on my ideas and writing style, but gave me an example of true and unselfish scholars. Other scholars who read and provided invaluable comments on various parts of the book include Nicholas Cafardi, Father James Conn, S.J., John Finnis, Mary Ann Glendon, Nicole Garnette, Monsignor Michael Heintz, and Mary Ellen O'Connell. Professor O'Connell introduced me to the editors at Oxford University Press. Chris Collins of Oxford guided me through the book proposal process, and together with Jessica Picone helped to bring the published work to completion. Monsignor David Malloy, Secretary of the United States Conference of Catholic Bishops, enabled me to have access to statistical information collected by the researchers of the John Jay Studies. While they were law students at Notre Dame, Nathanael Pollock, Christine Niles, and Paul Harold helped me with various parts of the research for the book. James Lee, Lidia Kim, and Jordan Smith proofread the manuscript. If it were not for the pains of all of the above persons, the book would contain many more substantive and stylistic errors than in fact remain.

Over the years of my teaching, I have developed the ideas in this study. In particular, I must express my gratitude to the students in my classes at Notre Dame for their keen interest in my ideas. At the same time, I wish also to thank my students at other institutions where I have been honored to teach. I first taught canon law at Saint Joseph's Seminary in Yonkers, New York. My first experience of teaching in a law school was also in New York at St. John's University in Queens. During the spring of 2009, I served as a Visiting Professor at the Pontifical Gregorian University in Rome where I was blessed to share parts of the final draft of the book with students from fourteen different countries with representation from all of the continents. Teaching at the Gregorian served as a reminder that the Roman Catholic Church is a global community of faith whose canon law transcends national, cultural, and linguistic boundaries. On a personal level, I confess that it was a bit of a thrill for me to return as a teacher to the place where two decades previously I had been privileged to study.

Some of the ideas and themes of this book have also appeared in my previous presentations and publications. I first wrote about the ideas of antinomianism, legalism, and the rule of law for a symposium on the clergy sexual abuse crisis sponsored by the Boston College Law School. The article, "The Clergy Sex Abuse Crisis and the Spirit of Canon Law," was published in 44 *Boston College Law Review* 977–97 (2003), and is the basis of some of the ideas expressed in chapters 2 and 3 of this book. In Chapter 2, I have also included material from my book review of Kevin E. McKenna's "The Battle for Rights in the United States," which appeared in *America*, January 21, 2008, 35–36. Chapters 6 and 7 of the book, which concern the denial of Holy Communion to Catholic public officials, are based on a talk that I gave at the National Press Club in Washington, D.C., at a conference sponsored by the Ave Maria Law School on September 16, 2004. My thoughts in the Introduction about canonical equity were first developed for an article "Canonical Equity," 30 *Studia Canonica* 403–35 (2001). An article, "Canon Law and the Human Person," 19 *Journal of Law and Religion* 1–58 (2003–2004), also represents a previous attempt to treat some of the theoretical issues that arise in comparative legal study. While none of the above-mentioned articles are reproduced entirely in this book, a number of paragraphs and sentences are taken from the articles, and are included with the permission of the respective publications.

As the project developed, the need to focus has led me to start writing another book about canon law from a comparative perspective, *Law, Person, and Community: Philosophical, Theological, and Comparative Perspectives on Canon Law*, which is presently under contract for publication by Oxford University Press. Considered together, the two monographs count as an attempt to express whatever modest insight has been afforded me from the opportunity of studying, teaching, and practicing both laws. I hope that I have not offended too badly against humility as I have tried to explain a bit about my reasons for writing this book and to express my gratitude in these prefatory remarks.

Collegio San Isidoro, Rome
May 2009

ABBREVIATIONS

AAS	Acta Apostolicae Sedis.
Am. J. Comp. L.	American Journal of Comparative law.
ASS	Acta Sanctae Sedis.
B.C. L. Rev.	Boston College Law Review.
C.	*Causa*, Decretum Magistri Gratiani (Concordia discordantium canonum). In Corpus Iuris Canonici. Vol. I. Frieburg, A., ed. Editio lipsiensis secunda. Graz: Akademische Druck-u.Verlagsanstalt, 1959.
Cath. U. L. Rev.	Catholic University Law Review.
CCEO	Codex Canonum Ecclesiarium Orientalim auctoritate Ioannis Pauli II promulgatus (Die 18 m. octobris a. 1990), 82 AAS 1033–1363 (1990).
CIC-1917	Codex Iuris Canonici Pii X Pontificis Maximi iussu digestus Benedicti Papae XV auctoritate promulgatus (Die 27 m. maii a. 1917), 9 AAS II, 3–521 (1917).
CIC-1983	Codex Iuris Canonici auctoritate Ioannis Pauli Pp. II promulgatus (Die 25 m. ianuarii a. 1983), 85 AAS II, 1–317 (1983).
Clem.	*Clementinae*. In Corpus Iuris Canonici. Vol. II. Frieburg, A., ed. Editio lipsiensis secunda. Graz: Akademische Druck-u.Verlagsanstalt, 1959.
CLSA Proceedings	Canon Law Society of America Proceedings.
CLSA-1985	James A. Coriden, Thomas J. Green, and Donald E. Heintschel, eds. The Code of Canon Law, A Text and Commentary. Commissioned by the Canon Law Society of America. New York and Mahwah, N.J.: Paulist Press, 1985.
CLSA-2000	John P. Beal, James A. Coriden, and Thomas J. Green, New Commentary on the Code of Canon Law, Commissioned by the Canon Law Society of America. New York and Mahwah, N.J.: Paulist Press, 2000.
CLSGB & Ireland	The Canon Law, Letter, and Spirit, A Practical Guide to the Code of Canon Law. Prepared by the Canon Law Society of Great Britain and Ireland in association with the Canadian Canon Law

	SOCIETY. Edited by Gerard Sheehy, et al. Collegeville, MN: Liturgical Press and Michael Glazier, 1996.
D.	*Distinctio*, DECRETUM MAGISTRI GRATIANI (CONCORDIA DISCORDANTIUM CANONUM). In CORPUS IURIS CANONICI. Vol. I. Frieburg, A., ed. Editio lipsiensis secunda. Graz: Akademische Druck-u. Verlagsanstalt, 1959.
ECC. L. REV.	ECCLESIASTICAL LAW REVIEW.
Extra. Ioannis	*Extravagantes Ioannis XXII*. In CORPUS IURIS CANONICI. Vol. II. Frieburg, A., ed. Editio lipsiensis secunda. Graz: Akademische Druck-u.Verlagsanstalt, 1959.
Extra. Com.	*Extravagantes communes*. In CORPUS IURIS CANONICI. Vol. II. Frieburg, A., ed. Editio lipsiensis secunda. Graz: Akademische Druck-u.Verlagsanstalt, 1959.
Gaudium et spes	Sacrosanctum Concilium Oecumenicum Vaticanum II. Constitutio pastoralis de ecclesia in mundo huius temporis, *Gaudium et Spes* (Die 7 m. decembris a. 1965), 58 AAS 1025–1120 (1966).
HARV. L. REV.	HARVARD LAW REVIEW.
ILL. L. REV.	ILLINOIS LAW REVIEW.
J. CONTEMP. HEALTH L. & POL'Y	JOURNAL OF CONTEMPORARY HEALTH LAW AND POLICY.
JURIST	THE JURIST.
Lumen Gentium	Sacrosanctum Concilium Oecumenicum Vaticanum II. Constitutio Dogmatica DE Ecclesia, *Lumen Gentium* (Die 21 m. novembris a. 1964), 57 AAS 5–89 (1965).
MICH. L. REV.	MICHIGAN LAW REVIEW.
NAVARRA-2004	EXEGETICAL COMMENTARY ON THE CODE OF CANON LAW, PREPARED UNDER THE RESPONSIBILITY OF THE MARTIN DE AZPILCUETA INSTITUTE, FACULTY OF CANON LAW, UNIVERSITY OF NAVARRE. Edited by Ángel Marzoa, Jorge Miras, and Rafael Rodríguez-Ocaña. Montreal: Wilson & Lafleur, 2004.
NOTRE DAME L. REV.	NOTRE DAME LAW REVIEW.
N.Y.U. L. REV.	NEW YORK UNIVERSITY LAW REVIEW.
OTTAWA-1993	CODE OF CANON LAW ANNOTATED. LATIN-ENGLISH EDITION OF THE *CODE OF CANON LAW* AND ENGLISH LANGUAGE TRANSLATION OF THE 5TH SPANISH LANGUAGE COMMENTARY PREPARED UNDER THE RESPONSIBILITY OF THE INSTITUTO MARTÍN DE AZPILCUETA. Edited by E. Caparros, M. Thériault, and J. Thorn. Montréal: Wilson & Lafluer, 1993.

PERIODICA	PERIODICA DE RE CANONICA. From 1927 to 1991, the title was PERIODICA DE RE MORALI, CANONICA, LITURGICA.
PG	Migne, J. P. PATROLOGIAE CURSUS COMPLETUS, SERIES GRAECA. Paris: 1857–1866.
PL	Migne, J. P. PATROLOGIAE CURSUS COMPLETUS, SERIES LATINA. Paris: 1844–1855.
ST	St. Thomas Aquinas, SUMMA THEOLOGICA. SANCTI THOMAE AQUINATIS. OPERA OMNIA, LEO XII, P.M. Romae: Ex Typographia Polyglota S. C. De Propaganda Fide, 1882. Vol. 4–12. English Translation by the Fathers of the English Dominican Province. Westminster, MD: Christian Classics, 1981.
TANNER	Tanner, Norman P., S.J. *Decrees of the Ecumenical Councils*. London and Washington, D.C.: Sheed & Ward and Georgetown University Press, 1990.
U.C. DAVIS L. REV.	UNIVERSITY OF CALIFORNIA AT DAVIS LAW REVIEW.
UCLA L. REV.	UCLA LAW REVIEW.
U. Tol. L. REV.	UNIVERSITY OF TOLEDO LAW REVIEW.
VI	*Liber Sextus*. In CORPUS IURIS CANONICI. Vol. II. Frieburg, A., ed. Editio lipsiensis secunda. Graz: Akademische Druck-u.Verlagsanstalt, 1959.
WISCONSIN L. REV.	WISCONSIN LAW REVIEW.
X	*Liber Extra, Quinque Libri Decrertalium Gregoriani IX.* In CORPUS IURIS CANONICI. Vol. II. Frieburg, A., ed. Editio lipsiensis secunda. Graz: Akademische Druck-u. Verlagsanstalt, 1959.
YALE L.J.	YALE LAW JOURNAL.

INTRODUCTION

The advent of the third millennium witnessed two seemingly unrelated events yielding contrasting images of the Roman Catholic Church. The first involved the sexual abuse of minors by Catholic clergy in the United States during the second half of the twentieth century. While the media had periodically reported on stories of clergy sexual abuse over the course of the past decades, the abuse became the object of sustained and intense national scrutiny in 2002. Media attention often focused on the failure of the church's internal system of governance to protect children from the abuse. Not limited to the United States, public scrutiny of the Catholic priesthood soon surfaced in other counties including, *inter alia*, Australia, Austria, Belgium, Brazil, Canada, Germany, Ireland, Italy, and Poland. The image was one of a suspect church in crisis whose priests posed a threat to the public good.[1] The second event entailed a transition at the highest level of leadership in the Catholic Church. On April 2, 2005, Pope John Paul II passed from this life, ending his twenty-six year pontificate. The pontiff's death set in motion a procedure for the government of the church during the interregnum and election of a new pope. In what is perhaps one of the longest applications of the collegial principle of "one man one vote," the College of Cardinals, in conclave at the Vatican's Sistine Chapel, elected Pope Benedict XVI on April 19, 2005. The image was of the church in an orderly transition, the rules of which were rooted in ancient tradition while cognizant of contemporary needs.[2]

1. The clergy sexual abuse crisis is discussed in Chapters 2 and 3. See Canon 1395 § 2, *CIC-1983*; and Congregatio pro Doctrina Fidei, *De delictis gravioribus eidem Congregationi pro Doctrina Fidei reservatis*, 93 AAS 785, 786–87 (2001). Both documents recognize the sexual abuse of a minor as a crime for which the penalty of dismissal from the clerical state might be imposed. The document from the Congregation for the Doctrine of Faith established that a minor is one who has not reached his or her eighteenth birthday.

2. The revision of the rules for the election of the pope had retained the central aspects of the tradition while introducing new measures to accommodate modern technology especially with regard to security for the Conclave and the medical health of the participants. *See* Ioannes Paulus Pp. II, *Constitutio Apostolica Universi Dominici Gregis* (Die 22 m. feb. a. 1996), 88 AAS 305–42 (1996). This law issued by Pope John Paul II had permitted election of the Roman Pontiff by the College of Cardinals by a simple majority vote after several days of inconclusive balloting. Pope Benedict XVI, by a *motu proprio*, dated June 11, 2007, amended the law so as to require a two-thirds majority for election in all cases. *See* Benedictus Pp. XVI, Litterae Apostolicae Motu Proprio Datae, *De Aliquibus Mutationibus in Normis De Electione Romani Pontificis* (Die 11 m. junio a. 2007), 99 AAS 776–81 (2007).

Although the two contrasting images arose from seemingly unrelated events, both could be attributed at least in part to canon law. The election of the pope represents the rule of law functioning in the life of the Roman Catholic Church. In contrast, I shall suggest that the sexual abuse crisis combined antinomian and legalistic approaches to canon law that defeated the rule of law. In 2010, the two events seemed to coalesce. A series of front-page *New York Times* stories alleged that, prior to his election as pope, Joseph Cardinal Ratzinger had facilitated a global cover-up of priest pedophilia.[3] His defenders responded that Cardinal Ratzinger had led the way to ensure that procedures designed to address cases of sexual abuse were observed by church officials.[4] Although not necessarily supported by a fair consideration of the evidence, the accusations against the pontiff were lent credibility in the atmosphere of suspicion generated during the 2002 U.S. crisis and its international spread. The crisis was based on the reality that the Catholic Church had a significant problem with clergy sexual abuse and that church authorities failed to employ canon law as a means of protecting victims of the abuse.

In this book, I discuss the ways in which antinomianism and legalism impact on canon law as the rule of law in the Roman Catholic Church.[5] Focusing on contemporary canon law, I examine several specific topics, including the sexual abuse crisis, the ownership of church property, and the refusal of Holy Communion to Catholic public officials. While they arise in the context of the United States, these specific topics raise larger theoretical issues that pertain to canon law as the universal law of the Catholic Church. As a way of affording a comparative perspective on the larger issues about the rule of law, I juxtapose canon law and Anglo-American legal theory. In this Introduction, I treat some concepts that are basic to the study as a whole. First, I define antinomianism and legalism in canon law and offer some historical examples of each. Second,

---

3. *See, e.g., Archdiocese Led by Pope Admits Error on Abuse*, N.Y. Times, Mar. 13, 2010, at A1 and A10; *Vatican Declined to Defrock U.S. Priest Who Abused Deaf Boys*, N.Y. Times, Mar. 25, 2010, at A1 and A15; *Priest Charged with Abuse Is Still Serving in India*, N.Y. Times, Apr. 6, 2010, at A1 and A12; *Pope Put Off Move to Punish Abusive Priest*, N.Y. Times, Apr. 10, 2010, at A1, A5, and A6. *See also* N.Y. Times, Editorial, Mar. 25, 2010, at A22. Prior to his election as pope, Ratzinger ordered "that bishops worldwide were to keep pedophilia secret under threat of ex-communication."

4. *See, e.g.*, John L. Allen, Jr., *A Papal Conversion*, N.Y. Times, March 28, 2010, at A11; Federico Lombardi, S.J., *Vatican Statement on* NY Times *Story on Abusive Wisconsin Priest*, 39 Origins 693–94 (Apr. 8, 2010); and George Weigel, *Scandal Time, Once More*, Denver Catholic Register, April 7, 2010, available at www.archden.org/weigel.

5. The phrase "canon law" may also refer to the law of the Anglican Church as well as to that of the Orthodox churches. *See generally* Eric Waldram Kemp, An Introduction to Canon Law in the Church of England (Hodder and Stoughton 1967); and Panteleimon Rodopoulos, An Overview of Orthodox Canon Law (W. J. Lillie trans., Orthodox Research Institute 2007).

I describe what I mean by Anglo-American legal theory, and discuss it in relation to comparative law. Finally, I pose a question about canon law as the rule of law in the church from the comparative perspective.

I. ANTINOMIANISM AND LEGALISM

Antinomianism diminishes or rejects the validity of law. For example, Marjorie Reeves has described the pervasive influence of Joachim of Fiore's antinomian thought from its eleventh-century origins to the fifteenth century.[6] In particular, the thirteenth-century Franciscan spiritualists adopted the thought of Joachim of Fiore, calling for a "spirit age," which was to abrogate institution, law, and sacrament. The spiritualists advocated a radical form of poverty that permitted little provision for the institutional structures of community life. Joseph Ratzinger observes that Joachim developed a trinitarian scheme in which the final triad or spirit age would follow upon the ages of the Father and Son.[7] Based upon Joachim's thought, the Franciscan spiritualists understood Saint Francis of Assisi as the eschatological prophet of the end times.[8] Their antinomian attitude imperiled the future of the Franciscan Order. As general of the Order, Bonaventure of Bagnoregio found it necessary to respond to the antinomian approach. He challenged the spiritualists to discern the presence of the spirit within the institutional structures of the Order and church. The Bonaventurian resolution evoked trust and respect for juridical structures even as it called for the institutional to remain *semper reformanda*. In the face of a vibrant antinomian movement, Bonaventure articulated an ecclesiological perspective that sought to restore the balance between spirit and law. Hans Urs von Balthasar describes Bonaventure's resolution as expressive of the medieval balance which longed to view both the juridical structure and its inner *intellectus* as in harmony.[9]

An antinomian strain may be detected in the thought of Martin Luther, who rejected the validity of canon law. Luther urged that canon law be "completely blotted

---

6. On the influence of Joachim's thought in the thirteenth century, *see* MARJORIE REEVES, THE INFLUENCE OF PROPHECY IN THE LATER MIDDLE AGES: A STUDY OF JOACHIMISM 3–228 (Clarendon Press 1969).

7. *See* JOSEPH RATZINGER, THE THEOLOGY OF HISTORY IN ST. BONAVENTURE 104–18 (Zachary Hayes trans., Franciscan Herald Press 1971).

8. See *id.* at 48–55, which discusses the identification of Francis and the Franciscan Order with the eschatological.

9. *See* HANS URS VON BALTHASAR, A THEOLOGICAL ANTHROPOLOGY 131–35 (Sheed & Ward 1967).

out from the first letter to the last especially in the decretals."[10] As I shall mention in Chapter 1, antinomianism was also evident in the approach of certain nineteenth-century biblical and legal scholarship, which painted a portrait of Jesus as in opposition to institutional and legal forms. Some interpretations of Vatican II fostered antinomianism in the life of the church during several decades that followed the Ecumenical Council.[11] Antinomianism views the law as an obstacle to individual freedom in the personal response to God.[12] The law may be understood as an instrument of oppression in the hand of the powerful against the powerless.[13] Antinomianism ignores the necessary and proper role of law in establishing the ecclesial order so that individuals and communities may grow and prosper. It fails to recognize the important function of the rule of law for individuals and the common good. When antinomianism flourishes, the institutional church tends to decline.

Legalism in canon law results from an approach that places the law above the person and community. Legalism tends to ignore the historical, philosophical, and theological dimensions of canon law viewing them as "meta-legal" and falling outside the parameters of law itself.[14] In the gospels, Jesus clearly rejects a legalistic approach to religion.[15] Legalism manifests itself in at least three forms. The first form of legalism sees law as an end in itself, and involves an abuse of reason. It often is expressed through an overwhelming body of technicalities and quibbles that detract from the deeper meaning that the law intends to convey. This form of legalism was sometimes present in the jurisprudence of fifteenth-century ecclesiastical courts, which recognized legalistic exceptions to the church's teaching on the indissolubility of marriage.[16] Michael Sheehan observes

---

10. MARTIN LUTHER, THREE TREATISES, ORIGINALLY PUBLISHED IN THE AMERICAN EDITION OF LUTHER'S WORKS 94–95 (Helmut T. Lehmann gen. ed., Fortress Press 1966). Of course, Luther also wrote *A Treatise Against the Antinomians.*

11. *See, e.g.,,* José Setién, *Tensions in the Church, in* 48 THE FUTURE OF CANON LAW, CONCILIUM 78 (Paulist Press 1969), which argues in favor of "the possibility of acting against the law in order to achieve what is right for the Church".

12. *See* Jan Rietmeijer, *The Competence of the Bishop in Matters of Dispensation, in* 48 THE FUTURE OF CANON LAW, CONCILIUM 101, 114 (Paulist Press 1969), which opines that bishops should dispense priests from celibacy and allow them to continue in ministry because "human beings cannot be sacrificed to general rules and systems".

13. *See* LEONARDO BOFF, CHURCH: CHARISM AND POWER 51 (John W. Diercksmeier trans., Crossroad 1986).

14. I am specifically concerned here with legalism in canon law. For a treatment of legalism from the perspective of secular legal theory, *see* JUDITH N. SHKLAR, LEGALISM: LAW, MORALS, AND POLITICAL TRIALS 1 (Harvard University Press 1964), which defines legalism as "the ethical attitude that holds moral conduct to be a matter of rule following, and moral relationships to consist of duties and rights determined by rules."

15. Luke 6:6–10; 12:37–52.

16. *See* Brian Tierney, *Canon Law and Church Institutions in the Late Middle Ages, in* RIGHTS, LAWS AND INFALLIBILITY IN MEDIEVAL THOUGHT, VII 66–68 (Variorum 1997);

that the marriage bond in the medieval canon law was vulnerable in cases of clandestinity but less so in cases of consanguinity and affinity.[17] From the Protestant Reformer's perspective, the tribunals' practice reinforced the perception of canon law's corruption. Luther rejected the tribunal practice as indicative of the hypocrisy of the church.[18] In response to the Reformation, the Council of Trent affirmed the theological teaching on marriage as an indissoluble sacramental union and clarified the juridical requirements for the free consent of the spouses.[19] In restoring the unity of theological teaching with canonical practice, Trent attempted to restore the balance in canon law. Following Trent, this first form of legalism could be detected in the abuse of casuistry. Sixteenth- and seventeenth-century Catholic moral theologians attempted to develop the art of an ethics, which avoided an excessive emphasis on universal rules and invariant principles. The casuist favored a method based on cases, circumstances, and individual conscience as understood by Thomas Aquinas.[20] However, as Blaise Pascal's critique made clear, casuistry was subject to abuse by applying canonical principles in such a way as to eviscerate the underlying purpose of the law.[21] This form of legalism then might be identified with the abuse of right reason, a kind of sophistry that obscures the inner meaning and purpose of law.

The second form of legalism manifests itself in authoritarianism. It emphasizes a kind of blind obedience to the law, and as such, represents a lack of respect for free will. This form of legalism might be described as voluntaristic. The authoritarian/voluntaristic form of legalism occurs when those who exercise the power of governance in the church resort to canon law to justify actions that disregard the fundamental rights of individuals and groups. Along with the antinomian strain of his thought, Luther argued that canon law had become "the arbitrary will of the pope." Canon law, he argued, "is not what is written in the books of law, but whatever the pope and his flatterers want."[22] As I shall discuss in Chapter 2, certain bishops in the United States during the nineteenth century were sometimes guilty of an

see also R. H. Helmholtz, The Spirit of Classical Canon Law 240–41 (University of Georgia Press 1996).

17. Michael M. Sheehan, C.S.B., *The Formation and Stability of Marriage in Fourteenth-Century England: Evidence of an Ely Register*, *in* Marriage, Family, and Law in Medieval Europe 38, 74–76 (James K. Farge ed., University of Toronto Press 1996).

18. *See* Martin Luther, The Christian in Society II, *in* 45 Luther's Works 36–37 (Walther I, Brandt & Helmut T. Lehmann gen. eds., Muhlenberg Press 1962).

19. *See* Council of Trent, *in* 2 Tanner 753–56 (Norman P. Tanner ed., Sheed & Ward, and Georgetown University Press 1990).

20. *See* Kenneth E. Kirk, Conscience and Its Problems: An Introduction to Casuistry 198–202, 207–11 (Westminster John Knox Press 1999).

21. *See* Albert R. Jonsen & Stephen Toulmin, The Abuse of Casuistry, A History of Moral Reasoning 11–15, 161–62 (University of California Press 1989).

22. Luther, Three Treatises, 95.

authoritarian legalism. Relying on canon law to assert authority such as the imposition of a penalty, the bishop would then overlook other provisions of the law which were intended to provide that the penalty be imposed only after a just process.

A third form of legalism calls for the strictest application of the letter of the law in all circumstances without regard to the dignity of the human person or the flourishing of communal life. The symbolic function of the law is lost in the primary and overriding requirement that the law be obeyed. This form of legalism contravenes the elasticity of canon law such as the generous role that canonical equity plays in canon law. I discuss the notion of canonical equity in Chapter 1. This third form of legalism may often yield an unintelligent bureaucratic approach to canon law. It sees canon law as the end itself, and manifests no understanding of the relation between the human person, community, and the salvific purpose of the law. The three forms of legalism have a thin positivistic character in the sense that the law is applied without regard to its deeper purpose. When legalism abides, it tends to stifle the spiritual essence of the church.

II. COMPARATIVE LAW AND ANGLO-AMERICAN LEGAL THEORY

My hope is that the comparative dimension of this study enhances the understanding of canon law. Comparisons of diverse legal systems enjoy a long history.[23] The vestiges of comparative legal scholarship may be traced to Greek antiquity.[24] Greek legal ideas in turn exerted a profound influence on the early Roman jurists when they developed the *ius gentium*.[25] During the republican period of Roman law, the *praetor peregrinus* engaged in legal comparisons to

23. For historical accounts of the emergence of comparative law as a scholarly science, *see* Walther Hug, *The History of Comparative Law*, 45 Harv. L. Rev. 1027 (1932); Neville Brown, *A Century of Comparative Law in England: 1869–1969*, 19 Am. J. Comp. L. 232 (1971); Konrad Zweigert & Hein Kötz, Introduction to Comparative Law 47–62 (Tony Weir trans., 2nd ed. rev. Clarendon Press of Oxford University 1992); Charles Donahue, *Comparative Law Before the "Code Napoléon," in* The Oxford Handbook of Comparative Law 3–32 (Mathias Reiman & Reinhard Zimmermann eds., Oxford University Press 2006).

24. Plato compared the laws of the Greek city-states, and on the basis of the comparison, he constructed the ideal constitution. *See* Plato, Laws, Book 1, *in* 2 The Works of Plato 407–31 (B. Jowett trans., Random House 1937). In his Politics, Aristotle compared the constitutions of various city-states. *See* Aristotle The Politics, Book II, Chapters 9–12, *in* The Complete Works of Aristotle: The Revised Oxford Translation 2014–19 (Jonathan Barnes ed., Princeton University Press 1984).

25. The *ius civile* applied only to Roman citizens. As the Roman Empire expanded to include diverse peoples and territories, the *ius gentium* developed from the need for a universal law. *See* Hug, *The History of Comparative Law*, 1030.

settle disputes to which a noncitizen was a party.[26] The eleventh- and twelfth-century renaissance of legal scholarship evoked a new methodology in which the medieval decretists culled, compared, and commented upon various and diverse texts.[27] Scattered instances of comparative law can be found in legal scholarship during the next several centuries.[28] For example, the *Utopia* of Thomas More, the chancellor of England, who was trained in both civil and canon law, contains elements of comparative law.[29] The great European codifications of the nineteenth

---

26. The *praetor peregrinus* relied on the *ius gentium* to settle cases between a citizen and a foreigner or between foreigners subjected to different laws. By adapting the accepted Roman law causes of action to foreign circumstances, the *praetor* responded to the circumstances of diverse cultures. *See* Cicero, *ad Att.*, VI, 1, 15 in *Letters to Atticus*, Volume II, *in* THE LOEB CLASSICAL LIBRARY 121 (D. R. Shackleton Bailey ed. and trans., Harvard University Press 1999). *See also* HERBERT H. JOLOWICZ & B. NICHOLAS, HISTORICAL INTRODUCTION TO THE STUDY OF ROMAN LAW 98 ff. (Cambridge University Press 1977); BARRY NICHOLAS, AN INTRODUCTION TO ROMAN LAW 23 (3rd ed. Clarendon Press of Oxford University 1962); Ladislas Örsy, S.J., *Book I, General Norms, in* CLSA-1985, 42–43.

27. *See generally* HAROLD BERMAN, LAW AND REVOLUTION, THE FORMATION OF THE WESTERN LEGAL TRADITION 120–224 (Harvard University Press 1983).

28. For example, Francis Bacon proffered that the object of scholarly judgment, a system of national law, cannot at the same time be the standard of judgment. He urged lawyers to free themselves from the bonds of their own national systems in order to conduct an objective evaluation. *See* FRANCIS BACON, DE DIGNITATE ET AUGMENTIS SCIENTIARUM, *in* 2 THE WORKS OF FRANCIS BACON 135 (James Spedding, Robert L. Ellis, & Douglas D. Heath eds., Herd and Houghton 1869). Hugo Grotius compared various systems of national law in his watershed work. *See* DE IURE BELLI AC PACIS LIBRI TRES, IN QUIBUS IUS NATURAE GENTIUM, ITEM IURIS PUBLICI PRAECIPUA EXPLICANTUR, I, 1, xi, 1, at 631 (H. Milford ed., Clarendon Press 1925). Gottfried Wilhelm Leibniz proposed a "Theatrum legale" which would compare the laws and customs of all peoples, times, and places. *See* GOTTFRIED WILHELM LEIBNIZ, NOVA METHODUS DISCENDAE DOCENDAEQUE IURIS PRUDENTIAE, *in* 3 GOTTFRIED WILHELM LEIBNIZ, OPERA OMNIA, NUNC PRIMA COLLECTA, IN CLASSES DISTRIBUTA, PRAEFATIONIBUS ET INDICIBUS EXORNATA, STUDIO LUDOVICI DUTENS 954 (Apud Fratres de Tournes 1768).

29. THOMAS MORE, UTOPIA, Book I, 23 (Cambridge University Press 1940). More considered canon law to be a collection of both divine and human commands. Positive law was no greater than its source, and could be dispensed or abrogated by the competent authority for just reason. Divine law, however, such as the prohibition of adultery, could not be dispensed from even by the pope. *See* UTOPIA, 8 THE YALE EDITION OF THE COMPLETE WORKS OF THOMAS MORE 598 (Yale University Press 1961). For a discussion of More's formal education and legal training, *see* WILLIAM ROPER, THE LIFE OF SIR THOMAS MORE, *in* TWO EARLY TUDOR LIVES 197–202 (Richard S. Sylvester & Davis P. Harding eds., Yale University Press 1962); *see also* RICHARD MARIUS, THOMAS MORE 14–33 (Vintage Books 1985); PETER ACKROYD, THE LIFE OF THOMAS MORE 53–64 (Nan A. Talese 1998); R. H. Helmholz, *Thomas More and the Canon Law, in* MEDIEVAL CHURCH LAW AND THE ORIGINS OF THE WESTERN LEGAL TRADITION, A TRIBUTE TO KENNETH PENNINGTON 375–88 (Wolfgang P. Müller & Mary E. Sommar eds., Catholic University Press 2006).

century occasioned renewed scholarly interest in legal comparisons.[30] Since the advent of the first scholarly publications and societies devoted to it in the nineteenth century, comparative law has emerged to constitute a distinct discipline of legal scholarship.[31]

In their well-known work about comparative law, Konrad Zweigert and Hein Kötz described the comparativist's method as comparing "one's own home system" to a "foreign system" of law.[32] This book focuses on canon law, which may therefore be termed the so-called "home system." As I have some familiarity with Anglo-American legal theory, I hesitate to refer to it as "foreign." At the same time, I am aware that the scope of Anglo-American legal theory, not to mention that of canon law, invites a certain humility. As Zweigert and Kötz observed: "[i]t is too much to say that one must systematically master all this knowledge and then keep it in mind before one is allowed to embark on any kind of comparative work."[33] The phrase "Anglo-American legal theory," has broad parameters with a primary and secondary meaning in this comparative study. Primarily, the phrase designates the jurisprudence of nineteenth- and

---

30. For example, perhaps the most influential code of the nineteenth century, the French Civil Code of 1804, amalgamated the "droit écrit" of Southern France with the more Germanic customs of the North. *See* P. Antoine Fenet, 1 Recueil complet de travaux préparatoires du Code civil, 481 (Dépot, rue Saint-André-des-Arcs 1827). In the area of private law, the General German Negotiable Instruments Law of 1848 and the General German Commercial Code of 1861 were both based on comparative studies. *See* Zeigert & Kötz, 50. In 1917, Pope Benedict XV promulgated the first modern codification of canon law, after an extensive study of various local laws and customs. *See* Petrus Card. Gasparri, *Praefatio*, Codex Iuris Canonici Pii X Pontificis Maximi iussu digestus Benedicti Papae XV auctoritate promulgatus (Die 27 m. maii a. 1917), 9 AAS II, xix–xxxviii (1917).

31. The year 1829 marked the appearance of the first periodical devoted to comparative law: 1 Kritische Zeitschrift für Rechtswissenschaft und Gesetzgebung des Auslandes, 1 (1829). In 1869 in Paris, the Société de Législation Comparée, and in 1898 in London, the English Society of Comparative Legislation, the first scholarly societies of comparative law, were founded. A few examples of the first scholarly and systematic studies include: Emerico Amari, Critica di una sciencia delle legislationi comparate (Tip. de R. I. de' Sordo-Muti 1857); Leone Levi, International Law, With Materials for a Code of International Law (Appleton Co. 1888); Edouard Lambert, *Conception général et définition de la science du droit comparé*, Congrès international de droit comparé, tenu à Paris du 31 juillet au 4 août 1900, *reprinted in* Rechtsvergleichung 30–51 (Konrad Zweigert & Hans-Jürgen Puttfraken eds., Wissenschaftliche Buchgesellschaft 1978); Roscoe Pound, *The Influence of French Law in America*, 3 Ill. L. Rev. 354 (1909). *See also* Roscoe Pound, *The Place of Comparative Law in the American Law School Curriculum*, 8 Tul. L. Rev. 161 (1943); Edward D. Re, *Comparative Law Courses in the Law School Curriculum*, 1 Am. J. Comp. L. 233 (1952); and Otto Kahn-Freund, Comparative Law as an Academic Subject 1–31 (Clarendon Press of Oxford University 1965).

32. Zweigert & Kötz, Introduction to Comparative Law, 32–34.

33. *Id.* at 32.

twentieth-century Anglo-American theorists such as John Austin, H. L. A. Hart, Lon Fuller, John Finnis, Joseph Raz, and Ronald Dworkin. These theorists, of course, do not speak in one voice. Austin's pristine legal positivism set the stage for Hart's modified positivism and Fuller's concerns about the separation of law from morality. In response, Finnis, Raz, and Dworkin have each made different contributions to the ongoing discussion. The phrase "Anglo-American legal theory" also has a secondary meaning in this book. The phrase takes into account the earlier theory of seventeenth- and eighteenth-century thinkers such as Thomas Hobbes, John Locke, and David Hume. This classical liberal political theory served as part of the philosophical foundation for the nineteenth- and twentieth-century legal theorists just mentioned. This meaning has also carried into the liberal political theory of such twentieth-century thinkers as John Rawls. The present study does not attempt to present a comprehensive summary of Anglo-American legal theory or the work of any particular theorist.

Rather, my choice of Anglo-American legal theory as the partner in this comparative study is due to the primary meaning of the phrase. These theorists have engaged in a sustained and sophisticated discussion about three basic and related questions: "What is law?"; "What is a system of law?"; and "What is the rule of law?". I am aware that Anglo-American legal theory is not a system of law that governs some particular nation, jurisdiction, or entity. Not only do parameters of Anglo-American legal theory transcend any particular system of law, but the theory encompasses a number of different responses to the basic questions. For example, in response to the first question ("What is law?"), the theory includes the legal positivism of Hart and the natural law approach of Finnis. Although legal positivists may arguably count as dominant, all of the twentieth-century Anglo-American theorists are concerned in some respect with the second question ("What is a system of law?"). In the words of Raz, "every law necessarily belongs to a legal system (the English, or German, or Roman, or Canon Law, or some other legal system)," and the comparativist is searching for a description that "is general in that it claims to be true of all legal systems."[34] While I rely heavily on Hart's legal positivism in this comparative study, my reliance is not intended as an endorsement. Rather, I present certain features of his theory because I believe that it proves a helpful analytical tool. Specifically, I ask whether canon law satisfies Hart's description of law and the legal system.

The response to the third question ("What is the rule of law?") is related to the first two questions. The rule of law obviously depends on the existence of law and a system of law as in their absence there could be no rule of law. Although this book examines particular canonical provisions pertaining to clergy sexual abuse, the ownership of church property, and the refusal of Holy Communion,

34. Joseph Raz, The Concept of a Legal System: An Introduction to the Theory of Legal System 1 (Clarendon Press of Oxford University 1980).

the comparative aspect of the study transcends a mere consideration of particular substantive and procedural laws. Describing "deep level comparative law," Mark Van Hoecke observes that "rules cannot be fully understood isolated from their legal and non-legal context."[35] Comparative legal study juxtaposes the theories that underpin diverse legal systems in order to enable a deeper understanding of the respective systems of law.[36] In speaking of "legal theory," I do not mean to suggest that law simply replicates some abstract, conceptual explanation. The making of particular law is, of course, a more complex phenomenon than the mere application of some theory. The deep level methodology suggests that an adequate understanding of canon law requires some consideration of its historical, philosophical, and theological context. Canon law remains a religious system of law that claims a strong metaphysical foundation. According to Marek Zirk-Sadowski, legal positivism, the dominant form of Anglo-American theory, "is almost inherently anti-metaphysical."[37] I turn to the deeper level methodology to ask whether canon law's metaphysical and theological foundation assists in meeting the substantive requirements of the rule of law as it is understood in modern democratic government.

III. CANON LAW AND THE RULE OF LAW

As a religious system of law, canon law guides the Catholic Church, but does it represent the rule of law? In offering a preliminary response to this question, permit me a few observations about the meaning of the rule of law. The rule of law may be formulated in a variety of ways. In its most pristine version, the rule of law means that those who exercise the power of governance do so through laws. While the rule of law in its various meanings enjoys a long historical development, the general principle is that "individuals should be governed by law rather than by the arbitrary will of others."[38] Aristotle wrote: "He who bids the law to rule seems to bid God and intelligence alone to rule, but he who bids that

35. Mark Van Hoecke, *Deep Level Comparative Law, in* Epistemology and Methodology of Comparative Law 167 (Mark Van Hoecke ed., Hart Publishing 2004).

36. *See, e.g.*, Charles Lefebvre, *Equity in Canon Law, in* Equity in the World's Legal Systems: A Comparative Study 93–109 (Ralph A. Newman ed., Établissements Émile Bruylant 1973); Mary Ann Glendon, Abortion and Divorce in Western Law, American Failures, European Challenges (Harvard University Press 1987); Javier Martinez-Torron, Derecho angloamericano y derecho canónico, las raices canónicas de la common law (Facultad de Derecho Universidad Compultense 1991).

37. Marek Zirk-Sadowski, *Legal Epistemology and the Transformation of Legal Cultures, in* Epistemology and Methodology of Comparative Law 21 (Mark Van Hoecke ed., Hart Publishing 2004).

38. Guri Ademi, *Legal Imitations: Michael Oakshott and the Rule of Law*, 1993 Wisconsin L. Rev. 839, 844 (1993).

man rule puts forth a beast as well; for that is the sort of thing desire is, and spiritedness twists rulers even when they are the best of men."[39] In his *History of the English Law*, Sir William Holdsworth observed that the rule of law "is derived directly from the medieval theory that law of some kind—the law either of God or man—rules the world."[40] F. A. Hayek offered a modern formulation that the rule of law "means that the government in all its actions is bound by rules fixed and announced beforehand—rules which make it possible to foresee with fair certainty how the authority will use its coercive powers in given circumstances, and to plan one's individual affairs on the basis of this knowledge."[41] However, conformity with the requirement of *rule by law* does not of itself guarantee justice. As Joseph Raz has indicated, the most oppressive of governments may nonetheless "excel in one respect: its conformity with the rule of law."[42]

As an aspect of his 1958 debate with Lon Fuller, H. L. A. Hart disputed the claim that Nazi law was not law. He rejected "the doctrine that the fundamental principles of humanitarian morality were part of the very concept of . . . legality and that no positive enactment or statute . . . could be valid if it contravened basic principles of morality."[43] He drew a distinction between "the bare fact that a rule may be said to be a valid rule of law" and "the final moral question: 'Ought this rule of law to be obeyed?'"[44] For Hart, the separation of law from morality protected morality by not permitting morality to be supplanted by law.[45] In his book, *The Concept of Law*, Hart argued that a legal system is composed of primary and secondary rules.[46] Primary rules are those that require or prohibit certain actions such as the rule that prohibits murder. Secondary rules function to underpin the legal system and include rules of recognition, change, and adjudication. These rules provide a test for identifying what counts as law, procedures by which rules can be changed, and authorization of officials to adjudicate disputes over the interpretation of rules. In Hart's view, the secondary rules are characteristic of a society with a valid legal system as opposed to the normative uncertainty, static character, and inefficiency of the customary rules that are characteristic of a prelegal society.[47]

---

39. Aristotle, Politics, III, 1287a, 29–34.

40. Sir William Holdsworth, 10 History of the English Law 647 (Methuen 1938).

41. Friedrich A. Hayek, The Road to Serfdom 54 (G. Routledge & Sons 1944).

42. Joseph Raz, The Authority of Law: Essays on Law and Morality 211 (Clarendon Press of Oxford University 2002).

43. H. L. A. Hart, *Positivism and the Separation of Law and Morals*, 71 Harv. L. Rev. 617 (1958).

44. *Id.* at 618.

45. *Id.*

46. *See* H. L. A. Hart, The Concept of Law 91–99 (Joseph Raz & Penelope Bullock eds., 2nd ed. Clarendon Press of Oxford University 1994).

47. *See id.* at 54–56 and 86–88, which discusses the rules of a prelegal group or society.

Responding to Hart, Lon Fuller described the legislative and administrative "monstrosity" of Nazi law. He contrasted his position that the German judges should have declared, "This is not law," with the position which he attributed to Hart: "This is law but it is so evil we will refuse to apply it."[48] In his 1967 book, *The Morality of Law*, Fuller stated that the attempt to create and maintain a system of law may fail by not meeting eight procedural requirements. Laws must be general and not *ad hoc*, publicized, prospective and not retroactive, clear, logical, capable of obedience in practice, stable and not subject to too frequent change, and administered in a way that is congruent with the rule as announced.[49] Fuller suggested that his requirements as part of due process of law constituted a procedural natural law which served as the internal morality of law.[50] Joseph Raz would add to this list other requirements such as an independent judiciary, fair hearings which are open to the public, review of elected officials, and limitations on the police power of the state.[51] Nonetheless, a law might satisfy all of Fuller's eight requirements, Raz's additions, and due process in general, and remain a substantively unjust law.

The German theorist, Jürgen Habermas, argues that the combination of procedural legality with democratic government offers the best possibility of the substantive law's legitimacy.[52] He contends that the rule of law "is only participation in the practice of politically autonomous lawmaking" when it "does not destroy the rational motives for obeying the law; it must remain possible for everyone to obey legal norm on the basis of insight."[53] This conception of the rule of law fits with his overall theory about the role of law in the development of democracy. As Habermas states it:

> informal public opinion-formation generates "influence"; influence is transformed into "communicative power" through the channels of political elections; and communicative power is again transformed into "administrative power" through legislation. This influence, carried forward by communicative power, gives law its legitimacy, and thereby provides the political power of the state its binding force.[54]

---

48. Lon L. Fuller, *Positivism and Fidelity to Law—A Reply to Professor Hart*, 71 Harv. L. Rev. 630, 655 (1958).

49. *See* Lon L. Fuller, The Morality of Law 39 (Yale University Press 1967).

50. *See id.* at 96–106.

51. *See* Raz, The Authority of Law, Essays on Law and Morality, 216–17.

52. *See* Jürgen Habermas, Beyond Facts and Norms 189 (William Rehg trans., MIT Press 1996).

53. *Id.* at 121.

54. Jürgen Habermas, *Three Normative Models of Democracy*, *in* 1 Constellation 8 (1994).

Habermas rejects the idea of natural law as providing a basis for political and social order in the modern democratic state.[55] In his approach to the rule of law, Habermas reinforces the description of state power and legal procedures with an account of public discourse. However, one may ask whether even his sophisticated theory can guarantee that the substantive law will be just.[56] Is it possible that law which meets the requirements for procedural legality might be adopted in a democratic process that denies fundamental human rights or significantly diminishes the common good, or that does both?

Canon law represents the rule of law in the pristine meaning of rule by laws. As I shall discuss in the subsequent chapters of this book, canon law arguably also fulfills the requirements of formal procedural legality identified by Anglo-American theorists such as Hyack, Fuller, Hart, and Raz. As the church is not a democracy, canon law does not meet the requirements for the rule of law as conceptualized by Habermas. However, if Habermas is correct that the rule of law depends on "rational motives" and "insight" as the basis for obedience to the law, canon law may fulfill the requirements of the rule of law even though it does not communicate democratic participation in the lawmaking process. Canon law is grounded in natural law and theology. Both of these fonts may be described as possessing a communicative power to the subject of the law about the rational motives that underpin the law. The practical reason of natural law in conjunction with the faith of the believer may communicate not only rational motive but lead to the insight necessary to convince the believer of the validity of the canon law.

For example, an approach to unjust laws, such as those considered by Hart and Fuller, might be informed by natural law and theology. In his treatment of unjust law, John Finnis observes that the natural law tradition based upon Thomas Aquinas does not embrace the slogan that "unjust laws are not laws."[57] Aquinas thought that unjust laws "do not bind in conscience, except perhaps in order to avoid scandal or disturbance."[58] Finnis sees in the exceptions a "collateral moral obligation" to safeguard the legal system as a whole, which must be accounted for in the moral calculus about whether or not to obey an unjust law.[59] Natural law thus serves as the measure of positive law, but does not automatically relieve one of the obligation to conform to the rule of law. The practical reason about just law is enhanced by theological considerations. Theological principles about the inviolability of individual human dignity, the sacredness of life, and the

---

55. *See id.* at 104–06.

56. *See* BRIAN Z. TAMANAHA, ON THE RULE OF LAW: HISTORY, POLITICS, THEORY 101 (Cambridge University Press 2004).

57. JOHN FINNIS, NATURAL LAW AND NATURAL RIGHTS 364 (Clarendon Press of Oxford University 1980).

58. ST, 96, 4, corpus.

59. FINNIS, NATURAL LAW AND NATURAL RIGHTS, 364.

just distribution of resources reinforce conclusions about justice available on the basis of practical reason. In his "Letter from a Birmingham Jail," Martin Luther King, Jr., appealed to the natural law tradition of Thomas Aquinas in order to justify his peaceful disobedience of unjust racial laws.[60] Although he was doubtful about natural law, Dietrich Bonhoeffer's death testifies to the theological basis for resistance to the unjust Nazi regime.[61] If fundamental substantive justice is to be counted as a requirement of the rule of law, canon law's adherence to principles drawn from natural law and theology may satisfy the requirement.

At the same time, theological and pastoral issues might function to diminish canon law's adherence to the rule of law. In his study of English medieval canon law, Robert E. Rodes argues that the pastoral element of canon law along with its eschatological goals prevented it from fulfilling the requirements of the rule of law. As Rodes puts it: "The problem in the system was not that it was administrative, pastoral, and legal at once; it had to be. The problem was that it failed to assign the respective aspects their proper places in a harmonious whole."[62] The problem identified by Rodes is evident in the long historical development of canon law. Antinomianism places the pastoral and theological elements above the legal, while legalism permits the legal element to obscure the pastoral and theological. Despite the manifestations of antinomianism and legalism, Stephan Kuttner concluded that the medieval canon law represented a systemic harmony between the "spiritual and temporal, the supernatural and the natural."[63] Contemporary canon law continues the attempt to incorporate the pastoral and theological elements into a coherent system of law. The question of how successful this attempt has proven is one of the issues explored in this book. As I shall discuss in the chapters that follow, antinomianism and legalism continue to present a problem for the rule of law in the life of the church.

Chapter 1 offers an overview of canon law as the "home system" in this comparative study. Through an exploration of the clergy sexual abuse crisis in the United States, Chapters 2 and 3 discuss the failure of the rule of law in preventing injury to individuals and the common good. Chapter 3 suggests that antinomian and legalistic approaches to canon law contributed to the crisis. Chapter 4 considers the canonical consequences of the failure of the rule of law. In refer-

---

60. *See* Martin Luther King, Jr., I Had a Dream: Writings and Speeches that Changed the World 89 (James Melvin ed., Harper Collins 1992). Dr. King explained: "To put it in the terms of St. Thomas Aquinas: An unjust law is a human law that is not rooted in eternal law and natural law. Any law that uplifts human personality is just. Any law that degrades human personality is unjust." *Id.*

61. *See* Dietrich Bonhoeffer, Letter & Papers from Prison 11–12 (Eberhard Bethge ed., Touchstone of Simon & Schuster 1997).

62. Robert E. Rodes, Jr., Ecclesiastical Administration in Medieval England, The Anglo-Saxons to the Reformation 150 (Notre Dame University Press 1977).

63. Stephan Kuttner, Harmony from Dissonance: An Interpretation of Medieval Canon Law 50 (The Archabbey Press 1960).

ence to the ownership of church property, Chapters 4 and 5 examine the unity of law and theology in the law of property. Chapter 4 compares the concept of property in canon law with that of liberal political theory. In contrast to antinomian and legalistic theories, Chapter 5 describes the correct canonical approach to the ownership of parish property and church property in general. The chapter focuses on the relationship between church property and the law of the secular state and the problem of the secularization of Catholic institutions and their property. Raising the indeterminacy claim in regard to canon law, Chapters 6 and 7 assess the arguments for and against the denial of Holy Communion to Catholic public officials. These two chapters consider the interpretation of Canon 915 as an easy or hard case, and the chapters identify antinomian and legalistic elements in the interpretation. Throughout this comparative study, I rely on salient aspects of Anglo-American legal theory in order to gain critical insight about canon law as the universal law of the Catholic Church. As the responses of ecclesiastical authorities to each of the three specific issues—the sexual abuse crisis, the ownership of church property, and the refusal of Holy Communion—have displayed antinomian and legalistic approaches to canon law, Chapter 8 presents concluding observations about the impact of these approaches on the question of the rule of law.

1. AN OVERVIEW OF CANON LAW

In Chapter 1, I offer an overview of canon law. The chapter starts by defining what canon law is not. It then traces the historical development of canon law from its origins in the early church to its flowering in the medieval period. Beginning with the twentieth century codifications of canon law, the second part of the chapter describes contemporary canon law. It discusses legislative, judicial, and executive acts of governance. It also distinguishes universal and particular law, as well as various other types of canon law and the related features of dispensation, exception, privilege, and canonical equity. I conclude the chapter with some thoughts about the relationship between canon law and theology. The chapter is not an exhaustive treatment of canon law. Rather, my intention is that the overview functions to provide an understanding of canon law as the "home system" in this comparative study.

I. EXAMPLES OF THE SCRIPTURAL AND HISTORICAL ORIGINS OF CANON LAW

During the nineteenth century, certain German theologians and legal scholars, such as Rudolf Sohm, argued that the ancient church was a spiritual and theological, rather than legal and juridical community.[1] The argument painted a picture of Jesus as a foe of the institutional church. It was an image of Jesus who repudiated cultic worship, transformed religion into morality, and championed the individual. The argument could be summarized by the famous dictum of Alfred Loisy: "Jesus foretold the Kingdom, and it was the Church that came."[2] In contrast to such liberal nineteenth-century thought, Stephan Kuttner observed that the argument failed to appreciate "the sacramental and juridic nature of the

1. Rudolf Sohm, Outlines of Church History 34 (May Sinclair trans., Macmillan 1895). *Cf.* Adolf von Harnack, The Constitution and Law of the Church in the First Two Centuries 210–11 (Williams & Norgate 1910).

2. Alfred Loisy, The Gospel and the Church 166 (Christopher Home trans., Charles Scribner's Sons 1904). John P. Meier indicates that an accurate assessment of the relation between Jesus and the law is a considerably more challenging task than the nineteenth-century liberal position might admit. The challenge, according to Meier, involves dealing with two "historical problems," that of the historical Jesus and that of the historical Torah, which is "akin to aiming at two distinct moving targets." John P. Meier, A Marginal Jew: Rethinking the Historical Jesus, Volume IV, Law and Love 40 (Yale University Press 2009).

primitive and ancient Church."[3] As Klaus Mörsdorf suggested, the necessity of canon law derives from the fact of the Incarnation. The Son of God, the Eternal Word, took on human flesh and entered into salvation history.[4] Through the Incarnation, the Son necessarily associated with institutional and legal forms.[5] Mörsdorf and Kuttner rejected the notion that canon law is inherently opposed to faith. Rather, they understood that canon law affords justice, order, stability, and permanence in the human community of the church even as it facilitates the supernatural goals of the church. The antinomian approach is an understandable, if misguided, response to a legalism that places canon law over and above sacred scripture. A more balanced approach understands canon law as fulfilling an auxiliary but nonetheless vital function in the life of the Church. As a preliminary step towards the balanced approach, I situate canon law in the proper context of the authority of sacred scripture and tradition. I then proffer examples of the seeds of canon law in sacred scripture and the early church which flowered in the medieval period.

A. Via Negativa

My description of canon law begins with a *via negativa*. First, canon law is not sacred scripture. In his comparison of the Bible and the U.S. Constitution, Jaroslav Pelikan noted that each "sacred text" is "not merely ancient and intellectually interesting . . . but each of them is, for its own community, 'normative' and authoritative."[6] Although canon law carries a certain normativity and authority in the Roman Catholic Church, it is not constitutive and foundational in the sense that sacred scripture is to the church. Nor does canon law represent a constitution in the sense that the federal constitution does for the United States. Rather, canon law's normativity is secondary and may never be inconsistent with the first level authority of sacred scripture. In writing his letters, Saint Paul claimed divine inspiration: "[W]e impart this in words not taught by human

---

3. Stephan Kuttner, *Some Considerations on the Role of Secular Law and Institutions in the History of Canon Law*, Paper delivered at the Conference on Law and the Humanities held by the American Council of Learned Societies, Dumbarton Oaks, April 12–13, 1950, *in* Stephan Kuttner, Studies in the History of Medieval Canon Law 351, 356–57 (Variorum 1990). Kuttner observes that, while the medievals first developed a systematic approach to canon law, the primitive and ancient church from its institution was both a spiritual communion and corporate society with the existence of a sacramental and jurisdictional law.

4. John 1:1.

5. *See* Myriam Wiljens, Theology and Canon Law, The Theories of Klaus Mörsdorf and Eugenio Corecco 28-39 (University Press of America 1992). *See also* Joseph Ratzinger, Milestones, Memoirs: 1927–1977, 49–50 (Rasmo Leiva-Merikakis trans., Ignatius Press 1998).

6. Jaroslav Pelikan, Interpreting the Bible and the Constitution 9 (Yale University Press 2004).

wisdom but taught by the Spirit."[7] The church considers sacred scripture to contain immutable divine revelation. I shall suggest that canon law acts as a bridge between immutable theological truths and practical action.

Canon law does develop in several ways.[8] One mode of development corresponds to the development of Christian doctrine. For example, the great Christological creeds pertaining to the fullness of Christ's humanity and divinity are not expressly defined in sacred scripture. Rather, the tradition developed on the basis of sacred scripture at a variety of ecumenical councils during the first several centuries of the church's existence. The development of tradition has continued throughout the history of the church.[9] In the sixteenth century, the Council of Trent expressed the correlation between sacred scripture and tradition in this way: "[F]ollowing the example of the orthodox fathers, [the council] receives and holds in veneration with an equal affection of piety and reverence the books both of the Old and New Testament, since one God is the author of both, and also the traditions themselves, those that pertain both to faith and to morals, as having been dictated either by Christ's own word of mouth or by the Holy Spirit, and preserved in the Catholic Church by a continuous succession."[10] When it directly flows from sacred scripture and tradition, canon law itself forms part of the tradition and claims its normativity. Another mode of development of canon law is change through its merely positive character. While no provision of canon law, ecumenical council, or papal definition may rescind the fundamental truths expressed in sacred scripture or tradition, canon law may be changed in its merely positive character through the legislative authority of the church. The U.S. Constitution may be amended through a legislative process which is a specification of the way in which law is generally enacted in the modern democratic state. Canon law has no such democratic legislative process for changes to the universal law of the church. Later in this chapter, I discuss the process for the modern codifications of canon law during the twentieth century.

Second, not only is canon law not sacred scripture, but it must also be distinguished from other normative sources of Christian belief such as moral theology. Just as it is not a summary of the Christian creed, canon law is not a compilation of all the moral doctrine of the church. Nonetheless, it remains true

---

7. 1 Corinthians 2:13. Scriptural quotations through this book are taken from HOLY BIBLE, REVISED STANDARD VERSION, CATHOLIC EDITION, prepared by the Catholic Biblical Association of Great Britain (Oxford: Oxford University Press 1966).

8. For a discussion of the transcendent and historical in the development of canonical equity, *see* John J. Coughlin, O.F.M., *Canonical Equity*, 30 STUDIA CANONICA 403–35 (1996).

9. *See* JOHN HENRY CARDINAL NEWMAN, AN ESSAY ON THE DEVELOPMENT OF DOCTRINE 29–30 (6th ed. University of Notre Dame Press 2005).

10. Council of Trent (April 8, 1546), no. 783, *in* HEINRICH DENZINGER, THE SOURCES OF CATHOLIC DOGMA 244 (Roy J. Deferrari trans., Loreto Publications 2001).

that in its long historical development canon law was often not distinguished from moral teaching.[11] Indeed, well into the twentieth century, it was not uncommon for canon lawyers and moral theologians to share the same kind of expertise and methodology. This is not surprising when one considers the fact that canon law and moral theology both flow from sacred scripture and natural law. With the promulgation of the twentieth-century codifications of canon law, the distinction between the church's moral teaching and law became more apparent. While the modern codifications often provide penalties for actions inconsistent with particular creeds and moral truths, the codifications were not designed as a summary of the church's doctrine. In a limited sense, the modern codification of canon law may have reflected a desire for the autonomy of law from other normative sources—an autonomy typical of the separation of law and morality called for by the twentieth-century legal positivists. However, in direct contrast to the separation of law and morality, canon law has remained faithful to its foundations in sacred scripture and natural law.

In canon law, a distinction may be drawn between doctrinal and disciplinary law. Doctrinal law contains some specific doctrinal point drawn directly from sacred scripture, natural law, or tradition. It was a methodological option in the design of the *CIC-1983* and the *CCEO* to start major sections and titles of the Codes with almost verbatim quotations of some doctrinal or pastoral provision from one of the sixteen documents of Vatican II. When a canon does articulate a doctrinal point, it is doctrinal law. For example, Canon 330, *CIC-1983*, quotes *Lumen Gentium*, 22: "Just as be the decree of the Lord, Saint Peter and the rest of the Apostles form one Apostolic College, so for a like reason the Roman Pontiff, the successor to Peter, and the Bishops, the successors of the Apostles, are united together in one." In contrast, disciplinary law sets forth some practical norm of action that explains and urges the spiritual good of the faithful. Book 4 of the *CIC-1983* contains many disciplinary laws that regulate the reception of the sacraments, such as the canonical form of, and certain impediments to, the celebration of Holy Matrimony.[12] Such disciplinary laws are necessary to the order of

11. The Catholic manuals regularly treated moral theology and canon law together. *See, e.g.*, Charles Laurent, The Busy Pastor's Guide to a Resume of Canon Law and Moral Theology (O. Dolphin 1924). *See also* John Mahoney, The Making of Moral Theology viii and 224–58 (Clarendon Press of Oxford University 1987). Mahoney discusses the emergence of moral theology as a distinct discipline in the sixteenth century and relation of law and moral theology in Roman Catholic thought.

12. In Western canon law, the spouses are the ministers of the sacrament of Holy Matrimony. Canon 1108 of the *CIC-1983* establishes the canonical form of the sacrament being celebrated in the presence of a bishop, priest, or deacon along with two witnesses. When there is a shortage of priest and deacons and with the vote of the Conference of Bishops and approval of the Holy See, Canon 1112 permits the diocesan bishop to delegate a layperson to assist at the sacrament in place of one in Holy Orders. The stipulation that the canonical form is necessary for validity is a positive law which the church

the ecclesial community and may be distinguished from doctrinal law that expresses what the community believes. Although canon law must be distinguished from sacred scripture and natural law, these fundamental sources of the church's belief and practice constitute the foundations of canon law.

B. The Juridical Form of Community, Sacrament, and Mission in the New Testament

My intention is not to provide an exhaustive account but rather to present a few examples of the seeds of canon law in the early church. First, the continuity of revelation in human history depends on an institutional form. The tradition of revelation does not float in time of itself, but its continuity in time is inexorably linked to the human community of the church. The kingdom preached by Jesus breaks into human history not only in the Incarnation as the primary revelation of God, but also in the community he gathers around himself. The original *communio* is the *ecclesia* of the New Testament.[13] The church is perfected in the cenacle of the upper room at Pentecost where Peter and the other Apostles are gathered in prayer with Mary, the mother of Jesus, the holy women, and the brethren.[14] Peter leads the Eleven in the selection of Matthias to replace Judas Iscariot.[15] The Holy Spirit descends upon them like the "rush of a mighty wind" and "tongues of fire."[16] They are "filled with the Holy Spirit" who enables them "to speak in other tongues" in order to proclaim to "every nation under heaven."[17] This Pentecostal gathering serves as a prototype for all subsequent ecclesial reality. It is not the apostolic college alone but the entire ecclesial reality that constitutes the form for the dynamic spread of the charism. Nonetheless, the proclamation of the charism is entrusted in a special way to Peter and the other Apostles. The apostolic tradition is public, not secret or private. Even before there was a written word, there was an oral tradition. The revelation of the Son in human history was tied to eyewitnesses, the Apostles, who continued preaching the gospel.[18] The oral tradition was recorded as sacred scripture. From the original Pentecostal gathering, the Apostles discerned the need to choose successors

---

theoretically could alter. The history of marriage shows that the canonical form has not always been required for a valid marriage. The same is true with regard to impediments to marriage. Certain impediments such as a prior valid marriage (Canon 1085) or impotence (Canon 1084) are aspects of the natural law and not subject to fundamental change bythe church. Other impediments to marriage such as affinity (Canon 1092) and adoption (Canon 1094) are not strictly speaking part of the natural or divine law, and therefore could be changed by the church.

13. Matthew 18:17; 1 Corinthians 1:2; Galatians 3:16, 26–29.

14. Acts 1:13–14.

15. Acts 1:15–26.

16. Acts 2:2–3.

17. Acts 2:4.

18. John 21:24; Acts 1:1–3.

who would function as the official witnesses passing on the tradition from age to age.[19] The inner meaning of Christ's passion, death, and resurrection as experienced at Pentecost is not separable from the outward ecclesial form of the apostolic ministry. The church structure entailed from the beginning an inner meaning, or *intellectus*, and an outward form.[20]

Second, certain structural and legal forms are associated with the sacramental life of the pristine church. The neophyte must not only acknowledge that Jesus is Lord, but must be baptized by the minister in the name of the Lord Jesus.[21] Jesus also commanded the Apostles to celebrate the Eucharist in his memory.[22] During the earliest phases of its development, the church understood more clearly the nature of Christ's mandate and set down formulae in response to it. The institution narratives in Mark, Matthew, Luke, and First Corinthians are essentially liturgical texts based on Jesus' actions at the Last Supper as practiced by the earliest Christian communities.[23] From the beginning, the sacramental life of the church has centered on the Eucharist, and the Eucharist has required an established order so that it might constitute the true sacrament of unity. There is a close association between the sacramental life and the social order of the

---

19. Acts 1:15–26; 1 Corinthians 11:23; 15:3; 2 Timothy 1:2.

20. *See* HANS URS VON BALTHASAR, A THEOLOGICAL ANTHROPOLOGY 162–63 (Sheed & Ward 1967). Balthasar attributes the word "intellectus" to Bonaventure's ecclesiology. Bonaventure actually speaks of the "logica." Applied to canon law, this would mean a grace-filled harmony between the outward structure and its inner *logica*. It is this *logica* that must inform the exercise of sacred power in the Christian community. From this internal *logica* flows the law's power to bind persons and communities, who are constituents of the Mystery which is the Church. According to Bonaventure, the superabundant love of the crucified Christ constitutes the source of the bond of charity that unites the members of the mystical Body to each other and the Head, forming a unified, living organism, the Church. *See* SAN BONAVENTURA, I *Sent.* d. 14, a. 2, q. 1, fund. 4, in 1 DOCTORIS SERAPHICI S. BONAVENTURAE OPERA OMNIA, EDITA STUDIO ET CURA PP. COLLEGII A S. BONAVENTURA 249 (EX TYPOGRAPHIA COLLEGII S. BONAVENTURAE 1882-1889), AND SAN BONAVENTURA *Brevil.* 3, 11, in 5 DOCTORIS SERAPHICI S. BONAVENTURAE OPERA OMNIA, EDITA STUDIO ET CURA PP. COLLEGII A S. BONAVENTURA 240 (EX TYPOGRAPHIA COLLEGII S. BONAVENTURAE 1882-1889). *See generally* PETER D. FEHLNER, THE ROLE OF CHARITY IN THE ECCLESIOLOGY OF ST. BONAVENTURE (Miscellanea Francescana 1965). In Bonaventure's ecclesiology, "the life of charity lies at the core of the Church's mystery, that living reality is embodied, at least in a limited way, in the visible relations, structures, offices, and sacraments of the historical community (church militant)." Zachary Hayes, O.F.M., *Bonaventure, Mystery of the Triune God, in* THE HISTORY OF FRANCISCAN THEOLOGY 102–03 (Kenan Osborne, O.F.M. ed., The Franciscan Institute 1994).

21. Acts 8:16; Acts 19:5; 1 Corinthians 1:13.

22. Luke 22:17–19; 1 Corinthians 11:26.

23. Mark 14:22–25; Matthew 26:26–29; Luke 22:18ff; 1 Corinthians 11–23. *See* RUDOLF SCHNACKENBURG, THE GOSPEL OF MATTHEW 266–67 (Robert R. Burr trans., Eerdmans 2002); and JOSEPH M. POWERS, S.J., EUCHARISTIC THEOLOGY 52–58 (Herder 1967).

church. The Acts of the Apostles states that the Twelve, not desirous of neglecting prayer and preaching, selected seven assistants to assist with the distribution of food to the needy.[24] These "seven men of good repute, full of the Spirit and of wisdom" corresponded to the college of seven elders (*presbyterium*) who exercised administrative authority in the local Jewish communities of first century Palestine.[25] The Letter to the Philippians starts with recognition of the bishops (*episkopoi*) and assistants (*diakonoi*).[26] The Greek word *episkopos* designated an important office holder who exercised supervisory authority or guardianship over some group of persons or geographic area on behalf of the central governing authority.[27] Although these offices were yet to be clearly defined, the later pastoral epistles annunciate the desirable qualities of bishops, presbyters (priests), and deacons who preside over and serve in the sacramental community of faith.[28]

Third, the mission of the church is expressed in an outward legal form. Matthew's Gospel records that Jesus "charged" the Apostles, and he "sent" them on mission as the Twelve."[29] In this sending the Apostles on mission for the first time, Jesus relied on the rabbinical legal form of the *schaliach*, which delegated one as an authoritative agent and official representative.[30] According to the Gospel of John, the risen Christ used a specific delegation to transmit his authority to the Apostles: "As the Father sent me, even so I send you."[31] The Apostles chose successors and also deacons for service in the church. The nature of this mission requires election and the laying on of hands.[32] The imposition of hands adopted another institution of Jewish Law, the *semikhah* through which the rabbi as teacher and judge installed his student to these same offices. It was an act that conferred divine power in an unrepeatable authorization.[33] The inner experience of believing in Christ is not sufficient for preaching. It was also necessary to be

---

24. Acts 6:1–6.

25. Acts 6:3. *See* C. K. BARRETT, A CRITICAL AND EXEGETICAL COMMENTARY ON THE ACTS OF THE APOSTLES, INTERNATIONAL CRITICAL COMMENTARY 312 (T & T Clark 1994).

26. Philippians 1:1. *See* RAYMOND E. BROWN, PRIEST AND BISHOP, BIBLICAL REFLECTIONS 21–39 (Paulist 1970).

27. *See* HENRY G. LIDDELL & ROBERT SCOTT, A GREEK-ENGLISH LEXICON 657 (Oxford University Press 1968); and A GREEK-ENGLISH LEXICON OF THE NEW TESTAMENT AND OTHER EARLY CHRISTIAN LITERATURE 379–80 (Frederick W. Danker ed., 3rd ed. University of Chicago Press 2000).

28. 1 Timothy 3:1–13; Titus 1:5–9. *See* BROWN, PRIEST AND BISHOP, BIBLICAL REFLECTIONS, 42.

29. Matthew 10:5.

30. *See* DOMINIQUE CUSS, IMPERIAL CULT AND HONORARY TERMS IN THE NEW TESTAMENT 134–40 (University Press 1974).

31. John 20:21.

32. Acts 6:1–6.

33. *See* RABBI J. NEWMAN, SEMIKHAH: A STUDY OF ITS ORIGINS, HISTORY, AND FUNCTION IN RABBINIC LITERATURE 10, 117, 125, 127, and 130 (Manchester University Press 1950).

commissioned by the risen Christ and filled with the Holy Spirit for the purpose of preaching to the nations to the end of the world.[34] Peter as head of the original college enjoys a primacy, and the Petrine ministry is to confirm the unity of the *communio*.[35]

C. Paul of Tarsus: Law and Spirit

The great missionary of early Christianity, Paul of Tarsus, has been described as an "Oriental lawyer."[36] Paul belonged to a class of scholars for whom knowledge of the Jewish Law was paramount. As a young man, Paul had trained under the tutelage of the esteemed rabbinical scholar, Gamaliel. Following his conversion to Christianity, Paul referred to the Jewish Law as a "curse," and urged the early Christians to live as justified in the spirit.[37] In the Letter to the Romans, Paul contrasted "the law of the spirit" with "the law of sin and death."[38] The Jewish Law for Paul included the entire corpus of pentateuchal rules and regulations which consisted of approximately 248 positive commands and 365 prohibitions. Although various rabbinical schools calculated the exact number of precepts of the Law differently, they agreed that the Law pronounced a curse on those who did not keep it in its entirety. However, Paul called the Law a curse not so much because it gave rise to legalism, but because he believed that it was a hopeless business to seek justification by the Law. For Paul, the Law told people what to do, but it imparted no power to do it. In contrast to the Law, Paul preached that the Gospel imparts power to live a new life in Christ. In Paul's theology, it is through faith and not observance of the Law that one is justified. The "law of the spirit" imparts the blessing which God promised to Abraham, his offspring, and all nations. This "new law" removes the curse pronounced on the lawbreaker. According to Paul, the curse is lifted and the new law established not through strict observance of the old Law but through Christ, the condemned one, who endured that Law in the manner of his passion and death.[39]

Nonetheless, much of Paul's thought was expressed in legal language and metaphors. Describing Saint Paul's "career as an administrator," the biblical scholar John Knox observes:

> Among the issues Paul might be called upon to handle were Jew-Gentile relations, threats of schism, disorders in services of worship, irregularities in the observance of the Lord's Supper, a misunderstanding between two

34. Acts 10:42; 1:8.

35. Matthew 16:17–19.

36. J. Duncan M. Derrett, Law in the New Testament 396–403 (Darton, Longmann & Todd 1970).

37. Galatians 3:13.

38. Romans 8:2.

39. *See* F. F. Bruce, *The Curse of the Law*, *in* Paul and Paulinism: Essays in Honour of C. K. Barrett 27–35 (Alden Press 1982).

> members of the local church, unhealthy excitement about the end of the world, litigation between Christians, occasional instances of serious immorality, the question of whether a Christian could eat food that had been consecrated by pagan rites, innumerable problems connected with marriage, the role of women in the church, various false teachings, the administration of charity by the churches, relations of Christians with their pagan neighbors and how Christian slaves and masters should treat each other.[40]

Paul understood that the Christian community could not be free from such issues and their legal aspects.

Perhaps, Paul's training in and concern for the Law is nowhere more evident than in his first letter to the Corinthians, one of the earliest New Testament texts.[41] Chapter 6 of First Corinthians combines antinomian and legal elements.[42] The antinomian is evident in Paul's concern with the imminent return of Christ rendering all worldly concerns "trivial."[43] Verses 7–8 served to remind the Corinthians that the ultimate court of appeal for Christian life is the teaching embodied on the cross of Christ.[44] Paul suggested that following Christ may sometimes require that one suffer some wrong or injustice for the sake of the community in the example of the Suffering Servant.[45] The eschatological perspective, however, did not prevent Paul from seeing the need for a juridic order in the early church.[46] He admonished the Christian community to avoid lawsuits in the civil courts.[47] When there is a dispute among you, Paul queried

---

40. *See* John Knox, Chapters in the Life of Paul 87 (Douglas R. A. Hare ed. Mercer University Press 1987).

41. "Paul himself tells us that First Corinthians was written in the spring from Ephesus (1 Corinthians 16:8), but the year is a matter of dispute. The suggested dates range from AD 52 to 57 with the majority opting for a date close to the middle of that span." The New Jerome Biblical Commentary 799 (Raymond E. Brown, S.S., Joseph A. Fitzmyer, S.J., & Roland E. Murphy, O.Carm. eds., Prentice Hall 1990).

42. For a general discussion of eschatology and ecclesiology in Pauline thought, *see* François Amiot, Les Idées Maîtresses de Saint-Paul 151–258 (Les Éditions du Cerf 1959).

43. *See* F. W. Grosheide, *Commentary on the First Epistle to the Corinthians, in* The New International Commentary of the New Testament 132–42 (Ned B. Stonehouse & F. F. Bruce gen. eds., Eerdmans Publishing 1974).

44. "To have lawsuits at all with one another is defeat for you. Why not rather suffer wrong? Why not rather be defrauded? But you yourselves wrong and defraud, and that even your own brethren." 1 Corinthians 6:7–8.

45. *See* Amiot, Les Idées, 209–13.

46. *See* Wilfred A. Knox, Saint Paul and the Church of Jerusalem 23–35 (University Press 1935).

47. "When one of you has a grievance against a brother, does he dare to go to the law before the unrighteous instead of the saints? Do you not know that the saints will judge the world? And if the world is to be judged by you, are you incompetent to try trivial cases? Do you not know that we are to judge the angels? How much more, matters pertaining to

the Corinthian community, why does one member of the community become a plaintiff and bring another Christian before the judgment of the civil magistrates?[48] Consistent with the rabbinical teaching that it was unlawful to plead a case before an idolatrous judge, Paul advocated the establishment of internal procedures to settle disputes among the members of the community.[49] Despite his admonition about avoiding the Roman courts, Paul resorted to the secular law to protect himself from his enemies. As a Roman citizen, Paul apparently utilized the imperial law and elected arrest and house custody in Rome.[50] Paul's travel to Rome served as the occasion of his second missionary journey, which proved significant to the spread of Christianity particularly among the Gentiles. The mystical missionary of the kingdom to come appears also to have been a man of practical action, knowledgeable in the Jewish Law, and by borrowing from that Law, intent on establishing a just legal order for the Christian community in the here and now.

D. The Council at Jerusalem

Paul's missionary activity resulted in the incorporation of many Gentile converts into the heretofore Jewish-Christian community. The tremendous growth of the early church was certain to raise legal issues.[51] Chapter 15 of the Acts of the Apostles discloses an example of the exercise of legislative power in the early

---

this life! If then you have such cases, why do you lay them before those who are least esteemed by the church? I say this to your shame. Can it be that there is no man among you wise enough to decide between members of the brotherhood, but brother goes to law against brother, and that before unbelievers?" 1 Corinthians 6:1–6.

48. The "judgment seat," or *bema*, was publicly located in the heart of the market place where the Roman civil magistrates heard all types of petty grievances. *See* Acts 18:12–17. For a general discussion of the role of magistrates and the exercise of executive power in Roman law, *see* BARRY NICHOLAS, AN INTRODUCTION TO ROMAN LAW 19–28 (Clarendon Press of Oxford University 1962).

49. *See* THE INTERPRETER'S BIBLE 69 (George A. Buttricks gen. ed., Abingdon-Cokesbury 1952).

50. *See id.*

51. Chapter 11 of the Acts of the Apostles recounts the origin of the controversy over the propagation of the Gospel to the Gentiles. *See generally* F. F. Bruce, *Commentary on the Book of Acts, in* THE NEW INTERNATIONAL COMMENTARY OF THE NEW TESTAMENT 298–316 (F. F. Bruce gen. ed., Eerdmans Publishing 1975); and F. F. Bruce, THE BOOK OF THE ACTS, REVISED EDITION 219-231 (Eerdmans Publishing 1988). Up to this point the events reported in Acts had concerned almost exclusively the Aramaic-speaking Jewish-Christians. The disciples from Cyrene and Cyprus relied on their knowledge of the Greek language, which enabled them to preach the gospel to Greek-speaking Gentile inhabitants of Antioch which was at that time the third largest city in the Roman Empire. When the church in Jerusalem learned that the Gospel had been preached in Antioch, they sent Barnabas there to investigate. Approving of the new venture in Antioch, Barnabas joined the missionary effort, and sought Paul to assist him with the work. *See* JOHANNES MUNCK,

church in response to the new pluralism. A vigorous controversy ensued as to whether the Gentiles were bound by the prescriptions of the Jewish Law, and in particular the circumcision requirement. Paul and Barnabas traveled to Jerusalem to present the issue to the Apostles. At the Council of Jerusalem, James, Paul, Barnabas, and Peter all spoke in defense of Gentile freedom from the Law. The weight of the apostolic authority resulted in the unanimous adoption by the Council of a decree which resolved the conflict.[52]

Two separate statements of the same decree are contained in Chapter 15. In both cases, the decree was introduced by a legal formula: "Therefore, my judgment," and "For it has seemed good to the Holy Spirit and to us."[53] The formula employed in the second version, in fact, imitates that of the official decisions of the Roman emperors.[54] Following the legal introductory-formulae, the decree next contained a prodesis. In James's speech, it is stated: "that we should not trouble those of the Gentiles who turn to God";[55] and in verse 28, it is stated: "to lay upon you no greater burden than these necessary things."[56] The decree determined that the Law did not have binding force for Gentile Christians.[57]

The third element of the decree was an apodesis. James urged that the Council "should write to them to abstain from the pollutions of idols, and from unchastity and from what is strangled and from blood."[58] Similarly, verse 29 required that "you abstain from what has been sacrificed to idols and from blood and from what is strangled and from unchastity."[59] The prohibitions reflected aspects of both the moral law and cultic practice of first-century Judaism. It was a

---

THE ACTS OF THE APOSTLES, *in* 31 THE ANCHOR BIBLE 105–08 (William F. Albright & David N. Freedman eds., Doubleday 1967).

52. KNOX, SAINT PAUL AND THE CHURCH AT JERUSALEM, 86–87.

53. The first can be found in verses 19–20 in the speech of James. He begins with the words: "διὸ ἐγὼ κρίνω . . ."; "Propter quod ego iudico . . ." Verses 28–29 contain the decree as it is pronounced by the Council starting with the words: "ἔδοξεν γάρ τῷ πνεύματι τῷ ἁγίῳ καὶ ἡμῖν. . ."; "Visum est enim Spiritui Sancto et nobis . . ." *See* F. J. FOAKES-JACKSON, THE ACTS OF THE APOSTLES 140 (Hodder and Stoughton 1960).

54. *See* ERNST HAENCHEN, THE ACTS OF THE APOSTLES: A COMMENTARY 453 (Westminster Press 1971).

55. Verse 19: "μὴ παρενοχλεῖν τοῖς ἀπὸ τῶν ἐθνῶν ἐπιστρέφουσιν ἐπὶ τὸν θεόν . . ."; "non inquietari eos qui ex gentibus convertuntur ad Deum . . ."

56. Verse 28: "μηδὲν πλέον ἐπιτίθεσθαι ὑμῖν βάρος πλὴν τούτων τῶν ἐπάναγκες"; "nihil ultra imponere vobis oneris quam haec necessario . . ."

57. The decree does not determine, nor did the Council consider, the question of the binding force of the Law on Judaic Christians. 7 NEW CATHOLIC ENCYCLOPEDIA 889–90, s.v. "Council of Jerusalem" by N. M. Flanagan.

58. Verse 20: "ἀλλὰ ἐπιστεῖλαι αὐτοῖς τοῦ ἀπέχεσθαι τῶν ἀλισγημάτων τῶν εἰδώλων καὶ τῆς πορνείας καὶ τοῦ πνικτοῦ καὶ τοῦ αἵματος." "Scribere ad eos ut abstineant se a contaminationibus simulacrorum et fornicatione et suffocato et sanguine."

59. Verse 29: "ἀπέχεσθαι εἰδωλοθύτων καὶ αἵματος καὶ πνικτῶν καὶ πορνείας . . ."; "abstinere ab idolothytis et sanguine et suffocatis et fornicatione . . ."

fundamental moral principle of Judaism that the sins of idolatry, murder, and fornication were intrinsically opposed to the law of God.[60] The prescriptions in the apodesis corresponded to this principle with the exception that the prohibition against murder was not included presumably because the Apostles did not think it a problem for the Gentile Christians at Antioch. The apodesis then was intended to balance the main point of the decree, which exempted the Gentiles from observance of the Law, by affirming the divine moral law. Moreover, Jewish Christians would have been offended by the partaking of food offered to idols or any other practice associated with the pagan cults. The decree of the Council can be said to represent the establishment of a general law intended to facilitate communal life between the new Gentile converts and the Jewish Christians.

The scriptural evidence suggests that early Christianity was far from inherently antinomian. To the contrary, the numerous examples culled from the New Testament indicate that the primitive Christian communities adopted specific norms and forms drawn from Jewish and Roman law in order to address pastoral needs. Consistent with the New Testament, the church of the first several centuries often relied on extra-ecclesial legal forms to fashion the order of the ecclesiastical community. Again, my method in this general overview is not to present a complete account of canon law's historical development.[61] Rather, I shall present two examples of the development. The first example consists of evidence that the Patristic church in Northern Africa sometimes adopted Roman legal concepts as part of the order ecclesiastical life. The second example discusses the emergence of canon law as a distinct science by the medieval canonists.

E. The Patristic Church of Northern Africa

A prominent figure in the Carthaginian Church was the cultivated Roman lawyer Tertullian (ca. 160–220).[62] After his conversion to Christianity, Tertullian devoted

---

60. Foakes-Jackson, The Acts of the Apostles, 140.

61. For some relatively recent histories of canon law, *see* James A. Brundage, Medieval Canon Law (The Medieval World) (Longman 1995); Ennino Cortese, Il diritto nella storia medievale, 1: L'Alto medioevo, 2: Il basso medioevo (Il Cingo Galileo Galilei 1995); Peter Erdö, Storia della scienza del diritto canonico: Una introduzione (Editrice Pontificia Università Gregoriana 2000); Brian E. Ferme, Introduzione alla storia del diritto canonico (Pontificia Università Lateranense 1998); Jean Gaudemet, Sources du droit de l'Église en occident du IIe au VIIe siècle. (Les Editions du Cerf 1985); Jean Gaudemet, Sources du droit de l'Église en occident du VIIIe au XXe siècle: Repères canoniques, sources occidentales (Les Editions du Cerf 1993); and Constant Van de Wiel, History of Canon Law (Peters Press 1991).

62. *See* Hubert Jedin & John Dolan, 1 History of the Church 248–52 (Burns & Oates 1980) [Jedin]. *See also* Jules Lebreton & Jacques Zeiller, 2 The History of the Primitive Church 214–15, n. 165 (2nd ed. trans. from the French, MacMillan 1949) [Lebreton].

all his considerable legal knowledge and skills to upholding Christianity against its pagan foes. He pleaded with the Roman proconsul attempting to mitigate cruelties against Christianity.[63] Adopting the substance and terminology of Roman law, Tertullian translated the Greek word *mysterion* with the Latin *sacramentum*, an accepted term in Roman law that carried multiple meanings. In ancient Roman law, one meaning of *sacramentum* was the sum which the parties to a lawsuit deposited in a sacred place pending the outcome of the suit. It could also mean an oath of allegiance, a solemn obligation, or the civil lawsuit and its process.[64] Borrowing from his legal knowledge, Tertullian introduced the notion of a sacrament into church life. He thus bequeathed a seminal legal concept that would shape the church's approach to the sacred.

Toward the middle of the third century, the church at Carthage produced an outstanding priest and bishop, Coecilius Cyprianus (d. 258). Like Tertullian prior to conversion, Cyprian had enjoyed renown as a successful lawyer and prominent member of Carthaginian society. Following Cyprian's election as Bishop of Carthage in the year 249 AD, the Roman Emperor Decius initiated a vicious persecution of the church during which numerous Christians lapsed into pagan practices. When the Decian persecution subsided, many of the lapsed wished to return to the church. Cyprian confronted the "lapsed controversy," with a response that integrated the theology of forgiveness with his legal expertise.[65] Responding to certain priests and deacons who requested some policy regarding the reception of the lapsed back into communion, Cyprian issued a letter which mandated that the lapsed perform a substantial period of penance. Cyprian's letter further provided that subsequent to the penance, the lapsed were entitled to obtain a certificate from a "confessor" indicating that they were now capable of being received back into full communion. The letter also permitted an exception to the certificate requirement in the case of danger of death where the imposition of a long period of penance might preclude the possibility of the lapsed Christian's return.[66] Five members of the presbyterate, who had opposed Cyprian's election

63. *See* LOUIS DUCHESNE, 1 EARLY HISTORY OF THE CHRISTIAN CHURCH FROM ITS FOUNDING TO THE END OF THE FIFTH CENTURY 286–87 (John Murray 1947) [DUCHESNE]; JEDIN, I, 219.

64. LEWIS & SHORT, A LATIN DICTIONARY 1611–12, s.v. "sacramentum" (Oxford University Press 1987).

65. In the year 250, the Roman Emperor Decius issued a decree requiring all citizens to manifest their loyalty by burning incense in front of temple images of the Roman deities. Many Christians refused to perform the idolatrous action and as a result went to martyrdom; many others, however, including two bishops acquiesced to the imperial demand. Although Saint Cyprian desired to wear the crown of martyrdom, the presbyterate of Carthage so highly valued his abilities that he was persuaded to go into hiding. In the midst of the period of fierce persecution, Saint Cyprian and other faithful Christians regarded defectors as apostates. *See* DUCHESNE, I, 383; JEDIN, I, 222–26.

66. *See* Cyprian of Carthage, *Epistolae*, 5, 6, 7, 10–19; 4 PL 235–46, 259–81.

as bishop, adopted a lax policy of readmission. The presbyters received the lapsed back into full communion, if the lapsed could produce a confessor's certificate, even when no prior penance had been undertaken.[67] The dispute led Cyprian to appeal to a higher authority for affirmation of the administrative practice established by his decree. Upon appeal to the Provincial Council, Cyprian's decree was affirmed, and ultimately, it received the approbation of Pope Cornelius, Bishop of Rome.[68]

Another convert to Christianity who had been trained in rhetoric and law was Augustine, Bishop of Hippo (354–430). Until the reign of Constantine and the establishment of Christianity as the official state religion in 318 AD, the decision of an ecclesiastical judge was binding only in conscience. It would be upheld by the public authorities, if at all, solely by prior stipulation of the parties. In the wake of the Constantinian establishment, the role of ecclesiastical judges changed in two dramatic ways. First, their jurisdiction was no longer limited to disputes between fellow Christians; now any party, believer or not, could bring a cause of action before an ecclesiastical court. Second, a successful litigant was able to obtain state enforcement of the ecclesiastical judgment.[69] In the words of one historian: "the State admitted that the episcopal procedure was simpler, more honest, and less costly than that of its own judges, offered to disputants special advantages, and it had no hesitation in securing these for them."[70] Shortly after Augustine's election as bishop in 395 AD, Hippo became a Christian city, and Augustine assumed a vital role as the episcopal administrator of justice.[71] Because he was known to offer a speedy and just settlement in cases, Augustine frequently functioned as a judge of both judicial and administrative controversies. He was regularly involved in activities such as reconciling disputes between landlords and tenants,[72] and visiting jails where his authority was recognized to protect criminals from torture and unjust execution.[73] Devoting long hours to his judicial and administrative cases, Augustine was often required to be in his court from early morning until late afternoon.[74] Like Tertullian and Cyprian, Augustine put his legal knowledge to good use in governing the local church in Northern Africa.[75]

---

67. *See* DUCHESNE, I, 293; JEDIN, I, 332–33.

68. *See* Cyprian of Carthage, *Epistolae*, 59–61; 4 PL 369–74.

69. *See* DUCHESNE, II, 525; JEDIN, II, 5–6.

70. *See* DUCHESNE, II, 525.

71. For a discussion of the role of Augustine as "administrator" and "arbiter," *see* PETER BROWN, AUGUSTINE OF HIPPO 195–97 (University of California Press 1969).

72. *See* Augustine of Hippo, *Epistola 247*; 33 PL 1062–64.

73. *See* Possidius, *Vita S. Augustini Episcopi*, 19; 32 PL 50.

74. *See id.*

75. Like Saint Cyprian, the Bishop of Hippo also turned to the authority of Rome when confronted with a severe crisis in the local church. Learning that a Synod of Eastern Bishops might approve the ideas of Pelagius, Saint Augustine, along with several other

F. The Medieval Canonists

Although the legal form is evident from the very origins of the church, it would be overstating the issue to suggest that canon law existed in the sense of a set of complete and coherent principles of law in the early church. Not until the third quarter of the eleventh century did canon law emerge as a distinct juridical science. This medieval development permitted the use of critical scholarly methods in the formation of church law. The rediscovery of the sixth-century legal writings compiled under the Roman Emperor Justinian afforded medieval canonists direct acquaintance with the classical Roman jurists.[76] The Justinian manuscript consisted of four parts, the most important of which was the Digest, a vast collection of the opinions of Roman jurists on a diverse array of legal matters including, *inter alia*, property, wills, torts, contracts, criminal law, and citizenship.[77] The Digest, together with the other three parts—the Code, the Novels, and the Institutes—began to be called the *Corpus Iuris Civilis*.[78] At the new law schools located in Bologna, Paris, and Oxford, teachers would read the texts of the Digest and explain them line by line.[79] These explanations or "glosses" were copied by students between lines of the text, and they often spilled over into the margins. Eventually, the written glosses, commentaries, and *summae* began to take on an authority of their own. Although the classical Roman law was no longer the positive law of any state or polity, it exerted a significant influence on the development of the newly emerging system of canon law. The new system of canon law, however, did not depend primarily on the glossators of the Roman law.

During the first half of the twelfth century, a jurist, jurists, or school thereof to be identified as Gratian, composed the *Concordance of Discordant Canons*.[80]

African bishops, appealed for support to the See of Peter. Pope Innocent responded by condemning the Pelagian heresies which held that human nature was not fundamentally flawed by original sin and that salvation was to be earned by human effort alone. Thus, Augustine, like Cyprian, recognized that the Bishop of Rome constituted the final authority in the church. *See* HENRY CHADWICK, THE EARLY CHURCH 230, 239–40 (Penguin Books 1967).

76. *See* HAROLD J. BERMAN, LAW AND REVOLUTION, THE FORMATION OF THE WESTERN LEGAL TRADITION 204 (Harvard University Press 1983).

77. The Digest had disappeared in the West. *See* NICHOLAS, AN INTRODUCTION TO ROMAN LAW, 40.

78. CORPUS IURIS CIVILIS (Paul Krueger, Theodor Mommsen, Rudolf Schoell, & Wilhelm Kroll eds., 1954–1959).

79. *See* HASTINGS RASHDALL, 1 THE UNIVERSITIES OF EUROPE IN THE MIDDLE AGES 87–267 (Oxford University Press 1936). *See also* JAMES A. BRUNDAGE, THE MEDIEVAL ORIGINS OF THE LEGAL PROFESSION, CANONISTS, CIVILIANS, AND COURTS 75–125 (University of Chicago Press 2008).

80. CONCORDIA DISCORDANTIUM CANONUM. DECRETUM MAGISTRI GRATIANI, *in* 1 CORPUS IURIS CANONICI (Aemilius Friedberg ed., Editio Lipsiensis Secunda, Akademische Druck-U. Verlagsanstalt 1959). Tradition holds that Gratian was a Camaldolese monk, who was born in Chaise and resided in the monastery of SS. Felix and Nabor. Although

This work, also known as Gratian's *Decretum*, built on the collections of earlier decretalists particularly those of Burchard, Bishop of Worms (1012),[81] and Ivo, Bishop of Chartres (1095).[82] Like his predecessors, Gratian culled scriptural texts, canons of ecumenical and local councils, decrees of the popes, rules contained in various penitentials, the rediscovered Roman law, and virtually any other source that pertained to some aspect of ecclesiastical law. He collected 3800 canonical texts which he analyzed in the light of patristic, conciliar, and papal authorities, reconciling the contradictions or indicating those which he found to be irreconcilable, offering generalizations and sometimes harmonizing the generalizations.[83]

Gratian's work exemplified the new canonical methodology.[84] Borrowing from secular and theological sources, he distinguished between divine, natural, and positive law. He systematically explored the legal implications of these distinctions, and arranged the various sources of law in hierarchical order.[85] According to Gratian, divine law is the will of God reflected in revelation, especially the sacred scripture. Natural law also reflects the divine will, but in distinction to revelation, it can be discerned through the right use of human reason. Positive law is manmade law which must always be in harmony with

---

the details of his life are uncertain, a biographical sketch of Gratian appears in Stephan Kuttner, *The Father of the Science of Canon Law*, 1 THE JURIST 2–19 (1941). More recent scholarship has called Gratian's identity into question. Anders Winroth argues that there were two different version of the *Decretum* authored by two different jurists. The first "recension" of the *Decretum* dates to sometime after 1139 while the second recension dates to 1150 at the latest. The second recension includes extracts from the CORPUS JURIS CIVILIS not included in the first recension which does not evidence great familiarity with the Roman law. *See* ANDERS WINROTH, THE MAKING OF GRATIAN'S DECRETUM (Cambridge University Press 2000).

81. Burchard made one of the earliest attempts to compile all the laws of the church into a single book. He arranged his vast collection not chronologically but according to various subjects such as the sacraments, crimes, spiritual and corporal works of mercy, and the contemplation derived from ascetic life. *See* Burchard of Worms, DECRETORUM; 140 PL 539–1058.

82. Like Burchard, Ivo compiled a vast collection of laws with commentary in order to unite canon law "into one body." Ivo, Bishop of Chartes, *Epistola XXXV;* 162 PL 46–47. An analysis of the canonists and theologians upon whom Gratian relied is provided in STANLEY CHODOROW, CHRISTIAN POLITICAL THEORY AND CHURCH POLITICS IN THE MID-TWELFTH CENTURY: THE ECCLESIOLOGY OF GRATIAN'S DECRETUM 2, n. 3 (University of California Press 1972).

83. *See* BERMAN, LAW AND REVOLUTION, 143–48.

84. For a study of the originality of Gratian's method in dealing with the sources of law and its connection to scholasticism, *see* Jean Gaudemet, *La doctrine des sources du droit dans le Decret de Gratien*, 1 REVUE DE DROIT CANONIQUE 6 (1951).

85. *See* D. IX, c. 1.

divine and natural law.[86] Custom must yield both to natural law and to positive law.[87] On the basis of these distinctions, Gratian differentiated between immutable principles of eternal validity and elements of law which had been suggested by the particular circumstances of time, place, and persons.[88]

The relation between medieval canon law and Roman law sheds further light on the methodology of the medieval canonists.[89] First, while the *Corpus Iuris Canonici* was to some extent patterned on the *Corpus Iuris Civilis*, the former differed from the latter in large part because it embraced the new scholastic methodology.[90] The schoolmen of the medieval universities, whether theologians, philosophers, or canonists, shared the *fides quaerens intellectum*.[91] United in the commitment to enhance the faith, the medieval thinkers sought to achieve a coherent system of general principles, concepts, and rules through the use of inductive and deductive reasoning.[92] In contrast, the Roman jurists, in the words of one scholar, had been primarily concerned with "the consistent and orderly treatment of individual cases . . . [and] [t]heir whole impulse was towards economy, not of language, but of ideas."[93] The glosses of the new centers of legal study of the eleventh and twelfth centuries formed a complex system of abstract concepts which the medieval canonists considered to be implicit in the narrow rules and settlements of particular cases offered by the classical Roman jurists.[94]

---

86. *See id.* Divine law may be either natural or positive. Thomas Aquinas held that human positive law is derived from divine or natural law in two ways: first, as a deduction from general principles, and second, through *determinatio*. Aquinas compared the process of *determinatio* to that of an architect building a house. The architect has a general idea of the house, and its particular specification could be reasonably built in a variety of different ways. *See* ST I–II, 95, 2, corpus; 99, 3, ad 2; 104, 1, corpus.

87. *See* D. XI, cc. 1–4.

88. *See* D. IX, dicta post c. 9.

89. *See generally* Berman, *Law and Revolution*, 120–64; Albert-M. Gauthier, O.P., *On the Use of Roman Law in Canon Law*, *in* Unico Ecclesiae Servitio: Canonical Studies Presented to Germain Lesage, O.M.I., on the Occasion of His 75th Birthday and of the 50th Anniversary of His Presbyteral Ordination 53–67 (Faculty of Canon Law, St. Paul University 1991). *Cf.* Robert E. Rodes, Jr., Ecclesiastical Administration in Medieval England: The Anglo-Saxons to the Reformation 66 (University of Notre Dame Press 1977), where Rodes argues that the method and substance of the new canon law was appropriated directly or indirectly from the Roman jurists.

90. *See* Charles P. Sherman, *A Brief History of Medieval Roman Canon Law*, 39 Canadian Law Times 638 (1919).

91. *See generally* David Knowles, O.S.B., The Evolution of Medieval Thought 153–84 (Helicon Press 1962).

92. *See* Stephan Kuttner, Harmony from Dissonance: An Interpretation of Medieval Canon Law 15–16, *passim* (Archabbey Press 1960).

93. John P. Dawson, The Oracles of Law 114 (University of Michigan Press 1968).

94. *See* Hermann Kantorowicz, *The Quaestiones Disputatae of the Glossators*, 16 Tijdschrift voor Rechtsgeschiednis/Revue d'histoire du droit 5 (1939).

The new method, for example, constructed a theory of contract law out of the particular Roman cases and rules that concerned contracts; it elaborated doctrines of justification for the use of force; and, it established the legal foundations for the necessity of private property. Consistent with the scholastic methodology, the medieval jurists would attempt to transform the classical Roman law into a comprehensive legal system.[95]

Second, Roman law was considered by its practitioners and adherents to be fixed, immutable, and finished; classical jurists did not recognize custom as a source of law, and even when it was recognized as such by Justinian, it played only a minor role in practice.[96] "The primary task of the Roman jurists as they conceived it was to provide solutions for cases that had arisen or might arise, testing and revising their central ideas by observing their effects on particular cases."[97] Canon law, instead, had the characteristic of organic development. Although canonists shared the classicists' deep respect for tradition, they continually attempted to incorporate into the juridic structure of the law the ecclesiological perspective of the church as mystical communion. Moreover, the canonists' task was necessarily an ongoing one as it was open to the dynamic action of divine grace in human history. The ability of the medieval canonists to assimilate both immutable principles and history into the corpus of law became the foundation of the modern Western legal tradition.[98]

The *Corpus Iuris Canonici* was established officially in 1580 by Pope Gregory XIII, as consisting of the following decretals: (1) Gratian's *Decretum* (c. 1140), (2) Pope Gregory IX's *Decretales* (1234), (3) Pope Boniface VIII's *Liber Sextus Decretalium* (1298), (4) Pope Clement V's *Clementinae* (1305–1314), and (5) those decretals issued by the Council of Vienne (1314), and transmitted to the universities by Pope John XXII in 1317. In addition, although not an official part of the text, John XXII's *Collectio Viginti Extravagantium* and the *Extravagantes Communes* (1316–1364) are usually considered to be part of the *Corpus Iuris Canonici*. In his treatment of the medieval canon law, Frederic W. Maitland described each of the decretals of Gregory IX, Boniface VIII, and John XXII as a "statute book deriving its force from the pope who published it, and who being pope was competent to ordain binding statutes for the catholic church and every part thereof . . ."[99]

---

95. *See* Gabriel Le Bras, *Canon Law, in* The Legacy of the Middle Ages 325–26 (C. G. Crump & E. F. Jacob eds., Oxford University Press 1926); Carl J. Friedrich, Transcendent Justice: The Religious Dimension of Constitutionalism 1–26 (Duke University Press 1964); Berman, Law and Revolution, 199–224.

96. *See* Herbert F. Jolowicz, Roman Foundations of Modern Law 21 (Oxford University Press 1957).

97. Dawson, The Oracles of Law, 117.

98. *See* Berman, Law and Revolution, 204–05.

99. Frederick W. Maitland, Roman Canon Law in the Church of England 3 (Burt Franklin 1968).

However, the canons of the decretals include more than statutory law. They are often papal decisions given in particular cases which were brought on appeal to the pope or papal responses to questions posed by bishops.

II. CONTEMPORARY CANON LAW AND THE RULE OF LAW

Until the twentieth century, the foundational body of canon law remained the medieval *Corpus Iuris Canonici*, a vast collection of canonical and theological materials that, even in the 1582 edition approved by Pope Gregory XIII, could hardly have been said to constitute a coherent unitary codification of law for the universal church. The modern form of canon law developed during the twentieth century. A twentieth-century commentator, Amleto Cardinal Cicognani, described canon law as "the body of laws made by the lawful ecclesiastical authority for the government of the Church."[100] Cicognani distinguished between the "strict sense" of canon law as the law enacted by the pope for the universal church and the "wide sense" as designating "laws which Bishops and other inferior legislators are empowered to make for the government of their own territory."[101]

A. Twentieth-Century Codifications

The nineteenth- and early part of the twentieth-century law of the European nation-states has been termed "the age of codification."[102] The modern development of canon law reflected the codification movement. On March 4, 1904, Pope Pius X announced the creation of a commission of cardinals to design one authoritative collection of canon law for the Latin Church. The monumental task of producing the first modern codification of canon law took thirteen years to complete. The drafting process included a series of consultations with bishops and religious superiors throughout the world as well as a method of examining the responses from the consultation and synthesizing them with the relevant provisions of the then extant ancient, medieval, and modern canon law. Cardinal Pietro Gasparri accomplished the lion's share of this prodigious work. The first modern codification of canon law was promulgated by the successor to Pius X, Pope Benedict XV, on Pentecost Sunday, May 27, 1917, and went into effect the following Pentecost, May 19, 1918. The so-called Pio-Benedictine Code consisted of 2414 canons that were divided into five books: *General Norms, Persons, Things, Procedures, and Penalties.* Consistent with the wider developments in approaches

---

100. Amleto Giovani Cicognani, Canon Law 43 (2nd ed. rev. Newman Bookshop 1934).
101. *Id.*
102. Manlio Bellomo, The Common Legal Past of Europe, 1 (Lydia G. Cochrane trans., Catholic University Press 1995), which traces the emergence and decline of the codification movement in European law.

to legal systems at the start of the twentieth century, the *CIC-1917* represented a central, coherent, and clear system of law for the Latin Church.

As with any system of codified law, the *CIC-1917* required periodic revision. Pope Benedict established the Pontifical Commission for the Interpretation of the Code of Canon Law to incorporate revisions, modifications, abrogations, deletions, and additions to the *CIC-1917.* Canon law evolves as it attempts to respond to concrete circumstances not contemplated or provided for by the legislative authority in the original codification. In the decades following the promulgation of the *CIC-1917,* new statutes along with interpretations and clarifications of the existing statutes grew so numerous that eventually the printed volume in which they appeared was more lengthy than the original 1917 statute. In 1932, for example, the Congregation for the Sacraments issued the Instruction *Provida mater,* which revised regulations on the annulment of marriage.[103] On February 2, 1947, Pope Pius XII established new law for the regulation of secular institutes.[104] By the midpoint of the twentieth century, canon law was once again developing into a somewhat confusing and unwieldy body of law. Not only changes in the law itself, but also new theological and pastoral insights called for a revised code.[105]

On January 25, 1959, at the Basilica of Saint Paul Outside the Walls, Pope John XXIII announced his intention to convoke an Ecumenical Council. At the same moment that he proposed Vatican II, the pontiff also called for the necessary revision of the Code of Canon Law. From the outset, the revision of the canon law was thus linked to the ecclesial reform set in motion by the Ecumenical Council. Although Pope John XXIII inaugurated the process when he established the Pontifical Commission for the Revision of the Code of Canon Law after the first session of Vatican II, the task of revision was delayed until the completion of the Ecumenical Council. A few days prior to the formal close of the Council in November 1965, Pope Paul VI appointed seventy consultors to assist the cardinal members of the Pontifical Commission. Pope Paul VI insisted that the revised Code of Canon Law would "accommodate canon law to the *new way of thinking* of Vatican II."[106] This new way of thinking concerned the nature and end of canon law. For Pope Paul VI, the nature of canon law was "to express more clearly the

---

103. *See* Sacra Congregatio De Disciplina Sacramentorum, Instructio, *Provida Mater* (Die 1 mensis iullii anno 1932), 28 AAS 313–72 (1936), although the Instruction is dated July 1, 1932, official publication in AAS occurred on August 15, 1936.

104. *See* Pius Pp. XII, Constitutio Apostolica, *Provida Mater Ecclesia* (Die 2 mensis febraurii anno 1947), 39 AAS 114–24 (1947).

105. *See* Paul Winniger, *A Pastoral Canon Law, in* 48 The Future of Canon Law, Concilium 51–65 (Paulist Press 1969).

106. Paulus Pp. VI, *Ad E.mos Patres Cardinales et ad Consultores Pontificii Consilii Codici Iurs Canonici recognoscendo* (Die 20 mensis novembris anno 1965), 57 AAS 985–89 (1965) ("scilicet accommodari debet novo mentis habitui, Concillii Oecumenici Vaticani Secundi proprio").

doctrinal and disciplinary thrust of the Council."[107] Canon law was to have a theological and pastoral nature. It was to reflect gospel charity and canonical equity. It was to serve as assistance to the people of God in knowing God's saving mysteries. Not only would the new law afford an ordered ecclesial life, but its ultimate end remained the salvation of souls.

The process for the revision of the new Code of Canon Law spanned two decades. It involved numerous consultations with bishops, religious superiors, theologians, and canonists throughout the church. It was informed by exegetical, historical, comparative, and textual criticism. The methodology was intended to incorporate the various theological and pastoral perspectives evident in the official documents of Vatican II. Although a great deal of this work was completed during the pontificate of Pope Paul VI, his successor, Pope John Paul II, guided the final years of the revision process. Shortly after he was elected to the Petrine ministry, John Paul II affirmed the nexus between Vatican II and the new Code of Canon Law. He desired that the church's law reflect the ecclesiology of Vatican II.[108] On January 25, 1983, twenty-four years to the date of John XXIII's announcement, John Paul II promulgated the revised Code of Canon Law for the Latin Church. The Code went into effect with force of law on the first Sunday of Advent, November 27, 1983. The *CIC-1983* consists of 1752 canons, organized into seven books: *General Norms, The People of God, The Teaching Function of the Church, The Sanctifying Function of the Church, The Temporal Goods of the Church, Sanctions in the Church, and Processes.* One notes how much better these titles reflect the mission of the church than did those of the *CIC-1917*, which were derived from the *Code Napoleon*. In a testament to the unity of law and theology, John Paul II referred to the *CIC-1983* as "the final document of Vatican II."[109]

Even as the revision for the *CIC-1983* was underway, Pope Paul VI had also called for a Code of Canon Law for the Eastern churches. Earlier in the twentieth century, the benefits of the *CIC-1917* encouraged discussion about a similar codification of Eastern canon law. In 1927, Pope Pius XI established a preparatory commission, and in 1935, the Pontifical Commission for the Redaction of Eastern Canon Law. Based upon a 1948 draft prepared by the commission, Pope Pius XII promulgated four parts of the new canon law for the Eastern churches, but the pontiff ultimately promulgated only 1574 of the proposed 2666 canons proposed by the commission. Pope John XXIII apparently elected not to promulgate the remaining canons in light of the desire that the Eastern canon law, in accord

---

107. Paulus Pp. VI, *Ad Praelotos Auditores et Officiales Tribunales Sacrae Romanae Rotae* (Die 29 mensis ianuarii anno 1970), 62 AAS 111–18 (1970).

108. *See* Ioannnes Paulus Pp. II, *Ad eos qui plenario coetui Pontificiae Commissionis Codici Iuris Canonici recognoscendo interfuere admissos* (Die 29 mensis octobris anno 1981), 73 AAS 720, 721 (1981).

109. Ioannes Paulus Pp. II, *Il Diritto inserisce il Concilio nella nostra vita,* 15 COMMUNICATIONES 128 (1983).

with its Western counterpart, reflect the ecclesiastical renewal of Vatican II. On June 10, 1972, Pope Paul VI established the Pontifical Commission for the Revision of the Code of Eastern Canon Law. The preparation of the Eastern Code involved a process of consultations and critical methodology similar to that employed for the *CIC-1983*. On October 18, 1990, Pope John Paul promulgated the *CCEO*. The *CCEO* acquired force of law on October 1, 1991. It contains 1546 canons that are divided into thirty *titles* in accord with the classical division of ancient Eastern canonical collections. The *CCEO* witnesses to the diversity and unity of the Catholic Church, which consists of the communion of particular churches. At the same time, the promulgation of the *CCEO* in the last decade of the twentieth century testifies to the church's continuing commitment to codifications of universal canon law.

B. Other Sources and Types of Canon Law

The *CIC-1983* and the *CCEO* constitute universal law in the Catholic Church. The very first canon of *CIC-1983* indicates that this Code is the universal law for the Latin Church.[110] Likewise, the *CCEO* constitutes universal law for all the individual churches that comprise the Eastern Church. Both of these Codes were promulgated by the Roman Pontiff, who is "the Supreme Legislator" in the church. Although the Western and Eastern Codes constitute the two major bodies of universal law in the Catholic Church, canon law also exists in a variety of other forms.

1. Legislative, Executive, and Judicial Power Legislative power in the Catholic Church is not limited to the Roman Pontiff. The bishops assembled at an Ecumenical Council may exercise the legislative power as a college with the Roman Pontiff at its head.[111] The diocesan bishop may promulgate law for his own diocese.[112] The general and provincial chapters of religious communities may also issue binding norms with regard to the life of the religious community.[113] Depending on the religious communities' own constitutions and statutes, major religious superiors may likewise issue norms for their subjects in the community.[114]

The broader meaning of canon law is also clear from the fact that the power of governance in canon law is not limited to legislative acts. Canon 135, Paragraph 1, of the *CIC-1983* states: "The power of governance is distinguished into legislative, executive and judicial."[115] The three functions are understood to flow from

---

110. *See also* Canon 12, § 1, *CIC-1983*, which states that this universal law of the Latin Church binds all Catholics for whom it was intended.

111. *See* Canon 337, § 1, *CIC-1983*.

112. *See* Canon 391, § 1 & 2, *CIC-1983* ("The bishop exercises legislative power himself."); & Canon 466 ("The diocesan bishop is the sole legislator in the diocesan synod.").

113. *See* Canon 631, § 1, *CIC-1983*.

114. *See* Canon 622, *CIC-1983*.

115. 1 Communicationes 83 (1969).

one sacred power of governance which is vested in a bishop.[116] Accordingly, canon law declines to adopt the modern democratic doctrine of the separation of powers.[117] Nonetheless, the distinction of functions has long been a feature of church governance. Historical evidence indicates that at least as early as the sixth century, bishops were delegating their judicial power to separate judges.[118] Likewise, the exercise of executive power by the vicar general on behalf of the bishop claims ancient historical roots.[119] When the *CIC-1917* stipulated the powers of governance that are proper to a bishop, it delineated legislative, judicial, and coercive powers.[120] The recognition of the tripartite distinction in

---

116. The question of who may exercise the power of governance is too theologically and canonically complex to be explored in this overview of canon law. Suffice it to mention that the *CIC-1983* provides for the following. In addition to the diocesan bishop, the priest who serves as the vicar general, episcopal vicar, or judicial vicar exercises a limited power of governance according to office. The priest who serves as an ordinary in a religious community may make law, posit acts of executive power, and judge cases. A lay person may serve as one of three judges of a collegiate tribunal.

117. This understanding conflicts with the modern secular political theory that assigns each of the three functions to a separate office or branch of the government. It should be noted, however, that given the complexities of modern government, a complete separation seems neither possible nor desirable. Thus, the executive branch of a government may routinely develop rules for the administration of certain entitlements. At the same time, the case decisions of the judicial branch may have binding force of law. *See* Peter L. Strauss, *An Introduction to Administrative Justice in the United States, in* 1 ADMINISTRATIVE LAW: THE PROBLEM OF JUSTICE, ANGLO AMERICAN AND NORDIC SYSTEMS 501 (Giuffrè 1991).

118. *See* JUSTINIAN, *Novellae,* 123, a cura di R. Schoell et G. Kroll, 3 CORPUS IURIS CIVILIS (Apud Weidmannos, 1929).

119. *See* X., Lib. I, Tit. 28, "De officio vicarii." Pursuant to *CIC-1983,* Canon 131, §§ 1–2 and Canon 134, § 1, the power of the vicar general is ordinary and vicarious.

120. *See* Canon 335, § 1, of the *CIC-1917,* specified the Latin terms "legislativa, iudiciaria, coactiva." The corresponding canon in the present Code replaces "coactiva" with "exsecutiva," thus reflecting the general norm on the distinction among the powers of governance expressed in Canon 135, § 1. *See also* Canon 391, § 1. The division in Canon 335, § 1 of the *CIC-1917* was not intended to be technical in nature, but rather descriptive of the power of governance proper to a diocesan bishop. *See* Zenon Grocholewski, *Atti e ricorsi amministrativi,* 57 APOLLINARIS 264 (1984). *See also* Francisco J. Urrutia, S.J., *La potestà amministrativa secondo il diritto canonico, in* PIO FEDELE, MOD., DE IUSTITIA ADMINISTRATIVA IN ECCLESIA 90 and note 35 (Officium Libri Catholici 1984). The same author has also noted that "[i]f it [Canon 335, § 1] stated the power of coercion alongside judicial and legislative powers, it was, in all probability, to assert those functions of episcopal power that were more contested by secular authorities for over one century." Francisco J. Urrutia, S.J., *Administrative Power in the Church According to the Code of Canon Law,* 20 STUDIA CANONICA, 254, note 2 (1986). Commentators on *the CIC-1917* developed various schema to delineate the distinction of functions. *See* BENEDICT OJETTI, S.J., DE ROMANA CURIA 18–24 (Apud Universitatem Gregorianam 1910); FELIX M. CAPPELLO, S.J., DE CURIA ROMANA IUXTA REFORMATIONEM A PIO X 40–52 (Fridericus Pustet 1911). In 1925, Pope Pius XI

the *CIC-1983* acknowledges that canon law encompasses more than statutory law derived from the exercise of legislative power.

Title 3, "General Decrees and Instructions," of Book 1 of the *CIC-1983* recognizes two types of general decrees rooted in the distinction between legislative and executive power. Canon 29 states that a general decree is a proper law given by a competent legislator to a community capable of receiving a law. A proper law may be described as a norm: (1) that is abstract and general in application, (2) that is not framed to provide an answer to a specific problem, and (3) that is adopted in anticipation of a future circumstance.[121] Issuing a general decree, which is proper law, requires legislative power. Canon 31 establishes a second type of general decree which does not require legislative power but executive power.[122] A general executive decree is issued by one who possesses executive power within the limits of his competency. This second type of general decree would include instructions, interpretations of law, protocols, guidelines, and policies to interpret and apply a proper law. These might be described as supporting documents, which, nonetheless, have obligatory effect since they constitute official explanations of what compliance with the law entails. While general decrees are legislative acts that constitute autonomous proper law, general executive decrees comprise auxiliary documents aimed at the maintenance of proper law in the community for which they are intended. In addition, canon law recognizes the exercise of executive power by hierarchical superiors through single administrative acts. For example, a single administrative act might involve the transfer of a parish priest to another parish by the diocesan bishop. This administrative act of executive power differs from an act of judicial power.

Title 2 of Book 7 of the *CIC-1983*, the "Different Grades and Kinds of Tribunals," establishes a system of courts, judges, trials, and appeals in the Roman Catholic Church. As with the legislative and judicial powers, canon law considers the judicial power of government to be vested in the office of bishop. Canons 1419, 1420, and 1421 require each diocesan bishop to establish a diocesan tribunal. The diocesan tribunal is presided over by the bishop's judicial vicar and a college of judges. Canon 1427 recognizes the judicial power of major religious superiors over their subjects. Canons 1438 through 1441 require the establishment of tribunals of second instance which hear appeals from the sentences of the diocesan tribunals. At the level of the Holy See, Canon 1442 refers to the

---

attributed to Christ a threefold royal power: legislative, judicial, and executive; *see Quas primas* (Die 11 mensis decembris anno1925), 17 AAS 599 (1925).

121. *See* Willy Onclin, *L'organisation des pouvoirs dans L'Église,* Actes du Congrés de Droit canonique: cinquantenaire de la Faculté de droit canonique, *Paris, 22–26 avril 1947* 371 (Letouzey et Ané, 1950); Willy Onclin, *The Church Society and the Organization of Its Powers,* 27 Jurist 13–14 (1967); Urrutia, *Administrative Power in the Church,* 255–56, and note 5.

122. *See* 9 Communicationes 232 (1977).

Roman Pontiff as the "Supreme Judge" of the universal church. According to Canon 1444, the Roman Pontiff exercises his judicial power through the Roman Rota, which hears appeals from the tribunals of second instance. Canon 1445 provides that appeals from the Roman Rota be heard by the Apostolic Signatura as the supreme tribunal in the church.

2. Universal and Particular Law In addition to the tripartite distinction of the powers of governance, canon law distinguishes between universal and particular law. The *CIC-1983* and *CCEO* are prototypical universal law but not the only examples. Universal law may be made by an Ecumenical Council, the Roman Pontiff, the College of Bishops with the Roman Pontiff at its head, the bishops of the Eastern Church with the approval of the Roman Pontiff, or arguably by a Dicastery of the Roman Curia acting in the name of the Roman Pontiff and with his approval.[123] In addition to the Codes, the Roman Pontiff promulgates other universal laws, such as the special law *Universi Dominici gregis*, a statute promulgated by John Paul II in 1996 which regulated the election of his successor.[124] In 1988, John Paul promulgated *Pastor Bonus*, which regulates the jurisdictional competencies of the various branches of the Roman Curia.[125] The 1998 document *Ad tuendam fidem* added a section to the text of Canon 750, *CIC-1983*, and Canon 598, *CCEO*, concerning the teaching authority of the church.[126] The *motu proprio*, issued by Pope Benedict XVI on July 7, 2007, which permitted the celebration of the Tridentine Mass, constitutes another example of universal law promulgated by the Roman Pontiff.[127]

Particular laws are laws directed to a specific portion of the people of God. Section 1 of Canon 13, *CIC-1983*, states the presumption that particular laws are geographic. A particular law is geographic if it pertains to all those persons who live in a particular geographic territory. For example, a particular law might

---

123. *See* Ioannes Paulus Pp. II, *Constitutio Apostolica Pastor Bonus* (Die 28 mensis jun. anno 1988), 80 AAS 1178–81 (1988). *Pastor Bonus*, 18, states that "[t]he dicasteries cannot issue laws or general decrees having force of law or derogate from the prescriptions of current universal law, unless in individual cases and with the specific approval of the Supreme Pontiff."

124. *See* Ioannes Paulus Pp. II, *Constitutio Apostolica Universi Dominici Gregis* (Die 22 mensis feb. anno 1996), 88 AAS 305–42 (1996). This law issued by Pope John Paul II had permitted election of the Roman Pontiff by the College of Cardinals by a simple majority vote after several days of inconclusive balloting. Pope Benedict XVI, by a *motu proprio*, dated June 11, 2007, amended the law so as to require a two-thirds majority for election in all cases.

125. *See Pastor Bonus*, 1178–81.

126. *See* Ioannes Paulus Pp. II, *Ad tuendam fidem Motu Proprio* (Die 1 mensis iul. anno 1998), 90 AAS 457–61 (1998). The new legislation also added disciplinary provisions to Canon 1371 of the *CIC-1983* and Canon 1436 of the *CCEO*.

127. *See* Benedictus Pp. XVI, *Summorum Pontificum Motu Proprio* (Die 7 mensis iul. anno 2007), 99 AAS 795–99 (2007).

modify the requirements of universal law with regard to holy days of obligation or for fast and abstinence in a specific geographic region. Although particular law tends to be geographic, some persons in the geographic area covered by the particular may be exempt from it. Consider, for example, a particular law for a Latin diocese that does not obligate Eastern Catholics who happen to live in the geographic area of the diocese. Alternatively, a particular law may be personal. Personal particular law pertains to the members of a special group. For example, juridic persons are entitled to establish their own statutes (particular law) that must be approved by the competent ecclesiastical authority.[128] The individual Eastern churches enjoy the right to make their own particular law. Likewise, diocesan bishops have the legislative power to promulgate particular law for their dioceses.[129]

3. Custom as a Source of Law Custom has long been recognized in the church as a valid source of canon law. The principal difference between promulgated law and custom is that promulgated law flows from a proper ecclesiastical authority who enjoys legislative power, while custom derives from the community.[130] Custom is often unwritten, but the fact that it is written down would not change its character as custom. Canon 26, *CIC-1983*, stipulates that a custom which is contrary to promulgated law obtains the force of law only after it has been observed for thirty continuous and complete years. The canon also permits a centenary (one hundred continuous and complete years) or immemorial custom (as long as anyone in the community can remember) to prevail against a provision of promulgated law even when the provision contains a clause that prohibits future customs. Any community that is capable of receiving law in the church is also capable of forming a custom. Although the clear development of canon law during the twentieth century has been through the process of codification, the fact that canon law continues to recognize custom as a legitimate source of law attests to the dignity that the canonical tradition attributes to the role of local communities.

4. International Law The Holy See is an international juridic person whose territory of the Vatican City State enjoys sovereignty under international law.[131] Canon 3, *CIC-1983*, recognizes the right of the Holy See to enter into treaties and pacts that enjoy force of law. An agreement between the Holy See and a sovereign state is known as a *concordat*. There are also partial agreements between the Holy See and other international bodies known as accords, *modi vivendi*, or protocols that enjoy the force of law. Such agreements may secure the rights of the church in a particular country to worship, education, property, and the

---

128. *See* Canon 117, *CIC-1983*.

129. *See* Canon 391, § 1, *CIC-1983*.

130. *See* Javier Otaduy, *Custom*, *in* 1 NAVARRA-2004, 393–96.

131. *See* Robert John Araujo, S.J., *The International Personality and Sovereignty of the Holy See*, 50 CATH. U. L. REV. 291–360 (2001).

regulation of marriage. Pursuant to a concordat with the Holy See, a national government may enjoy the right to be notified of the appointment of a bishop prior to its official announcement. While they may be properly described as constituting valid law, such agreements, nonetheless, do not depend for their validity on the Code of Canon Law.

5. The Canonization of Civil Law Canon 22, *CIC-1983*, recognizes that canon law yields to civil law in certain instances. This is known as the limited "canonization" of the civil law.[132] To mention but one example, Section 1 of Canon 1282, *CIC-1983*, requires that state statutes of labor law and policy be meticulously observed together with the church's own social teaching in the employment policies of church organizations and agencies. The church entity as an employer is thus bound by canon law to follow the civil legislation that might, for example, establish a minimum wage or social security. Of course, it may well be the case that the social teaching of the church requires even greater benefits than those required by the law of the state. Canon law does not yield to civil law in general, but only in certain matters defined by the canon law itself. Canon 22, *CIC-1983*, requires that the effects of civil law be observed in canon law with the same effects, and in this sense, the effects of the civil law are "canonized." In other words, the effects of the specific civil law become part of the canon law. However, the canon law sometimes defers to the effects of civil law without incorporating the civil law into canon law. For example, Canon 110, *CIC-1983*, requires canon law to respect the civil effects of adoption. This means that all the effects of the parent-child relationship are recognized in canon law such as the capacity of minors and their legal domicile, the responsibility of parents for the child's reception of the sacraments and education, and the impediments to marriage that arises from a familial relationship.[133] Although respecting the civil effects of adoption, the canon law is not incorporating the entirety of state policy and its adoption law into the law of the church.

The relation between canon law and civil law is complex, and here I shall mention only a few further aspects of the complexity. If the civil law conflicts with canon law based upon divine or natural law, the civil law obviously is not canonized. However, even when a particular application of canon law, which reflects divine law, conflicts with civil law, the nature of the obligation may determine which of them is followed. Consider the question: "Should I drive on a suspended license if that is the only way to go to Church in order to fulfill the Sunday Mass obligation?"[134] The civil law requiring a valid license is not contrary to divine law; rather, it is a reasonable requirement directed toward the common

---

132. *See* Robert T. Kennedy, *Contracts and Especially Alienation, in* CLSA-2000, 1493.

133. *See* Canons 98, § 2; 105, § 1; 851 §2; 855; 867; 869, § 3, 872, 874, § 1; 890, 891, 1136, 793, 795–98, 774, § 2; 1252, 1094; & 108, *CIC-1983*. *See also* Amadeo de Fuenmayor, *The Canonical Status of Physical Persons, in* 1 NAVARRA-2004, 735–36.

134. *See* Canons 1246–48, *CIC-1983*.

good. Although the Sunday obligation reflects divine law, it does excuse one from the obligation of the civil law requiring a driver to have a valid license. If canon law and civil law conflict, and the canon law is merely ecclesiastical law, the canon law would not oblige in the case when obeying it would cause grave inconvenience. Again, neither the conflicting civil law itself nor its effects would be canonized.

6. Liturgical Law The *CIC-1983* and *CCEO* contain some, but not all, of the rules that govern the celebration of the church's liturgy and sacraments.[135] Book 4 of the *CIC-1983* and Title 16 of the *CCEO* contain rules that pertain to the celebration of the sacraments with regard to issues such as who is a qualified minister, who is an eligible recipient, the matter and form, and under what circumstances the sacraments may be celebrated.[136] The rules and rubrics found chiefly in the official Roman liturgical books also govern the celebration of the sacraments. There are also non-Roman rites in both the Eastern and Latin churches with their own proper liturgical laws. The liturgical books themselves are considered to form part of canon law and to constitute norms with full canonical force. However, it must be kept in mind that some of the liturgical norms are facultative in that they offer a variety of options or nonpreceptive in that they are only directive guidelines. This variety is one of the reasons why the liturgical norms are not encoded in the universal law. Such norms do not easily fit into the meaning of proper law as it is described in Canons 29–34, *CIC-1983*.

C. Canonical Equity, Dispensation, Exception, and Privilege

1. Canonical Equity The *Dictionnaire de Droit Canonique* offers various descriptions of the concept of equity. Equity is "the application of objective justice to a concrete case." It arises because "the rules that a society imposes on its members, in order to protect the common good and promote justice, figure as too general in conception to deal with all the particular instances that fall under their scope." "Justice is the ideal," and "equity serves as the means for the realization of the ideal in practice." Equity is constituted from "the benevolent interpretation of written law by judges, administrators, and superiors." It is "a relative notion which reckons a superior principle of justice or of moderation in the application of law."[137] In connection to canon law, the same source defines

---

135. *See* Canon 2, *CIC-1983*.

136. *See* Eloy Tejero, *The Sanctifying Office in the Church, in* 3/1 NAVARRA-2004, 382–89.

137. (". . . l'application de la justice objective à un cas concret.") (". . . la vie de société impose à l'homme la détermination de certaines lois positives destinées à assurer, en tenant compte des nécessités de l'ordre [bonum], cette même justice [aequum]. Mais ces règles, forcément générales, négligent par le fait même les circonstances particulières dans lesquelles s'en opérera l'application.") ("La justice est l'idéal; l'équité la réalise dans la pratique . . .") (". . . l'équité sera l'interprétation bienveillante de la loi écrite par les

equity as "a superior justice to the positive law, which on account of the spiritual general or particular well-being mitigates the severity of law."[138]

Canonical equity enjoys a rich historical development. For the purpose of this general overview, suffice it to mention that the notion of canonical equity includes both the ideals of natural justice and evangelical mercy. Canonical equity points to the limits of the law. Attempting to convey the law's inner meaning, the outer juridical formulation of the law may fall short in a given instance. Canonical equity is the juridical principle that functions to bridge the gap between the letter and the spirit of the law.[139]

Canonical equity may be written or unwritten. Written equity is expressed in the statute itself, and the *CIC-1983* contains seven instances of expressed written equity.[140] For example, Canon 19 of the *CIC-1983* identifies canonical equity as a source of suppletory law when a *lacuna* of law exists. Written equity may also be implied from the meaning of a statute. Implicit written equity is referred to as the equitable character of the statute. Unwritten canonical equity is an appeal to the intent of the legislator when a literal application of law would violate that intent. Canon law presumes that certain qualities remain characteristic of the mind of the lawgiver. Among these characteristics are the intention to be intelligent and humane, to act in conformity with the common good, to follow divine law on the basis of faith, to conform with the requirements of natural law through the use of practical reason, and to imitate the charity, mercy, and love of Christ. Confronted with an unjust or uncharitable result from the application of law, canonical equity permits one vested with governing power to correct the problem on the ground that such a correction reflects the intent of the lawgiver. Unwritten equity also informs those who are vested with discretion in the exercise of the governing power.

Both Canon 20, *CIC-1917*, and Canon 19, *CIC-1983*, stipulate that canonical equity ought not to be utilized as a suppletory norm in a penal matter. There would seem to be at least two reasons for the exception of the penal law. First, Book 6 of the *CIC-1983* envisions the imposition of a penalty as a last remedy, after all other pastoral and juridical options have been exhausted. Such an occasion generally calls for a rigorous and strict justice. Indeed, it has been suggested that if one resorted to an application of canonical equity, rather than

---

magistrats, juges ou supérieurs . . .") (". . . une notion relative . . . ils tiennent compte dans l'application d'une loi d'un principe supérieur de justice ou de modération.") Charles Lefebvre, "Équité," in 5 Dictionnaire de Droit Canonique col. 394 (sous la direction de R. Naz Letouzey et Ane 1953).

138. ("L'équité consiste dans une justice supérieure qui, en raison d'un bien spirituel général ou particulier, adoucit les droits stricts . . .") Lefebvre, "Équité," col. 400.

139. *See* Coughlin, *Canonical Equity*, 403–35.

140. *See* Canons 19, 221, § 2, 271, § 3, 686, § 3, 702, § 2, 1148, § 3, and 1752, *CIC-1983*.

soften the rigor of law, it would "sometimes increase certain penalties."[141] Second, when a penalty must be imposed, it should be the one prescribed by law. Pursuant to the *CIC-1983*, Canon 1314, the law prefers *ferendae sententiae* to *latae sententiae* penalties. The requirement that the penalty be imposed attests to the legislator's intent that the matter be clear and no suppletory norm be necessary. Finally, the exclusion of canonical equity as a suppletory norm for penal matters does not eliminate justice, mercy, and compassion from the consideration. The purpose of the ecclesiastical penal law is not to punish, but to protect the integrity of the faith community and to urge the offender to reform.[142]

The stipulation of canonical equity as a suppletory source to fill a *lacuna legis* is not to suggest that it should serve as a general norm for the interpretation of all laws. Neither Canon 17, *CIC-1983*, nor Canon 18, *CIC-1917*, which concern the general interpretation of law, mention canonical equity. At the same time, both of these canons recognize the mind of the legislator as a valid source for the interpretation of law. To be sure, it seems fair to surmise that the tradition of authentic canonical equity comports with the mind of the Supreme Legislator. Thus, there is a tension present in the *CIC-1983* between the fact that the lawgiver has omitted to identify canonical equity as a source for the interpretation of the law and the fact that canonical equity must be said to constitute an aspect of the mind of the lawgiver. It seems correct, however, to surmise that the lawgiver intends an interpretation of law in accord with the requirements of natural justice, evangelical love, and historical consciousness of the tradition. The incorporation of evangelical mercy into the notion of canonical equity differentiates canon law from systems of law that view equity as based only on natural justice.

2. Dispensation, Exception, and Privilege This difference between canon law and secular systems of law is further evident in the canonical system of dispensation, exception, and privilege.[143] First, Canon 85, *CIC-1983*, defines a dispensation as a relaxation of a merely ecclesiastical law in a particular case. One may never be dispensed from the requirements of divine and natural law. In the *Decretum* of Gratian, a dispensation is considered the relaxation of law on account of the mercy and common good of the church.[144] Section 1 of Canon 87, *CIC-1983*, provides that the diocesan bishop may dispense for his territory or his subjects from universal and particular laws promulgated by the supreme authority of the church unless the dispensation has been reserved by law to the Apostolic See. This is a change from Canon 81 of the *CIC-1917*, which held that ordinaries inferior to the Roman Pontiff could not dispense general laws of the church

---

141. Paulus Pp. VI, Allocution to the Tribunal of the Sacred Roman Rota, *Aequitas Canonica* (Die 8 mensis feb. anno 1973), 65 AAS 98–99 (1973).

142. *See* Juan Arias, *Sanctions in the Church, in* Ottawa-1993, 817.

143. *See* John A. Alesandro, *General Introduction, in* CLSA-1985, 1, 13.

144. *See* C. 1, q. 7, c. 5; & C. 1, q. 7, c. 23.

unless they had received the power to dispense. Section 2 of Canon 87, *CIC-1983*, permits any ordinary, not just the diocesan bishop, to dispense from the same universal and particular laws of the church if recourse to the Holy See would be difficult, delay would result in grave harm, and the Holy See customarily grants a dispensation in the same circumstances even if the dispensation is reserved to the Holy See. Pursuant to Section 2, an ordinary would include not only the diocesan bishop and those equivalent in law to him, but also the vicar general, episcopal vicar, and major superior of a clerical religious institute or clerical society of apostolic life of pontifical right.[145] The dispensation is a formal acknowledgment that the application of canon law should conform to the benign mind of the lawgiver.[146]

Second, Canon 18, *CIC-1983*, calls for a law that grants an exception to be interpreted strictly. The concept of strict interpretation of a law that grants an exception must be distinguished from a restrictive interpretation of law pursuant to Canon 16, *CIC-1983*. A strict interpretation does not go beyond the plain meaning of the words of the canon while a restrictive interpretation results in an actual restriction or new law.[147] It is also important to note that Canon 18 calls for a strict interpretation of a law that prescribes a penalty or restricts the exercise of a right as well as of a law that grants an exception. This reflects the traditional canonical principle attributed to the mind of the lawgiver that the odious is to be restricted and the favorable amplified (*odiosa restrigenda, favorabilia amplianda*). Nonetheless, the exception that exaggerates the intention of the lawgiver would conflict with the strict interpretation contemplated by Canon 18. For example, an interpretation of a law that permits an extraordinary minister of a sacrament under certain conditions which resulted in the extraordinary minister to be the same as, or more preferable than, the ordinary minister would contradict the meaning of strict interpretation required by Canon 18.[148] It is also a characteristic of the lawgiver's mind not to undermine the law by granting exceptions so liberally that the exception overcomes the law. Section 1 of Canon 1536, *CCEO*, refers to exceptions in terms of the common good.

Third, Section 1 of Canon 76, *CIC-1983*, describes a privilege as a favor to a real or juridic person granted by one who has legislative power. Traditionally, a privilege has been viewed as a private law granted with a benevolent intention.

---

145. *See* Canon 134, § 1, *CIC-1983*.

146. *See* Eduardo Baura, *Dispensations, in* 1 NAVARRA-2004, 644–51, which notes that dispensation must be distinguished from *epikeia*, excuse, and privilege.

147. *See* Javier Otaduy, *Ecclesiastical Laws, in* 1 NAVARRA-2004, 388.

148. *See* Congregatio de Culto Divino et Disciplina Sacramentorum, Instructio, *Redemptionis sacramentum, De quibusdam observandis et vitandis circa Sanctissimam Eucharistiam* (Die 25 mensis martii anno 2004), 147, 96 AAS 549–601 (2004), which confirms the strict interpretation for an extraordinary minister when there is a *deficientibus ministris*.

However, pursuant to Canon 76, the legislator may also delegate one who has executive power to grant a privilege. A privilege is presumed to be perpetual, in the sense that it continues as long as the beneficiary exists on earth.[149] Canon 79, *CIC-1983*, permits the authority who granted a privilege to revoke it. Generally, a privilege does not cease when the office of the grantor ceases, unless in granting the privilege the grantor has expressly stated such a limitation.[150] Canon 84, *CIC-1983*, states that one who has abused the power of a privilege deserves to be deprived of the privilege. For example, the Holy See might grant the diocesan bishop the privilege to permit sentences of nullity of marriage from his diocesan tribunal, which have been confirmed by the provincial tribunal of second instance, to be reviewed by the metropolitan tribunal rather than by the Roman Rota. The privilege is granted due to state restrictions on the church which forbid the diocesan tribunal from presenting evidence outside the nation to a foreign tribunal. It would be an abuse of the privilege if the metropolitan tribunal abrogated the norms of evidentiary proof stipulated in the *CIC-1983* in favor of a more relaxed approach to the evidence.[151]

Although they represent distinct canonical forms, the dispensation, exception, and privilege have been said to function either apart from the law (*praeter legem*) or against the law (*contra legem*). At the same time, each is a feature of the system of canon law. As with canonical equity, these canonical forms attest to the legislator's intent to imbue canon law with the justice, mercy, and love of Christ.

D. The Unity of Law and Theology

The principle for the revision of canon law that new law should reflect the theology of Vatican II, which culminated in the promulgation of the *CIC-1983* and *CCEO*, leads to the unity of law and theology. This unity may be detected in Mörsdorf's observation, noted at the outset of this chapter, that canon law is the logical outgrowth of the Incarnation in which the divine necessarily associated with human legal forms and institutions. A student of Mörsdorf's, Eugenio Corecco, developed the position in describing canon law as the "unity of law and theology."[152] In calling for the unity of law and theology, Corecco is not denying the important place of natural law and history in shaping canon law. To the contrary, the problem of canon law requires the proper resolution between "faith and reason."[153] Faith and its divine law are not only transcendent but also immanent and therefore not isolated from reason, nature, and history. Natural law

149. *See* Canon 78, § 1, *CIC-1983*.

150. *See* Canon 81, *CIC-1983*.

151. *See* María J. Rocca, *Privileges, in* 1 NAVARRA-2004, 642.

152. EUGENIO CORECCO, THE THEOLOGY OF CANON LAW: A METHODOLOGICAL QUESTION 108–12, 127–28 (Francesco Turvasi trans., Duquesne University Press 1992).

153. *See id.* at 107.

derived from practical reason remains an important source of canon law. Likewise, canon law cannot be divorced from the historicity that recognizes the relation between universal principles and particular applications of such principles.

The unity of law and theology properly understood checks against antinomianism and legalism by maintaining fidelity to canon law's *intellectus*, or inner meaning. First, theology without law results in antinomianism. It deprives the ecclesiastical community of the instrument that functions to secure an ordered, just, and peaceful life. Second, the separation of canon law from its inner theological meaning sets the conditions for legalism. Such a law is bereft of the Gospel meaning and fails to assist individuals and the church in knowing the saving mystery of God. Third, canon law should retain its status as a distinct discipline from theology. Although it is a distinct discipline from theology, canon law as the church's juridical science remains always closely related to theology and at the service of the church. Canon law functions as a bridge between theology and norms for practical action. It relies on practical reason and juridical methodology to design the external language of the law that expresses its inner theological meaning. The inner theological meaning is meant in a broad sense. It encompasses not only the transcendence but also the immanence of all the best qualities of what it means to be human.

2. CANON LAW AND THE SEXUAL ABUSE CRISIS
Antinomianism, Legalism, and the Failure of the Rule of Law

Chapters 2 and 3 discuss antinomian and legalistic approaches to canon law. Specifically, they explore these approaches to canon law by ecclesiastical authorities in dealing with the sexual abuse of minors by Catholic priests in the United States. Revelations of instances in which a Catholic priest sexually abused a minor have been documented by the media since at least the early 1980s.[1] Media attention has often been prompted by civil litigation brought on behalf of victims by plaintiffs' attorneys seeking to recover financial damages from the Catholic Church for emotional distress resulting from the abuse. Starting in the late 1980s and through the following decades, church officials attempted to respond to the problem by implementing a variety of sexual abuse policies.[2] In 2002, the media directed months of sustained local and national coverage to the "sexual abuse crisis" in the Roman Catholic Church. The intense media coverage, unequaled in American religious history, depicted Catholic priests as sexual predators and church officials as enablers of the priests in their crimes. These chapters are not intended as a general treatment of the complex multifaceted issues of a substantive and interpretative nature raised by the sexual abuse crisis. Rather, the more modest focus of the chapters is on the failure of canon law to protect victims, ensure a just ecclesiastical order, and communicate a sense of justice to the larger secular society.

In discussing antinomian and legalistic approaches to canon law, Chapter 2 consists of two major parts. The first part reviews the canonical provisions that were in place to respond to allegations of sexual abuse and to impose the penalty of dismissal from the clerical state on a guilty priest. In this part, I also present statistical information about the sexual abuse of minors by Catholic priests in the United States from 1950 until 2006. In light of the information, I argue that canonical action could have been taken against guilty priests, especially those who were serial child abusers. The second part offers an explanation for the failure of church authorities to utilize canon law in dealing with cases of sexual

1. *See generally* Boston Globe Investigative Staff, Betrayal, The Crisis in the Catholic Church 38 (Little Brown Back Bay Books 2003).

2. *See, e.g.*, Joseph Cardinal Bernadin, *Statement Announcing Policy on Clerical Sexual Misconduct with Minors*, 22 Origins 282, 282–83 (Oct. 1, 1992); United States Bishops' Meeting, *Twenty-Eight Suggestions on Sexual Abuse Policies*, 24 Origins 443, 443–44 (Dec. 8, 1994); *see also* Raymond C. O'Brien, *Pedophilia: The Legal Predicament of the Clergy*, 4 J. Contemp. Health L. & Pol'y 91, 151–52 (1988), which calls on churches to develop procedure for dealing with allegations of child abuse against clergy.

abuse. After reviewing some examples of antinomianism and legalism on the part of nineteenth-century bishops in the United States, I discuss how these approaches led to the failure of canon law in dealing with cases of clergy sexual abuse. I suggest that, when a psychological model replaced the rule of canon law, the conditions were set for great harm to individuals and the common good. In Chapter 3, I shall address the canonical consequences of antinomianism and legalism. These include the injury to the victims, alleged link between priesthood and sexual deviancy, disruption of the unity of law and theology, and diminishment of canon law as law properly understood.

I. THE FAILURE OF CANON LAW IN RESPONDING TO CLERGY SEXUAL ABUSE CASES

The discipline of the clergy for sexual offenses is not something novel in the history of the church. The rule of canon law has long included structures to address the problem.[3] From 1917 until the present time, there have been statutory provisions in canon law which establish that the sexual abuse of a minor by a cleric constitutes a grievous sin and grave crime. Complementing the substantive procedures, canon law contains various procedures through which guilt may be ascertained and the penalty of dismissal from the clerical state may be imposed.

A. Canonical Provisions for the Investigation, Adjudication, and Resolution of an Allegation of Clergy Sexual Abuse of a Minor

After its promulgation in 1917, the so-called Pio-Benedictine or *CIC-1917* remained in effect until 1983.[4] Section 2 of Canon 2359 of the *CIC-1917* provides that if a cleric (deacon, priest, or bishop) should "engage in a delict of the sixth precept of the Decalogue with a minor below the age of sixteen," he may be "suspended, declared infamous, and deprived of any office, benefice, dignity, responsibility, whatsoever, and deposed in more serious cases."[5] In canon law, a "delict," is a criminal offense. The Sixth Commandment states: "You shall not commit adultery."[6] The moral tradition of the Catholic Church considers the

---

3. *See* R. H. Helmholz, *Discipline of the Clergy: Medieval and Modern*, 6 Ecc. L. J. 189, 191–96 (2002), which presents various examples of prosecution of clergy in the medieval ecclesiastical courts for sexual offenses and other types of crimes; John W. O'Malley, S.J., *The Scandal: A Historian's Perspective*, 186 America 14, 16 (May 27, 2002), which explains that while scandals are not new in church history, the role of the media in developing the crisis is a new and significant factor.

4. Technically, *the CIC-1917* was in effect from 1918 until 1983.

5. *See* Stephen W. Findlay, Canonical Norms Governing the Deposition and Degradation of Clerics: A Historical Synopsis and Commentary 111–246 (The Catholic University of America 1941).

6. Exodus 20:14; Deuteronomy 5:18.

Sixth Commandment's prohibition to encompass any thought, word, or action against the virtue of chastity.

The Catholic tradition is based on the words of Jesus in the Gospel of Matthew, which have long been understood to internalize the external requirements of the law of the Decalogue: "You have heard it was said, 'You shall not commit adultery.' But I say to you that every one who looks at a woman lustfully has already committed adultery with her in his heart."[7] In the tradition, even unchaste thoughts may be seriously sinful. However, canon law does not punish immoral thoughts. Rather, the delict must be external and verifiable. Such a delict is committed when a cleric sexually abuses a minor through word or action. The delict constitutes an external violation of the divine and natural law encoded in the Decalogue. Canon law's requirement that the sin be "external" presents little difficulty in the case where a church official learns about the sexual abuse of a minor. As discussed later in this chapter, such knowledge renders the sin external, as opposed to a private matter kept in the internal forum.

The serious penalties provided for in Section 2 of Canon 2395 reflect the gravity of the delict committed when a cleric sexually abuses a minor. When this provision states that the guilty clerical may be "deposed," it means permanent removal from the clerical state, which is the most serious penalty available against a priest in canon law. *Crimen sollicitationis*, a 1962 Instruction issued by the Congregation of the Holy Office and confirmed by Pope John XXIII, stated that a cleric "who in any way attempts or perpetrates any obscene, external act, which is gravely sinful with a prebuscent child of either sex" is guilty of a delict "equated with the worst crime."[8] The Instruction directed that such a crime carried the penal effects provided for in Section 2 of Canon 2359. Although substantively the Instruction added nothing to the provision of Canon 2359, it confirmed the intent of the legislator with regard to the gravity of the crime when a cleric sexually abuses a minor.

Pope John Paul II promulgated the *CIC-1983*, abrogating the *CIC-1917*. The *CIC-1983* constitutes universal law for the Roman Catholic Church, and this law is binding on all Latin Rite Catholics. Section 2 of Canon 1395 of the *CIC-1983* replaces Section 2 of Canon 2359 of the *CIC-1917*. Consistent with the former statute, Section 2 of Canon 1395 establishes that sexual contact between a cleric and a minor counts as one of four classifications of sexual offences for which a penalty, including suspension and/or permanent removal from the clerical state, may be imposed upon deacon, priest, or bishop. The other three grounds include any form of coerced sex, a public offense against the Sixth Commandment of the

7. Matthew 5:27–28. The reference is directly to the Sixth Commandment of the Decalogue, and the tradition also encompasses the Ninth Commandment: "You shalt not covet thy neighbor's wife."

8. Suprema Sacra Congregatio Sancti Officii, *Crimen sollicitationis* (Die 16 mensis mar. anno 1962), 5, 72. This document was never officially published in AAS by the Holy See.

Decalogue, and continued open concubinage with a woman after an official warning.[9]

In 1990, Pope John Paul II promulgated the *CCEO*, which binds all Eastern Rite Catholics. Section 1 of Canon 1453 of the *CCEO* provides that a cleric "who commits an external sin against chastity with scandal is to be punished by permanent suspension, and if he persists in the delict, he may incur additional penalties up to and including being deposed." In comparison to the Latin Rite *CIC-1983*, the *CCEO* does not explicitly mention a sexual offense with a minor, but such an offense is, of course, included in the phrase "sin against chastity." The substantive differences between the two Codes are the *CCEO*'s conditions that the offense is "with scandal" and the offender "persists in the delict." In contrast, Section 2 of Canon 1395 of the *CIC-1983* simply provides for "dismissal from the clerical state if the case so warrants." In the Latin Rite, the injury and scandal of even a single incident of sexual abuse of a minor may result in permanent removal of the offending priest from the clerical state. In terms of the substantive law, the *CIC-1917*, *CIC-1983*, and *CCEO* all treat the sexual abuse of a minor as a grave crime to be punished by severe canonical penalty.

In November 1993, Pope John Paul II addressed a public letter to the bishops of the United States in which he affirmed that the sexual abuse of a minor by a priest constitutes a "crime" to which "[t]he canonical penalties . . . give a social expression of disapproval for the evil that are fully justified."[10] Under all three Codes, a minor is defined as a person who is under the age of sixteen. Canon law applies to the universal law of the church and is therefore an international and transcultural statute. The idea of who is a minor in national law varies from one national jurisdiction to another and, as in the United States, may vary within the nation according to state and local law. In April 1994, the Holy See promulgated special law for sexual abuse cases in the United States that raised the age of a minor as until the person reaches the eighteenth birthday. In a 2001 letter sent to the bishops throughout the entire Catholic Church, the Congregation for the Doctrine of the Faith extended this provision to the universal church.[11]

As was the case with the *CIC-1917*, the *CIC-1983* and *CCEO* also afford processes through which their respective substantive provisions for dealing with

9. The penalty is considered of such severity that prior to the 1917 Code, it was the common opinion among canonists that such a penalty was reserved exclusively to the Holy See, except when the common law of the church attached the penalty, and both of the twentieth-century statutes confirm that opinion. *See* X 5.40.27 *de verborum significatione.*

10. John Paul II, *Clergy Sexual Misconduct, Vatican–U.S. Bishops' Committee to Study Applying Canonical Norms*, 23 ORIGINS 102 (1993). *See also* National Conference of Catholic Bishops, *Canonical Delicts Involving Sexual Misconduct and Dismissal from the Clerical State* (United States Catholic Conference 1983).

11. *See* Congregatio pro Doctrina Fidei, *De delictis gravioribus eidem Congregationi pro Doctrina Fidei reservatis* (Dei 18 mensis maii anno 2001), 93 AAS 785, 786–87 (2001).

sexual abuse may be implemented.[12] The Ordinary (bishop or religious superior) bears the responsibility, through his delegates, to initiate, pursue, and bring to closure the initial investigation of an allegation against a priest of his diocese or religious community. In accord with the present canonical procedure, the investigation of an allegation of abuse begins with an informal administrative process.[13] Most dioceses and religious communities have established advisory boards consisting of clerics and laypersons to assist in the administrative investigation. If the initial investigation indicates that the allegation is credible, the Ordinary must refer the case to the Congregation of the Doctrine for the Faith pursuant to special law promulgated in 2001.[14] The Congregation then either calls the case to itself or directs the Ordinary to commence a trial.

The canonical trial or contentious penal process is the regular process for the determination of guilt or innocence and the imposition of a penalty in canon law. Cases that may result in permanent removal from the clerical state would normally require the contentious penal process to protect the rights of the accused cleric given the finality of the penalty that may be imposed. However, in clear or notorious cases, permanent dismissal may be imposed on a guilty cleric through a simple administrative procedure conducted under the authority of the Congregation for the Doctrine of the Faith and confirmed by the pope.[15]

The contentious penal process afforded by canon law is a variation of the contentious marriage process that is followed when a diocesan tribunal considers an annulment case. The contentious processes in canon law differ in significant ways from the jury trial of Anglo-American law. In the canonical process, a college of three judges, and not a jury, decides the case. The contentious penal process does not involve the lawyers for the opposing sides who examine and cross-examine witnesses. Rather, in the canonical process, all the questions are posed by a judge or other tribunal official who interviews witnesses privately. These interviews are recorded in notarized affidavits that form part of the evidence, which is known in canon law as the "acts of the case." The accuser and accused as well as any other person in possession of relevant information may be interviewed. The canonical process requires a promoter of justice, who acts as the prosecutor of the case, and a defendant's advocate, both of whom may suggest witnesses to be interviewed and present written questions to the judge. Once the acts have been collected by the judges, the promoter of justice and

---

12. *See generally* William H. Woestman, O.M.I., Ecclesiastical Sanctions and the Penal Process, A Commentary on the Code of Canon Law (Saint Paul University 2003).

13. *See* Canon 1717–19, *CIC-1983*.

14. *See* Congregatio pro Doctrina Fidei, *De delictis gravioribus idem Congregationi pro Doctrina Fidei riservatis* (Die 18 mensis mai. anno 2001), 93 AAS 785–87 (2001).

15. *See CIC-1983*, Canons 1341 and 1718. *See also* Gregory Ingels, *Dismissal from the Clerical State: An Examination of the Process*, 33 Studia Canonica 169, 190 (1999).

defendant's advocate study the acts, and then they present written arguments for their positions to the tribunal. After carefully considering the arguments in light of all the evidence of the case, the judges render a determination of guilt or innocence. Either side has the right of appeal.[16]

The canonical contentious process might seem similar to the documentary administrative process in Anglo-American law. However, canon law considers the contentious process in either its penal or its marriage annulment variation to be an exercise of the judicial and not the executive power of government. In contrast to the contentious penal process of canon law, the Congregation for the Doctrine of the Faith may resolve a case of clergy sexual abuse through an extrajudicial or administrative process. The administrative process does not contemplate that less proof of guilt is required than in the judicial process. Nor does it mean that the rights of the parties are to be any less respected. The Congregation sometimes relies on the administrative process in urgent cases when there is already clear evidence of guilt established on the record submitted by the diocese or religious community against the offender.

From Vatican II until the 2002 sexual abuse crisis, contentious penal processes in the United States for priests accused of sexual abuse of a minor were, in the words of one expert, "nonexistent."[17] Prior to 2002, unofficial sources suggest the administrative process of dismissal had been employed by the Holy See in only about a dozen cases against priests in the United States in exceptional circumstances at the request of a diocesan bishop.[18] Even in the absence of accurate data, it does seem clear that over the course of several decades, many bishops and religious superiors declined to implement and enforce the rule of canon law. This failure violated not only the positive law of the church, but also the normative principles of natural and divine justice.

B. Statistical Evidence and Canon Law

In 2002, the United States Conference of Catholic Bishops commissioned the first comprehensive sexual abuse study of any religious or professional group. The work was entrusted to the John Jay College of Criminal Justice. The landmark study, *The Nature and Scope of the Problem of Sexual Abuse of Minors by Catholic Priests and Deacons in the United States*, was published in 2004 (2004 John Jay Study).[19] The allegations during this fifty-two-year time period covered

---

16. *See* Canon 1717, *CIC-1983*.

17. William H. Woestman, O.M.I., Ecclesiastical Sanctions and the Penal Process, A Commentary on the Code of Canon Law, xv.

18. *See* Ingels, *Dismissal From the Clerical State*, 169–70, which states knowledge of four such administrative cases from the United States in 1998.

19. John Jay College, the Nature and Scope of Sexual Abuse of Minors by Catholic Priests and Deacons in the United States (United States Conference of Catholic Bishops 2004).

by the 2004 John Jay Study involved 4,392 priests and 10,667 victims.[20] This study was followed by a series of annual reports conducted by the John Jay College, the most recent of which was issued in 2006 (2006 John Jay Study).[21] The 2006 John Jay Study found that approximately 4.2 percent of all diocesan priests and 2.7 percent of all religious priests who served in ministry during this time period from 1950 to 2006 had been accused of the sexual abuse of a minor.[22] The statistical information contained in these reports contains critical evidence about the failure of canon law to address the problem of clergy sexual abuse of minors in the United States that led to the crises of 2002.

First, of the total number of allegations of sexual abuse brought against Catholic clergy from 1950 to 2006, more than two-thirds of the allegations were reported to church officials for the first time after 1992, and more than one-third were reported for the first time in 2002–2006.[23] Obviously, there was no possibility of canonical action against a member of the clergy until the allegation had been presented to church officials. The canonical failure remains that in those cases when church officials had received an allegation of abuse, the provisions of the relevant Code of Canon Law were often neglected.

Second, 3.5 percent of the accused priests were accused of abusing more than ten victims, and this small subset of priests was responsible for 26 percent of all allegations.[24] The subset of serial child molesters includes priests such as Louisiana's Gilbert Gauthe, Fall River's James Porter, and Boston's John Geoghan and Paul Shanley. In the words of the 2004 John Jay Study, "a very small percentage of accused priests are responsible for a substantial percentage of the allegations."[25] In the case of a serial child abuser, it would have been more likely that church officials were aware of the abuse than in a case of a single allegation. For example, the records of the Archdiocese of Boston indicate that diocesan officials were in fact aware of allegations against serial child abusers, John Geoghan and Paul Shanley.[26] Prompt canonical action against a serial molester, which would have permanently removed such a priest from ministry in the church, was not taken. The 2002 clergy sexual abuse crisis focused on the

20. The *New York Times* estimates that there were approximately 5,000 priests accused of abuse involving approximately 13,000 victims. *See* Alexandra Stanley, N.Y. Times, Apr. 18, 2008, at A1.

21. Karen Terry & Margaret Leland Smith, 2006 Supplementary Report to the Nature and Scope of Sexual Abuse of Minors by Catholic Priests and Deacons in the United States, *available at*: http//www.nccbuscc.org/ocyp/JohnJayReport.pdf.

22. *Id.* at 4.

23. 2004 John Jay Study, 7.

24. *Id.* at 8.

25. *Id.*

26. For accounts of the Goeghan and Shanley personnel files from the Archdiocese of Boston, *see* Boston Globe, Jan. 2, 2002, at A1; *Signs of the Times*, America, Apr. 22, 2002, at 3; and *Signs of the Times*, America, Apr. 14, 2003, at 5.

profile of the priest as serial child abuser. As I shall discuss in greater detail in the following section, canonical action could have been taken in cases of serial abuse.

Third, 75 percent of all the alleged events occurred between 1960 and 1984.[27] Although the wave of media reports reached a crest at the beginning of the twenty-first century, the vast majority of cases of priest sexual abuse occurred several decades earlier during the twentieth century. The highest level of incidents in which priests abused minors commenced after Vatican II and abated shortly after the promulgation of the 1983 Code of Canon Law. Relative to the number of cases from the mid-sixties to the mid-eighties, the time period from 1950 until 1960 shows a low number of alleged incidents per year, and the time period from 1985 to 2006 reveals a similar relatively low number of cases. However, one must be cautious in concluding that the low incidence of reports for the period from 1985 to 2006 means that there was necessarily a low incidence of child abuse by Catholic clergy during the last two decades. Victims and mental health professionals indicate that it may take years for a victim to summon the courage to bring such a complaint. At the same time, the sharp decline in incidents during the 1980s is statistically significant. For cases in which the abuse stopped twenty years ago, one would now expect a relatively high degree of reporting. This seems especially so in the environment following the 2002 sexual crisis, which fostered more favorable conditions for victims reporting to religious and secular authorities. The 2006 John Jay Study went even further in concluding: "The decline in cases in the 1990s . . . is confirmed to be not simply a decline in reporting cases, but in the incidence of unreported events."[28]

C. Difficulties with the Canonical Process

In the wake of the revelations of 2002, it has been suggested that the procedural safeguards intended in canon law to protect the rights of all the parties prevented the imposition of canonical penalties on accused priests. In other words, it is argued that canon law itself was the problem and not the failure of church authorities to utilize canon law.[29] In the decades prior to the 2002 crisis, canon lawyers in the United States were advising bishops that the statute of limitations

27. 2004 John Jay Study, 8.

28. 2006 John Jay Study, 24.

29. A document issued by the United States Conference of Catholic Bishops, titled *USCCB Efforts to Combat Clergy Sexual Abuse Against Minors: A Chronology 1982–2006*, 2, states that in 1989: "With regard to canonical remedies to deal with priests who would not return to ministry, NCCB/USCC officers and key staff begin discussing alternative approaches to existing provisions of the Code of Canon Law with representatives of the Roman Curia, especially the Code's *statute of limitations* and its treatment of *culpability*. Discussions focus on ways to streamline the penal provisions of the Code and the possibility of an administrative process to remove a priest from the clerical state." (emphasis added). *Available at* http://www.usccb.org/comm./combatefforts.shml.

(prescription) and difficulty in meeting the requisite standard of proof to establish guilt (culpability) rendered it difficult if not impossible to impose a penalty on a guilty priest.[30]

The statute of limitations or as it is referred to in canon law, "prescription," did bar prosecution of certain but not all cases of clergy sexual abuse. Pursuant to the *CIC-1983*, the statute of limitations for the commencement of a canonical penal process in a diocese was five years from the commission of the crime.[31] In 1994, the Holy See promulgated a special law for the United States that altered the statute of limitations to extend for ten years from the victim's eighteenth birthday.[32] According to the 2006 John Jay Study, two-thirds of the cases were not reported to dioceses until 1994, and one-third of the cases were not reported until 2002.[33] Since many of the incidents had been perpetrated decades prior to their reporting, the 1994 change in the statute of limitations to run until the victim's twenty-eighth birthday did not permit the imposition of a canonical penalty in such cases. The cases were already too old to fall within the canonically prescribed period. Thus, the canonists were correct that in many instances canonical prescription did prevent church authorities from prosecuting a case pursuant to the canonical penal process.

However, the facts suggest that even the original five-year statute of limitations should not have prevented canonical action against a priest who was a serial child molester. As the Geoghan and Shanley cases illustrate, church authorities were aware of multiple allegations against such priests well within the five-year prescription period.[34] Until the church's response to the 2002 scandal, I am not aware of any case in the United States in which a priest was dismissed from the clerical state as a result of the diocesan penal process stipulated in canon law. In the wake of the 2002 crisis and the failure of diocesan bishops to utilize the penal process, the Congregation for the Doctrine of the Faith has routinely been rescinding the prescription requirement for cases handled through the diocesan penal process and through the administrative process.[35]

---

30. *See, e.g.*, Francis G. Morrisey, *The Pastoral and Juridical Dimensions of Dismissal from the Clerical State and of Other Penalties for Sexual Misconduct*, 53 CLSA PROCEEDINGS 221–39 (1991); and John P. Beal, *Doing What One Can: Canon Law and Clerical Sexual Misconduct*, 52 JURIST 642–83 (1992).

31. *See* Canon 1362, § 1, 2°, *CIC-1983*.

32. The "derogation" was specific to the United States. *See* United States Conference of Catholic Bishops, *USCCB Efforts to Combat Clergy Sexual Abuse Against Minors: A Chronology 1982–2006*, at 2, sub "April 1994."

33. 2004 John Jay Study, 7.

34. *See* note 28 *supra*.

35. *See* Canon 20, *CIC-1983*, which identifies the praxis of the Roman Curia as a suppletory source of law.

The 1962 Instruction, *Crimen sollicitationis*, had reserved cases of clergy sexual abuse to the Holy See.[36] Pursuant to Canon 1555, Section 1, of the *CIC-1917*, the reservation had the effect of suspending canonical prescription.[37] Canon 1402 of the *CIC-1983*, which requires deference to the special law governing the tribunals of the Holy See, arguably sustained the 1962 Instruction's suspension of prescription. If this analysis is correct, there was no statute of limitations in effect from 1962 until the Holy See's promulgation of the special law of 1994. Although this interpretation is technically correct, it is problematic for two reasons. First, the Instruction was never officially published by the Holy See, and it only seems to have come to light because it was mentioned in a footnote in the 2002 Document from the Congregation for the Doctrine of the Faith.[38] Whatever

36. *See* Brian E. Ferme, *"Graviora delicta": The Apostolic Letter M.P. sacramentorum sanctitatis tutela*, *in* IL PROCESSO PENALE CANONICO 365, 369 (Zbigniew Suchecki ed., Laternan University Press 2003).

37. *See* NICHOLAS P. CAFARDI, BEFORE DALLAS, THE U.S. BISHOPS' RESPONSE TO CLERGY SEXUAL ABUSE OF CHILDREN 30–32 (Paulist Press 2008).

38. *See* Congregatio pro Doctrina Fidei, *De delictis gravioribus*, 3. There was a somewhat similar document issued by the Holy See in 1922. Although the documents were never officially promulgated, it could be argued that there was constructive notice of them. The Instruction itself calls for distribution to bishops throughout the world who were to keep it in the diocesan archives. However, the documents were apparently distributed by the Holy See on a need to know basis to bishops and to a limited number of canonists. Although the 1962 Instruction permitted the religious superior to conduct a judicial or administrative trial of the case of sexual abuse of a minor, it is also not clear that the Instruction was circulated to religious superiors. Constructive notice occurs when the law's existence is known, or should be known, by the subject(s) of the law. For example, the famous decree of the Council of Trent, *Tametsi*, was to be promulgated locally in each diocese throughout the church. Due to a variety of historical circumstances such as opposition from the Protestant government of a given geographic area, the local promulgation did not always occur. Some canonists argued that *Tametsi's* requirement of canonical form for the validity of marriage between baptized persons was law by constructive notice. However, constructive notice necessitates that there is at least some generally available form of notice of a law's existence as in the case of *Tametsi* where the law was not promulgated in a particular diocese, but the law's existence was evident from its promulgation and implementation in other dioceses. The total absence of public promulgation of the 1962 *Crimen sollicitationis* and its 1922 predecessor mitigate against constructive notice. Unlike *Tametsi*, which was a public document of an Ecumenical Council with widespread, everyday, continuous application to the celebration of marriage throughout the universal church, there was no guaranty that a bishop of a given diocese either had actual notice or should have known of the 1922 and 1962 Instructions about the relatively rare cases of solicitation in the confessional—not to mention the Instruction's brief mention of the sexual abuse of a prepubescent child. To suggest that there was constructive notice of *Crimen sollicitationis* is tantamount to saying that a law is given juridical effect without promulgation, that the lawgiver does not inform the diocesan bishop of the law's content or even existence, that the law about one crime—solicitation in the confessional—also happens to mention briefly

force of law it may have once enjoyed, it was largely forgotten until 2002. The fact that in 1994 the Holy See issued special law for the United States that extended prescription to the victim's twenty-eighth birthday indicates that even the Holy See had forgotten the 1962 Instruction or at least overlooked its suspension of prescription. Second, Canon 1402 notwithstanding, the Instruction was arguably abrogated with the promulgation of the *CIC-1983* which, as just discussed, contained its own procedural provisions.

The 1962 Instruction was primarily concerned with the crime of solicitation by a priest confessor of a penitent. The sexual abuse of a prepubescent child (*cum impuberibus*) is mentioned only briefly at the end of the document comparing the abuse to the "worst" or "most injurious" crime. A solicitation case involves an accusation that a priest solicited a penitent for a sexual act during sacramental confession. Based upon a rough English translation that appeared in the wake of the sexual abuse crisis, the Instruction was interpreted by some to require the same level of confidentiality in sexual abuse cases as in solicitation cases.[39] This led to the assertion that the Instruction proved that the church adopted a procedure for the cover-up of sexual abuse.[40] However, from a legal perspective, there are numerous problems with this assertion.

First, an examination of the original Latin text of the Instruction reveals that the reference to child abuse is limited to abuse of "prepubescent children." Even if it had been an attempt at a cover-up, it would not have pertained to the vast majority of clergy sexual abuse cases in the United States which involved adolescent males. Second, the Instruction expressly required anyone who knew about the abuse of the child to make a denunciation of the cleric to the appropriate church official under pain of excommunication.[41] The Instruction was not attempting to discourage the denunciation of a priest, rather it expressly required it under penalty. Third, Number 72 of the Instruction contains a *mutatis . . . mutandi* clause, which differentiates the process for the prosecution of a crime for the abuse of the prepubescent child from that for a solicitation in the confessional case.[42] The latter involves the inviolability of the seal of sacramental

---

another crime—the sexual abuse of a prepubescent child, and that the diocesan bishop is nonetheless bound by the law. I know of no fair and reasonable system of law that would endorse such an approach. *See* Lon L. Fuller, The Morality of Law 39 (Yale University Press 1967), which recognizes publication as a factor necessary to the validity of law.

39. This English translation is available at http://news.bbc.co.uk/1/shared/bsp/hi/pdfs/28_09_06_Crimen_english.pdf. *See* Canon 88, § 2, *CIC-1917*, which established the age of puberty for males at 14 and females at 12.

40. *See* Thomas P. Doyle, A. W. R. Sipe, & Patrick J. Wall, Sex, Priests, and Secret Codes 47–51 (Volt Press 2006).

41. *See Crimen sollicitationis*, n. 15. This seems to expand the requirement of Canon 904, *CIC-1917*, which referred only to the penitent.

42. *See* John P. Beal, *The 1962 Instruction 'Crimen Sollicitationis': Caught Red-Handed or Handed a Red-Herring*, 41 Studia Canonica 199, 231 (2007), which explains that one of

confession, and it therefore requires a process of strict confidentiality. The case of clergy sexual abuse, unless the abuse was also a solicitation in the confessional case, would be addressed to the ordinary processes in canon law with certain modifications specified in the Instruction. All canonical cases, whether they involve marriage annulments, contentious penal trials, or some other judicial or administrative procedure, are treated with a certain level of confidentiality. Confidentiality in canonical cases serves the following purposes: (1) it permits parties to the action and other witnesses to testify freely, (2) it sets the conditions in which the accuser might testify to the crime without undue publicity, and (3) it protects the good reputation of the accused until a judicial finding of guilt and imposition of a canonical penalty. Fourth, although canon law stipulates confidentiality in the process, the penalty of removal from the clerical state is not a confidential matter in canon law but an external and verifiable act. Moreover, the obligation of confidentiality referred only to the canonical process of the case, and in my view, it would not have prohibited reporting a crime to civil authorities. In addition to all the above problems with the assertion of international cover-up on the part of church hierarchy, it is also questionable as to whether the Instruction ever enjoyed force of law in the church due to its lack of promulgation. Certainly, the Instruction fails to prove that the Holy See intended to cover-up cases of clergy abuse.

The second alleged obstacle to the prosecution of a clergy sexual abuse case involved the issue of culpability. Canonists advised bishops that the psychological state of a priest who committed an act of sexual abuse of a minor would mitigate the priest's culpability in a canonical trial.[43] In other words, psychological factors were thought to pose difficulty in meeting the standard of proof required by canon law in a case of a priest accused of abusing a minor. The standard of proof in the penal process for a determination of guilt is "moral certainty." This is the same standard for nullity of marriage cases. In a 1942 Allocution to the Roman Rota, Pope Pius XII distinguished moral certainty from the extremes of "absolute certainty" and "greater or lesser probability." Absolute certainty requires that "all possible doubt as to the truth of the fact and the existence of the contrary is entirely excluded." Greater or lesser probability "leaves a foundation for the fear of error." In contrast, moral certainty "is characterized . . . by the exclusion of well founded or reasonable doubt."[44] The ecclesiastical tribunal

---

the most significant differences would be that a sexual abuse case would be adapted so as not to conflict with the secular law of the particular jurisdiction.

43. *See, e.g.*, Morrisey, *The Pastoral and Juridical Dimensions of Dismissal from the Clerical State and of Other Penalties for Sexual Misconduct*, 232; and Beal, *Doing What One Can: Canon Law and Clerical Sexual Misconduct*, 679–80.

44. Pius Pp. XII, *Allocutio adstantibus Praelatis Auditoribus ceterisque Officialibus et Administris Tribunalis Sacrae Romanae Rotae necnon eiusdem Tribunalis Advocatis et Procuratoribus* (Dei 1 mensis oct. anno 1942), 34 AAS 338–43 (1942); English translation

relies on the moral certainty or beyond a reasonable doubt standard in issuing a judicial decision that a marriage is null. The reasonable doubt standard is similar to that which is required in American criminal trials when a person has been accused of sexually abusing a minor. Likewise, canon law requires that the reasonable doubt standard be met in sexual abuse cases prior to pronouncing the guilt of the priest and imposing the penalty of permanent removal from the clerical state. The conclusion that meeting the moral certainty standard would prove too difficult in the penal process that deals with a priest accused of sexually abusing a minor must be evaluated in light of the significant judicial structures and procedures functioning in virtually every diocese in the United States.

Canon law requires each diocese to establish a tribunal in which judicial cases may be heard and resolved.[45] Diocesan tribunals were routinely finding moral certainty in nullity of marriage cases at the same time that church authorities were receiving credible allegations of sexual abuse against priests. Since Vatican II, the diocesan tribunals in the United States have functioned successfully to process hundreds of thousands of marriage annulments. Over the ten-year period from 1985 until 1994, the contentious process was utilized to grant decisions declaring the nullity of marriage in average of over 40,000 cases per year in the diocesan tribunals of the United States. Each case included a first instance contentious trial, the sentence of which was confirmed by second instance independent appeals tribunal. In comparison, all other diocesan tribunals combined throughout the rest of the world utilized the contentious process to grant annulments in an average of less than 14,000 cases per year over the same ten-year period.[46] Given the diocesan tribunals' record of success in adjudicating marriage cases, there is no reason why diocesan tribunals could not have been utilized to adjudicate an allegation of sexual abuse against a priest.

Critics of the diocesan tribunals have charged that from the late 1960s through the early 1990s, the tribunals misused psychological evidence in granting marriage annulments.[47] On numerous occasions, Pope John Paul II expressed similar concern about excessive deference to psychological factors in the contentious process for marriage cases.[48] The excessive deference being shown to psychological factors in marriage cases may have influenced bishops into thinking that

---

in William H. Woestman, O.M.I., Papal Allocutions to the Roman Rota, 1939–2002, at 17–22, at 18 (Saint Paul University 2002).

45. *See* Canons 1420 and 1421, *CIC-1983*.

46. *See* Robert H. Vasoli, What God Has Joined Together: The Annulment Crisis in American Catholicism 4–5 (Oxford University Press 1998).

47. *See id.* 5.

48. *See, e.g.*, Ioannes Paulus Pp. II, "Allocutiones: I. *Ad Rotae Romanae Auditores coram admissos* (Die 5 m. februarii a. 1987)," 79 AAS 1454–58 (1987). For a complete English language collection of John Paul II's annual talks to the Roman Rota, see William H. Woestman, O.M.I., Papal Allocutions to the Roman Rota, 1939–2002 (Saint Paul University 2002).

the moral certainty standard could not be met in a penal process against a priest for child abuse. Such excessive deference would mitigate the culpability of the crime on the ground that the accused possessed a diminished capacity to control his impulses.[49] In 1988, Paul John Paul II observed that "only the most severe forms of psychopathology impair substantially the freedom of the individual . . . psychological concepts do not always correspond with canonical . . . the categories that belong to psychiatry or psychology are not automatically transferred to the field of canon law."[50] In canon law, culpability enjoys the presumption of law when the offender has in fact committed an external violation of the law.[51]

Thus, the claim that the canonical penal process rendered it difficult or impossible for an Ordinary to prosecute all cases of clergy sexual abuse of a minor possesses only limited support. With regard to the statute of limitations, an allegation made several decades after the abuse is alleged to have taken place would have been barred by the original five-year period of prescription. This would also be true even under the present statute, which permits the initiation of a case within ten years of the victim's eighteenth birthday. However, the statute of limitations was unlikely to have been a problem in prosecuting a priest who committed serial acts of child abuse when there were ongoing multiple allegations against the priest. Likewise, the moral certainty standard of proof required in the penal process should not have presented a problem, especially in a case that involved multiple independent allegations of sexual abuse against a priest. It remains true that the moral certainty standard might be difficult to meet in a case in which only one allegation is brought without other corroborating evidence. This is not a problem unique to canon law but to any just legal process in which conviction of a serious crime requires sufficient evidence that the crime was committed.

Neither prescription nor culpability barred the imposition of canonical penalties on priests who were guilty of serial child abuse. A small number of serial abuser priests accounted for a significant percent of the child abuse covered by the John Jay studies. Taking canonical action against such priests would have prevented a great deal of injury to the victims. Canonical action against serial abusers would also have conveyed that the Catholic Church was acting responsibly to prevent future abuse.

---

49. Canon 1321, § 1, *CIC-1983*.

50. Ioannes Paulus Pp. II, Allocutiones: XII, *Ad Romanae Rotae Auditores simul cum officialibus et advocatis coram admissos, anno forensi ineunte* (Die 25 mensis ianuarii anno 1988), 80 AAS 1178, 1180–81; English translation in William H. Woestman, O.M.I., Papal Allocutions to the Roman Rota, 1939–2002, 200 (Saint Paul University 2002).

51. Canon 1321, §3, *CIC-1983*.

II. THE FAILURE OF THE RULE OF LAW: ANTINOMIAN AND LEGALISTIC APPROACHES

Canon law functions to set the conditions for a just ecclesial order, protect individual rights while respecting the common good, facilitate the mission of the church in preaching the gospel and administering the sacraments, encourage acts of charity, and promote peace and security in the here and now even as it points to the ultimate justice of the life hereafter and the consummation of time. These objectives of the rule of law in the life of the church are diminished by antinomian and legalistic approaches. Antinomianism undervalues the significance of canon law in the life of the church, and it is often accompanied by an authoritarian legalism on the part of hierarchical superiors. In the antinomian absence of the proper appreciation of canon law, superiors may feel free to use their lawful power in an authoritarian manner. By disrupting the rule of law in the life of the church, antinomianism and legalism hinder canon law from fulfilling its objectives.

A. Antinomianism and Legalism during the Nineteenth Century

The history of the Catholic Church in the United States during the nineteenth century offers a historical context for understanding the failure of canon law to address cases of clergy sexual abuse. Both antinomian and legalistic approaches to canon law in the United States were evident during the nineteenth century. In his book, *Defending Rights in the Church,* Kevin E. McKenna offers some prominent examples.[52] For forty years during the second half of the nineteenth century, James McMaster, a Catholic layman heavily influenced by the Oxford movement, published the *Freeman's Journal and Catholic Register,* which was at the time "the most widely read Catholic newspaper in the country," and read by "more than 85% of the English speaking diocesan clergy of the United States." McMaster utilized this forum to lament the inapplicability of canon law in the United States due to the country's missionary status.[53] Writing in the *Freeman's Journal and Catholic Register,* Eugene O'Callahan, a parish priest in Ohio, employed a *nom de plume* to complain that certain bishops exploited the missionary status of the United States to avoid establishing proper parishes entrusted to permanent pastors with definite rights and responsibilities under canon law.[54] McMaster, O'Callahan, and a group of like-minded priests sought to bring their concerns about this antinomianism to Vatican I, where some American

52. *See* Kevin E. McKenna, Defending Rights in the Church 49–164 (Paulist Press 2007).

53. *See id.* at 49–70. *See also* Robert F. Trisco, Bishops and Their Priests in the United States 157–158 & 175–176 (Graland Publishing 1988).

54. *See id.* at 70–85. *See also* Trisco, Bishops and Their Priests, 157–59.

bishops like Rochester's Bernard J. McQuaid successfully blocked the endeavor.[55] In an example of how an antinomian attitude to canon law sometimes leads to an authoritarian legalism, the Bishop of Alton, Illinois, Peter J. Baltes, went so far as to ban publication of the *Freeman's Journal and Catholic Register*, but he eventually retracted the censure when other bishops refused to join him in a united front.[56]

Richard L. Burtsell, a priest and expert in canon law in New York City during the postbellum period, shared the concern about the plight of canon law in the United States. When it was published in 1887, Burtsell's book, *The Canonical Status of Priests in the United States*, elicited a strong critical response from many bishops.[57] Consistent with the positions of McMaster and O'Callahan, Burtsell maintained that bishops in the United States routinely flouted canon law. In his view, certain bishops acted in an authoritarian manner in the appointment, transfer, and removal of parish priests, in the manner of imposing penalties, and in denial of appeals against the arbitrary exercise of episcopal authority. A member of the so-called *New York Academia*, Burtsell joined fellow priests such as Edward McGlynn in advocating an Americanism that called for the adoption of democratic principles by the Catholic Church in the United States.[58] When New York's Archbishop Michael A. Corrigan disciplined McGlynn by removing him from his parish and imposing the penalty of excommunication for his strong pro-socialist political activities, Burtsell rose to the defense.[59] He also served as a canonical advocate for Louis Lambert, a priest of Rochester, New York, whose ministerial faculties had been severely restricted by Bishop McQuaid.[60] In response to Burtsell's advocacy, Archbishop Corrigan removed him from his office as Defender of the Bond at the Archdiocesan Tribunal and as founding pastor of Epiphany Parish on the East side of Manhattan, transferring him to a rural parish upstate. Obedient to the church, Burtsell accepted the transfer despite its apparent inequity.[61] Corrigan's removal of Burtsell from his offices in retaliation for his representation of McGlynn exemplifies a mix of antinomianism and legalism. The antinomian element in the archbishop's actions corresponded to the inapplicability of canon law that established permanent pastors who possessed canonical rights. The authoritarian use of his

55. *See id.* at 60–63. *See also* TRISCO, BISHOPS AND THEIR PRIESTS, 189–90.

56. *See id.* at 63–69. *See also* TRISCO, BISHOPS AND THEIR PRIESTS, 187.

57. *See id.* at 87. *See also* TRISCO, BISHOPS AND THEIR PRIESTS, 252–253 & 257–258.

58. *See id.* at 88–90. *See also* Robert Emmett Curran, S.J., *The McGlynn Affair and the Shaping of the New Conservative Catholicism, in* THE AMERICAN CATHOLIC RELIGIOUS LIFE: SELECTED HISTORICAL ESSAYS 183-201 (Joseph M. White ed., 1988).

59. *See id.* at 92–94. *See also* TRISCO, BISHOPS AND THEIR PRIESTS, 251.

60. *See id.* at 94–98. *See also* TRISCO, BISHOPS AND THEIR PRIESTS, 257.

61. *See id.* at 105–06. *See also* TRISCO, BISHOPS AND THEIR PRIESTS, 257–58.

legitimate power of church governance, which sacred power itself was verified in canon law, reflected legalism.

Another nineteenth-century priest with expertise in canon law, Peter A. Baart, defended Dominic Kowalski, a Polish-born priest ministering in Detroit who was at the center of an immense intraparish conflict with tragic consequences. Spanning the years from 1885 to 1897, the conflict included the issue of trusteeism, allegations of Kowalski's sexual impropriety with adult women, questions over financial accountability, intractable disagreement between rival Polish factions of the parish community, and a parish riot which resulted in the death of one of the rioting parishioners. Baart appealed Kowalski's suspension and removal as pastor to the Congregation for the Propagation of the Faith on the grounds that the bishop had removed Kowalski without notice or a hearing and that the charges against him had never been proven.[62] Notice of the charges and the opportunity to be heard by an impartial judge remain fundamental procedural guarantees of natural law. The imposition of a canonical penalty in the absence of these natural rights represented another example of how an authoritarian legalism may stem from antinomianism.

Toward the end of the nineteenth century, in 1893, Pope Leo XII appointed Archbishop Francesco Satolli as the first Apostolic Delegate to the United States.[63] Satolli not only facilitated the reconciliation of Father Kowalski but he also lifted the excommunication imposed on Father McGlynn.[64] The appointment of an Apostolic Delegate, cessation of missionary status, and eventual promulgation of the 1917 Code of Canon Law contributed to a more balanced functioning of canon law in the Catholic Church in the United States. These examples from the nineteenth century are not intended to suggest that every American bishop vacillated between antinomian and legalistic approaches to canon law. However, the examples demonstrate that antinomianism and authoritarian legalism had already posed problems for the rule of canon law in the United States during the nineteenth century. Nineteenth-century antinomianism and legalism seem helpful in explaining the failure of the rule of canon law in dealing with clergy sexual abuse in the United States during the second half of the twentieth century.

B. Post–Vatican II Antinomianism: The Psychological Approach

The approach to canon law throughout the worldwide Catholic Church during the several decades preceding and following Vatican II also assists in understanding the 2002 sexual abuse crisis in the United States. It is fair to describe the

62. *See id.* at 114–19. *See also* E. Brooks Holifield, God's Ambassadors: A History of the Christian Clergy in America 192–194 (Wm. B. Eerdmans Publishing Co. 2007).

63. *See id.* at 145, 161–64.

64. *See id.* at 121–22. *See also* Trisco, Bishops and Their Priests, 260–61.

approach to canon law in the several decades immediately prior to Vatican II as sometimes manifesting characteristics of legalism. This preconciliar legalism reflected the view of canon law as an end in itself, separated from its spiritual underpinning. The separation may result in casuistical and authoritarian manifestations of legalism.[65] In 1959 Pope John XXIII announced his intention to convoke an Ecumenical Council, and simultaneously, the pontiff called for the revision of the 1917 Code.[66] Pope John had urged a general renewal (*aggiornamento*) in the church.[67] The desire to revise the 1917 Code stemmed from the realization that the legalism of the preconciliar period needed to be corrected in light of recent developments, especially in the areas of theological anthropology and ecclesiology.[68] These developments at the Ecumenical Council led Pope Paul VI to endorse a much needed "new habit of mind" (*novus habitus mentis*) with regard to church law and discipline.[69]

The process of the revision of the 1917 Code commenced at the conclusion of the Council and continued throughout the pontificates of Pope Paul VI and John Paul I with the hope that the new legislation would reflect the theology of Vatican II.[70] Over the course of almost three decades of revision, although theoretically still the universal law of the church, the 1917 Code fell into general disuse.[71] It was in many instances abrogated in favor of postconciliar innovations

---

65. *See* Ladislas Örsy, Theology and Canon Law 96–100 (Liturgical Press 1992), which discusses the separation between canon law and substantive values from after the Council of Trent until Vatican II.

66. *See* Giuseppe Alberigo & Joseph A. Komanchak, 1 History of Vatican II, at 1 (Orbis Books 1995), which describes Pope John XXIII's announcement at the Basilica of St. Paul Outside the Walls on January 25, 1959 of the Ecumenical Council, Synod for the Diocese of Rome, and the "desired and awaited modernization of the Code of Canon Law."

67. *See id.* at 504–05, which discusses Pope John's "spirit of search for '*aggiornamento*.'"

68. *See* Yves Congar, 1 I Believe in the Holy Spirit 66 (David Smith trans., Seabury Press 1983), which recalls his thought at the start of Vatican II that the desired renewal in the life of the Church would flow from a Christian anthropology that entails a new understanding of the human person.

69. Paulus Pp. VI, *Allocutiones*, (Die 20 mensis nov. anno 1965), 1 Communicationes 41 (1969).

70. *See* Paulus Pp. VI, *Allocutiones: Ad Romanae Rotae Auditores simul cum officialibus et advocatis coram admissos, Aequitas Canonica*, (Die 8 mensis februarii anno 1973), 65 AAS 95, 98 (1973), which calls for the revision of the new Code of Canon Law to be guided by the principle of canonical equity. *See also* John J. Coughlin, O.F.M., *Canonical Equity*, 30 Studia Canonica 403, 421–33 (1996), which compares the *CIC-1917* and the *CIC-1983* concluding that the present statute has an enhanced sense of the canonical equity that was already evident in the former statute.

71. *See* Andrew Greeley, *Canon Law and Society*, *in* The Future of Canon Law, 48 Concilium 130, 131 (N. Edelby, T. Urresti, & P. Huizing eds., 1969), which concludes from a sociological perspective that canon law "*in its present form* has become largely irrelevant."

ad experimentum.[72] In retrospect, the ecclesial ambiance in the wake of Vatican II represented a swing of the pendulum from the preconciliar legalism toward the antinomian. While it would overstate the matter to claim that the juridical structures of the church disintegrated during the postconciliar years, it seems accurate to observe that proper function of law in the church became unbalanced. The legalism of the past had been supplanted not only by openness to the new spirit but perhaps also by the tendency to underestimate the need for a healthy ecclesial order. The culture of canon law was reduced, with the effect that law was seen as an obstacle to the manifestation of the spirit in the church.

Three factors in particular seem to have contributed to the failure of canon law in addressing clergy sexual abuse. First and most important, the years following Vatican II witnessed a decreased emphasis on the traditional spiritual discipline of Christian life. In seminary formation, religious life, and diocesan priesthood, individualism and the desire for personal fulfillment displaced the asceticism traditionally associated with being a disciple of Christ. The traditional Catholic asceticism values a daily commitment to celebration of the Mass, frequent confession, communal and private prayer, fasting, self-denial, and acts of charity. In an insightful study of the sexual abuse crisis, *After Asceticism: Sex, Prayer and Deviant Priests*, the Linacre Institute attributes the large number of priests who sexually abused minors during the post–Vatican II period to a breakdown in traditional asceticism.[73] This is not to suggest that the reform of canon law based upon Vatican II degraded traditional spiritual values. On the contrary, Vatican II represented a dissipation of legalism, a call to retrieve the authentic inner meaning of the law, and openness to developments in the secular realm especially concerning the protection of human rights.[74] The breakdown in traditional spiritual discipline together with an antinomian approach to canon law were among the conditions that coincided with increased levels of clergy sexual abuse in the United States during the post–Vatican II years.

Second, canonists advised bishops in the United States to adopt a pastoral approach rather than to utilize the canonical process. As Nicholas P. Cafardi indicates, concern for "fraternal correction and pastoral solicitude" led canon lawyers to counsel "that the bishop's first response should be pastoral and not punitive."[75]

---

72. *See* Paul Winninger, *A Pastoral Canon Law, in* THE FUTURE OF CANON LAW, 48 CONCILIUM 51, 59 (N. Edelby, T. Urresti, & P. Huizing, eds., 1969), which calls for an "experimental law" to replace the 1917 Code.

73. *See* LINACRE INSTITUTE, AFTER ASCETICISM: SEX, PRAYER, AND DEVIANT PRIESTS 3 (Author House 2006).

74. *See* Walter Kasper, *The Theological Foundations of Human Rights,* 50 JURIST 152–53 (1990), which states that from the Enlightenment through the nineteenth century, the church sometimes expressed hostility to the new human rights language.

75. CAFARDI, BEFORE DALLAS: THE U.S. BISHOPS' RESPONSE TO CLERGY SEXUAL ABUSE OF CHILDREN, 21.

Setting pastoral concerns over against the rule of canon law typifies antinomianism. This approach ignores the reality that justice in the community depends on a communal order protected by the rule of law. The pastoral solicitude shown to the priest guilty of abuse was often not matched by pastoral solicitude for the victim(s) injured by the priest's conduct.

Third, the bishops opted for a therapeutic approach to the exclusion of correcting the grave injury through the rule of law. Statistical information in the John Jay studies reveals that from the end of Vatican II to the early 1980s, there was a dramatic increase in the number of allegations of sexual abuse against priests.[76] It was also during this time period that the infamous crimes of priests, such as Boston's John Geoghan and Paul Shanley, first came to the attention of diocesan officials.[77] In response to these kinds of allegations, bishops routinely sought psychological evaluations and treatment for the offenders. The church's emphasis on a psychological model reflected a general trend in American society, and many mental health professionals believed at the time that a sexual abuser could be reformed with proper treatment.[78] Although the psychological and canonical approaches have never been mutually exclusive, the focus shifted from punishment for the crime to the rehabilitation of the priest through therapy. It is fair to observe that the bishops were not acting in malice. As pastors of the church, they believed the psychological approach to be proper. No doubt, lawyers and insurances companies also advised them that placing an accused priest in psychological treatment would be necessary to demonstrate an absence of negligence in civil lawsuits brought by victims against the diocese.[79]

When the psychological model replaced the canonical order, the conditions were set for great resulting damage to individuals and the common good. My point is not that post–Vatican II antinomianism caused an increased level of sexual abuse by Catholic priests. As the 2004 John Jay Study revealed, in every year for the period covered by the study (1950–2002), there were incidents of sexual abuse of minors by priests reported. The incidence of reported abuse increased nearly threefold starting in the late 1960s and throughout the 1970s in

---

76. *See* 2004 John Jay Study, 28.

77. *See* Pam Belluck, *Depositions Show Cardinal Was Notified Early of Abuse*, N.Y. TIMES, Nov. 20, 2002, at A16, which states that in depositions given in civil suit against the Archdiocese of Boston, Cardinal Law acknowledged that he transferred abusive priests on the basis of psychological and medical opinion that the priests had been effectively treated and would not likely repeat their crimes.

78. *See* D. Kelly Weisberg, *The "Discovery" of Sexual Abuse: Experts' Role in Legal Policy Formulation*, 18 U. C. DAVIS L. REV. 1, 2–10 (1984), which discusses the shift from criminalization to the psychological approach with regard to pedophilia during the 1970s.

79. *See* Adam Liptak, *Religion and the Law*, N.Y. TIMES, Apr. 14, 2002, at 1, 30, which observes that insurance companies and not bishops often selected lawyers and legal tactics in sexual abuse cases.

relation to the other decades covered by the study.[80] There is no statistical available evidence to demonstrate that from 1950 until the late 1960s cases of clergy sexual abuse were addressed through the canonical process and that in the late 1960s the canonical process was abandoned. Rather, my point is that when the incidence of sexual abuse perpetrated by priests began to increase sharply in the late 1960s, the canonical process if utilized properly could have served to check the abuse. According to the 2004 John Jay Study, the incidents of abuse decreased dramatically starting in the early 1980s and continued to decrease until 2002. The decreased level of abuse coincided with the promulgation of the *CIC-1983* and the implementation of sexual abuse policies by diocese and religious communities starting in the late 1980s. The statistical evidence suggests the inference that the rule of canon law expressed in the universal law of the church and the policies of American dioceses and religious communities has proved effective in decreasing the incidence of sexual abuse of minors by priests. Even if antinomianism had no direct causal relationship to increased levels of abuse, it nonetheless mitigated against an adequate canonical response to the problem.

Contrary to antinomianism, the statistical evidence points to the importance of penal sanctions in canon law. The 2004 John Jay Study reveals that from 1950 to the mid-1960s, there was a relatively low incidence of clergy sexual abuse. The low incidence of abuse corresponded with a strong respect for canon law, which sometimes morphed into authoritarianism on the part of church superiors. Unfortunately, there is apparently no available statistical evidence of the number of clergy sexual abuse cases dealt with by the canonical process from 1950 to the mid-1960s. Even if there were no trials during this time period, a proper respect for canon law, not to mention the legalistic exaggeration of its importance, would have communicated to clergy that the commission of a grave delict such as sexual abuse of a minor carried serious canonical consequences. Consistent with post–Vatican II antinomianism, any hint at a coercive element in canon law was viewed as contrary to the spirit of renewal. Canonists argued that the new post–Vatican II law did not favor the imposition of penalties on priests through the penal process. In regard to priests who were guilty of the sexual abuse of minors, Francis G. Morrisey stated "the imposition of penalties, and particularly a return to the lay state, should be a last resort, a measure not applied until all other possibilities are exhausted."[81] The Catholic Church is a community based on faith, and the canon law which orders the community of faith is not defined primarily by the coercive element. However, the failure to prosecute clergy sexual abuse cases and to impose the permanent penalty of dismissal from the clerical state on guilty priests demonstrates that the coercive element retains significance

80. 2004 John Jay Study, 24.
81. Morrisey, *Pastoral and Juridical Dimensions*, 227.

in maintaining a just order in the church. Predictability is an essential element of any system of law. In terms of clergy sexual abuse, it warns the abuser that his actions will have serious consequences. It assures the victims that the canon law is designed to prevent future harm. It communicates to the church and to society that the sexual abuse of minors by priests will not be tolerated in the church.

Vatican II was never intended to usher in an antinomian age. Following his election as the Successor to Saint Peter in 1978, Pope John Paul II was determined to check the antinomianism that had surfaced during the postconciliar years. When he promulgated the new Code on the first Sunday of Advent in 1983, John Paul II expressly acknowledged that the legislation was a response to the "insistent and vehement demands of the bishops throughout the world."[82] Joined with the Successor to Peter, the college of bishops had discerned the pressing need to restore the rule of canon law in the church. Referring to the 1983 Code as the "final document of Vatican II," the Supreme Legislator intended the revised universal law of the church to express in juridical terms the dynamic theological perspective of the Council.[83] While the new Code had the general goal of restoring the balance between law and spirit in the life of the universal church, it also affirmed the significance of the church's penal order in dealing with cases of the sexual abuse of minors by clergy. Antinomianism in the United States defeated these general and specific goals of the rule of canon law.

C. The Legalist Response

The antinomianism of the second half of the twentieth century was met with a legalistic response by the U.S. bishops at the start of the twenty-first century. Confronted with the crisis of 2002, the bishops abrogated the psychological model in favor of an absolute rule. In the spring of 2002, Pope John Paul II summoned the American cardinals to the Vatican and urged them to deal with the problem.[84] Although several of the American cardinals had impressive backgrounds in canon law, the Rome meeting failed to result in unanimity about the rule of law.[85] When the U.S. bishops assembled in Dallas in June 2002, the atmosphere might fairly be described as one of extreme urgency, if not

---

82. *See* Ioannes Paulus Pp. II, Constitutio Apostolica *Sacrae Disciplinae Leges* (Die 25 mensis ian. anno 1983), xvi, 75 AAS II xi (1983).

83. Giovanni Paolo II, *Il Diritto Canonico inserisce il Concilio nella nostra vita*, 15 Communicationes 128 (1983).

84. *See* John Paul II, *Address to Summit of Vatican, U.S. Church Leaders*, 31 Origins 757, 759 (2002) ("[T]here is no place in the priesthood and religious life for those who would harm the young.").

85. *See* Adam Liptak, *Scandals in the Church: News Analysis; Damage-Control Mode*, N.Y. Times, Apr. 26, 2002, at A1, which states that the cardinals' statement following the Vatican meeting exhibited classical signs of damage control by an institution in crisis.

bordering on the hysterical.[86] Clearly under enormous pressure from the media and victims groups, the bishops adopted a so-called "zero-tolerance" policy.[87] Pursuant to the Dallas policy, any priest with an admitted or proven act against him at any time was to be expelled from the clerical state or banned from public ministry for life.[88] The bishops elected to correct the decades-long absence of a canonical response to the problem with a rule of strict criminal liability.

Law hastily framed runs the risk of abrogating any semblance of fundamental fairness and justice. In the months following Dallas, it was not uncommon for a priest with a single allegation against him, which was placed in his diocesan personnel file twenty or more years ago, to be summarily dismissed from an active and fruitful ministry. Following years of faithful service, the priest suddenly found himself deprived of his life's work and with his reputation irreparably damaged. Placed on indefinite administrative leave without adequate notice or opportunity to be heard, he received the same penalty as a serial child abuser. The implementation of the zero-tolerance approach in certain instances stunned priests and their parishioners and caused attorneys for the accused to raise questions about a lack of fundamental due process.[89]

The due process concerns for the rights of the accused included, *inter alia*, the following issues: the lack of notice of the precise nature of the allegation; the imposition of indefinite administrative leave with no legal recourse; the vagueness of the definition of the offense of sexual abuse in the Dallas policy; the disregard of the statute of limitations, which special canon law has established as ten years running from the victim's eighteenth year; the denial of the opportunity to be heard and offer a defense; the absence of proportionality in penalties; and the retroactive application of law.[90] Few if any American or canon lawyers would dispute that these issues pertain to the fundamental human rights of

---

86. *See* Bishop Wilton Gregory, *Presidential Address Opening Dallas Meeting*, 32 ORIGINS 97, 101 (2002), which describes media coverage as sometimes "hysterical and distorted".

87. *See Essential Norms for Diocesan/Eparchial Policies Dealing with Allegations of Sexual Abuse of Minors by Priests, Deacons, or Other Church Personnel: Pending "Recognitio,"* 9A, 32 ORIGINS 107, 108 (2002), which mandates that "even for a single act of sexual abuse of a minor—past, present or future—the offending priest or deacon will be permanently removed from ministry."

88. *See Charter for the Protection of Children and Young People*, Art. 5, 32 ORIGINS 102, 104 (2002). The Charter stipulates: "If the penalty of dismissal from the clerical state has not been applied (e.g., for reasons of advanced age or infirmity), the offender is to lead a life of prayer and penance. He will not be permitted to celebrate Mass publicly, to wear clerical garb or to present himself as a priest." *Id.*

89. *See* Laurie Goodstein, *Call for Revision Means More Priests Are Likely to Fight Zero-Tolerance Dismissals*, N.Y. TIMES, Oct. 20, 2002, at A14.

90. *See* John P. Beal, *Hiding in the Thickets of Law, Canonical Reflections on Some Disturbing Aspects of the Dallas Charter*, 187 AMERICA 15, 15–19 (Oct. 7, 2002), which identifies and discusses many of the canonical problems with the policy.

an accused person.[91] The lack of concern to frame a fair and just policy that would protect the rights of the accused displayed a strange combination of both antinomian and legalistic approaches. On the one hand, the bishops seemed simply to ignore many of the requirements of the natural law as expressed in canon law. On the other hand, the bishops adopted an absolute rule that permitted little or no discretion.

The Holy See declined to grant approval (*recognitio*) to the Dallas policy even on an experimental basis.[92] A mixed commission of representatives from Rome and the American bishops was formed to suggest revisions. It is perhaps ironic that the Vatican found itself in the position of raising questions about the Dallas policy, which violated quite elementary principles of American justice. However, these same basic principles are shared by the church's canon law.[93] In response to the recommendations of the mixed commission, it was necessary for the bishops to reconsider the policy approved at Dallas. Assembled in Washington in November 2003, the bishops affirmed the zero-tolerance approach but provided for it to be implemented in accord with the procedural requirements of canon law.[94] The rule of law is intended to set the conditions for a just ecclesial order in which the rights of the individual are balanced with the requirements of the common good. Antinomianism stifled the rule of law in permitting the grave crime to go unpunished, while legalism undermined confidence in canon law by creating the impression of a lack of justice for victims and accused alike.

---

91. *See* James H. Provost, *Book II, The People of God, in* CLSA-1985, 117, 134–37, which discusses the development of a list of fundamental rights for the 1983 Code and the similarities with the Bill of Rights and United Nations Declaration on Human Rights.

92. *See Letter of the Cardinal Prefect of the Congregation for Bishops*, 32 ORIGINS 341 (Oct. 31, 2002).

93. *See* Provost, *Book II, The People of God*, 134–38.

94. *See Charter for the Protection of Children and Young People, Revised*, 32 ORIGINS 409, 412 (2002) (the revision contains emphasis on the importance of adhering to Canons 1468–1477 of the 1983 Code); *see also Vatican Approves Plan on Sexual Abuse by U.S. Priests*, N.Y. TIMES, Dec. 17, 2002, at A28.

3. CANON LAW AND THE SEXUAL ABUSE CRISIS CONTINUED

The Consequences of the Failure of the Rule of Law

The primary consequence of the lack of balance in the bishops' approach to canon law was the damage suffered by the victims. When Bernard Cardinal Law, then the Archbishop of Boston, claimed that canon law prevented him from protecting the victims, they responded clearly: "Canon law was irrelevant to us. Children were being abused. Sexual predators were being protected. Canon law should have nothing to do with it. But they were determined to keep this problem, and their response to it, within their culture."[1] Given the failure of the rule of canon law to protect them, the victims quite understandably might attach little value to it. While injury to the victims remains the primary harm, the failure of canon law also held other consequences for the church and society. As with the defined parameters of the previous chapter, I shall discuss some of the ways in which antinomianism and legalism have disrupted the proper functioning of canon law.

I. THE CANONICAL REQUIREMENT OF CELIBACY AND THE SEXUAL ABUSE OF MINORS

A. Clerical Celibacy: Witness to Faith or Threat to the Public Good?

Canon 277, Section 1, of the *CIC-1983*, requires that priests in the Western branch of the Catholic Church observe celibacy. In the Eastern branch, the value of clerical celibacy is affirmed, but priests are permitted to marry in accord with a long-standing practice tracing its roots to the primitive church.[2] Since the 1950s in the West, the church has sometimes permitted an exception to mandatory celibacy for married former Protestant clergymen who became Catholic priests.[3] Although the celibacy requirement in the West is technically considered to be a disciplinary norm and not inherent in the nature of ordained priesthood, the canonical requirement reflects theological reasons of ancient tradition.[4] In his study of the historical development of the canonical requirement of celibacy for

---

1. Boston Globe Investigative Staff, Betrayal: The Crisis in the Catholic Church 153 (Little Brown Back Bay Books 2003).

2. *See* Canon 373, CCEO.

3. *See* R. Hill, *Ordination of Married Protestant Ministers*, 51 Canon Law Society of America Proceedings 95–100 (1989).

4. *See* R. Garrity, *Spiritual and Canonical Values in Mandatory Priestly Celibacy*, 27 Studia Canonica 217–60 (1993).

priests, Stefan Heid presents significant evidence that the celibacy requirement may be traced back through the centuries to spiritual values that originated in the primitive church.[5]

From the church's perspective, the discipline of clerical celibacy functions as an important witness both within the church itself and to the larger society. Clerical celibacy means that a man who would otherwise be married and the father of a family chooses to sacrifice this fundamental human good in testimony to his faith in Christ and dedication to the church. In Philip Jenkins's words, the sexual abuse crisis reversed this witness by presenting "a picture of a Catholic priesthood heavily influenced by perverts and child molesters, whose activities were treated so mildly by their superiors that the bishops themselves were virtual accomplices."[6] Thus, the failure to apply canon law facilitated a misunderstanding in the popular imagination that linked the canonical requirement of priestly celibacy with sexual deviance.

The antinomian failure of the rule of canon law supplied the reality upon which the canonical requirement of celibacy for priests was linked to the sexual abuse of minors. During the 2002 sexual abuse crisis, intense media focus and government responses seemed to reflect two assumptions. First, the Catholic priesthood contains a disproportionate number of sexual abusers as compared to the percent of sexual abusers in the general population and other professional groups. The investigative staff of the *Boston Globe* stated: "[I]n the wake of relentless revelations about sexually abusive priests, even the most conservative defenders of the Church have abandoned the argument that the priesthood is no worse than any other profession in which adults work with children."[7] Second, the widespread problem of sexual abuse among Catholic priests and cover-up by church authorities pose a threat to the public good which required a response from the secular government. State attorney generals and district attorneys in places such as Massachusetts, Philadelphia, Cincinnati, and Suffolk County, New York, impaneled grand juries to investigate the issue of the sexual abuse of minors by Catholic priests and the possibility of criminal cover-ups by church authorities.[8] Numerous state legislatures either repealed or debated repealing the statute of limitations in order that victims might bring civil suits against the

5. *See* Stefan Heid, Celibacy in the Early Church: The Beginnings of a Discipline of Obligatory Continence for Clerics in East and West 347–50 (Ignatius Press 2000). *See* also Christian Cochini, S.J., The Apostolic Origins of Priestly Celibacy 429–39 (Ignatius Press 1990); and Alfons Cardinal Stickler, The Case for Clerical Celibacy, Its Historical Development and Theological Foundations 83–103 (Ignatius Press 1995).

6. Philip Jenkins, Pedophiles and Priests: Anatomy of a Contemporary Crisis 133 (Oxford University Press 1996).

7. Betrayal, The Crisis in the Catholic Church, 166.

8. *Id.* at 112–13.

church. Such government actions were apparently seen as necessary to check the threat posed by the Catholic hierarchy and priests to the public good.

It seems fair to ask whether or not these assumptions are supported by the factual evidence. Does the Catholic priesthood in the United States contain a disproportionate number of sexual abusers as compared to the percent of sexual abusers in the general population and other professional groups? Does the canonical requirement of priestly celibacy pose a threat to the public good such that it justified the intense media focus of the 2002 crisis and the use of government power against the Catholic Church to check the threat?

First, the Catholic priest sexual abuse crisis needs to be considered within the context of the general problem of the sexual abuse of minors in the United States. Recent studies measuring the incidence of the sexual abuse of minors in the general population of the United States vary widely. David Finkelhor's *Child Sexual Abuse: New Theory and Research*, published in 1984, remains a frequently cited theory of child sexual abuse.[9] On the basis of what he considered to be conservative estimates of child sexual abuse (10 percent of girls and 2 percent of boys), Finkelhor concluded that over 210,000 new cases of sexual abuse occur in the United States each year.[10] A scientifically controlled study led by Finkelhor in 1990 that was based upon a control sample of 2,626 citizens aged 18 or older from all fifty states found that 27 percent of females and 16 percent of males had been sexually abused as minors.[11] Based on data collected from the National Child Abuse and Neglect Data System, Finkelhor and Lisa M. Jones determined the number of child abuse cases actually reported in the United States reached a peak of 149,800 cases in 1992 followed by annual declines to a low level of 89,355 cases in 2000.[12] In the fifty-two year period covered by the 2004 John Jay Study, the average number of minors abused per year is 205,[13] and the average number

9. *See* David Finkelhor, Child Sexual Abuse: New Theory & Research (Free Press 1984).

10. *See id.* 2.

11. *See* David Finkelhor, Gerard Hotaling, I. A. Lewis, & Christine Smith, 14 Child Abuse and Neglect 19–18 (1990).

12. Lisa Jones & David Finkelhor, *Explanations for the Decline in Child Abuse Cases*, OJJDP Bulletin, Office of Juvenile Justice and Delinquency Program, Office of Justice Program, U.S. Department of Justice, Washington, D.C., 2004, cited in 2004 John Jay Study, 25.

13. The mean average of victims per year is calculated by dividing the total number of victims, 10,667, by the total number of years, 52, covered in the 2004 John Jay Study, with the result of 205.134 victims per year from 1950 until 2002. As the 2006 John Jay Study indicates dioceses and religious communities continued to receive allegations of clergy sexual abuse from the period of 1940 to 2002 after the 2004 John Jay Study was complete. The mean average of 205 minors per year is derived from the 2004 John Jay Study and does not include allegations reported after 2004. Any study of sexual abuse, whether of Catholic priests, Protestant clergy, or some other group, shares the phenomena

of priests accused per year is 85.[14] By date of first instance, there were 421 priests accused of having committed the sexual abuse of a minor in 1970, the highest number of incidents for any year covered by the study. For the year 1984, the 2004 John Jay Study reports 204 priests by date of first instance. In 2002, by date of first instance, there were twenty-four priests who allegedly were guilty of abuse for that year.[15] Even if one takes the low number of 89,355 actual reported cases of the sexual abuse of minors per year in the United States, the average of 205 cases perpetrated by Catholic priests is less than one-quarter of one percent of the larger societal problem.

Second, the 2006 John Jay Study found that 4.2 percent of diocesan priests and 2.7 percent of religious priests, who had served during the fifty-four year period covered by the study, had been accused of the sexual abuse of a minor. These percentages were derived by comparing the number of priests accused to the total number of priests in the United States during the period covered by the study. In the absence of reliable statistical reports of the number of adult males in the United States accused of sexual abuse in a given year as compared to the total number of adult males in the United States for that year, it is impossible to know with certainty how the percentage of priest abusers compares to the percentage of abusers in the general population.

Third, it is possible to compare the rate of abusers among the celibate Catholic clergy to the rate of sexual abusers in the general population according to marital status. Another scientific study of the general problem of sexual abuse of minors in the United States published in 1996 by Douglas W. Pryor found that 70 percent of sexual offenders who abused minors were married.[16] The Pryor study also found that 23 percent of the incidents of sexual abuse were perpetrated by the victim's biological father; and another 38 percent of the abuse was perpetrated by the minor's stepfather, adoptive father, or mother's boyfriend.[17] In other words, married men and men in other heterosexual adult relationships account for the vast majority of the sexual abuse problem in the United States. The fact that married men account for a much higher percent of the societal problem of the

---

of previously unreported allegations of sexual abuse being reported after the study is complete as the number of incidents of abuse which may go unreported at all. This is the additional issue raised by false positive reports when no sexual abuse actually occurred.

14. The mean average of priest per year is calculated by dividing the total number of accused priests, 4392, by the total number of years, 52, covered in the 2004 John Jay Study, with the result of 84.48 priests per year from 1950 until 2002.

15. These statistics of the annual breakdowns with regard to the number of priest abusers were provided to me directly upon my request from the John Jay College through the U.S. Conference of Catholic Bishops. The annual numbers of accused priests may also be confirmed by reference to the 2004 John Jay Study, 30, fig. 2.3.2.

16. *See* Douglas W. Pryor, Unspeakable Acts: Why Men Sexually Abuse Children 23–24 (New York University Press 1996).

17. *See id.*

sexual abuse of minors than do celibate priests does not rule out the possibility that priestly celibacy might lead some men to sexually abuse minors. However, the possible link between celibacy and the sexual abuse of a minor is far from substantiated on the basis of the available statistical evidence.

Fourth, due to the absence of comprehensive studies of the sexual abuse of minors by clergy other than the John Jay studies, there is no reliable means of ascertaining how the problem among Catholic priests compares to that among other groups of religious ministers. The total number of cases included in the 2004 John Jay Study over the fifty-two year period results in an average of approximately 205 minors a year who report abuse by Catholic clergy. In comparison to Protestant clergy, the *New York Times* reports that "the three major companies that insure the majority of Protestant churches receive upward of two hundred sixty reports a year" of sexual abuse of minors by church ministers.[18] It is not clear from the *New York Times* article whether 260 represents the number of minors who claim to have been sexually abused or the number of ministers who allegedly perpetrated the abuse. It is also important to keep in mind that a given Protestant denomination's definition of who counts as an official minister may be broader and less carefully regulated than the Catholic Church's understanding of an ordained priest. Of the three insurance companies, one kept records for the past twenty years, another insurer was reporting on the basis of its records covering the past fifteen years, and the third of the major insurers reported on the basis of its ten-year records. The reports of the three insurance companies do not include all allegations against Protestant ministers but only those recorded by the three major insurers. Unlike the Catholic Church, none of the Protestant denominations have a requirement of celibacy for their ministers.

Fifth, juxtaposing the rates of abuse by Catholic priests and public school teachers may also offer a helpful comparative context from which to evaluate the claim that the celibacy requirement poses a threat to the public good. On the basis of a 1998 survey of nationwide newspaper articles, *Education Week* found that over a six-month period there were 244 reported cases of sexual abuse of public school students perpetrated by teachers.[19] As is the case for Protestant clergy mentioned above, it is not clear from the *Education Week* article whether 244 represents the number of minors who claim to have been sexually abused or the number of public school teachers who allegedly perpetrated the abuse. For the entire year 1998, the 2004 John Jay Study reports forty events of clergy sexual abuse of minors which started in that year.[20]

---

18. N.Y. TIMES, June 16, 2007, at A11.

19. *See* PHILIP JENKINS, THE NEW ANTI-CATHOLICISM: THE LAST ACCEPTABLE PREJUDICE 144 (Oxford University Press 2003).

20. As noted above in regard to the mean average number of victims per year over the 52-year period covered by the 2004 John Jay Study, allegations received after the year 2004 are obviously not included in the study. Again, given the nature of sexual abuse, previously

Legitimate questions may be raised about the reliability of specific child abuse studies, methodologies, and estimates based upon the studies. As the 2006 John Jay Study indicates, dioceses and religious communities continued to receive allegations of clergy sexual abuse from the period of 1940 to 2002 after the 2004 John Jay Study was complete. Any study of sexual abuse, whether of the general U.S. population, Catholic priests, Protestant clergy, or some other group, shares the phenomena of previously unreported allegations of sexual abuse being reported after the study is complete. The nature of these kinds of statistical studies produces a snapshot and cannot go beyond formulating a hypothesis about the future.

Again, I was unable to find any reliable statistical studies that would report the percentage of abusers among the general population, Protestant ministers, or public school teachers. However, the available statistical evidence suggests the following: (1) Catholic priests account for only a very small percent of the total number of cases of sexual abuse of minors that occur in the United States each year; (2) the vast majority of sexual abusers in the general population of the United States are married males or males living in some type of adult heterosexual union; (3) the average per year number of victims of abuse perpetrated by Catholic priests is no greater or less than that perpetrated by Protestant clergy; and (4) the average per year number of victims of abuse perpetrated by Catholic priests is no greater or less than that perpetrated by public school teachers. In other words, there is no conclusive evidence that proves that Catholic priests pose a special threat to the public good.

Based on the available statistical evidence, it is also impossible to know with certainty whether or not the rate of sexual abusers among Catholic priests is greater than, the same as, or less than the rate of abusers among Protestant clergy, public school teachers, or the general population. The statistical evidence also suggests that the percentage of Catholic clergy accused of abuse from the mid-1960s through the mid-1980s may well be higher than that of the percent of abusers in the general population, clergy of other denominations, and public school teachers. This is particularly true in certain geographic areas such as that covered by the Archdiocese of Boston.[21] It seems less true for other geographic areas such as that covered by the Archdiocese of New York.[22] The evidence also

---

unreported allegations of abuse being reported after the study is complete would also be probable for the survey of public schools.

21. *See* Report of the Attorney General on the Sexual Abuse of Children in the Archdiocese of Boston, Office of the Attorney General Commonwealth of Massachusetts, July 23, 2003, which reports on page 12 that from 1940 to 2003, the records of the Archdiocese of Boston indicated 789 victims of priest sexual abuse in the Archdiocese of Boston.

22. *See* John J. Coughlin, O.F.M., *Restoring the Faith: Responding to Clergy Sexual Abuse through Justice, Redemption, and Reconciliation*, Jurist, Nov. 11, 2002 (*available at* http://jurist.law.pitt.edu), which reports that records of the Archdiocese of New York as of 2002

indicates that prior and subsequent to the balloon in the statistical curve of Catholic clergy abusers (from 1950 until the mid-1960s and from the mid-1980s until 2004) the percentage of child abuse cases among Catholic clergy may be the same as or less than that of the general population, other clergy, and public school teachers.[23] If there were a statistical link between the canonical celibacy requirement and elevated instances of the sexual abuse of minors among Catholic priests in the United States, one would expect at least somewhat consistently elevated rates in the population of priests in comparison to the general population and other groups of professions over the period of the study. The statistical evidence from the John Jay studies suggests that the opposite is true. Over the five-plus decades encompassed in the studies, there are two periods of lower rates of clergy sexual abuse (1950 to the mid-1960s and the mid-1980s to 2004) and one period of higher rates (mid-1960 to mid-1980s).

Raising the question of whether the link between clerical celibacy and child abuse is supported by the factual evidence is in no way intended to diminish the significance of the problem among Catholic priests. However, it does seem helpful to put the problem in perspective. The antinomian failure to take canonical action against serial abusers provided the reality which led to the 2002 sexual abuse crisis in the Catholic Church. The rule of canon law would have served to dismiss serial sexual abusers from the priesthood. For reasons discussed, neither the statute of limitations nor culpability was likely to have presented insurmountable issues in prosecuting the case against the priest who was a serial child abuser. Neither canon law nor any other system of law can alter the reality that certain adults are prone to commit serial child abuse. However, the rule of canon law would have communicated that such priests were the exception and not the norm in the Catholic priesthood. It would have prevented much injury to many individuals and to the common good. To the extent that the 2002 sexual abuse crisis was about the complicity of the bishops, the crisis was facilitated by the failure of the bishops to honor the rule of canon law in dealing with cases of serial child abusers.

B. The Sexual Abuse Crisis and American Anti-Catholicism

Given the lack of proof that priests pose a unique threat to the public good as compared to the clergy of other denominations, public school teachers, and the general population, what might explain the fascination of the media and the response of government officials to take special action against the church? In the 1996 book, *Pedophiles and Priests: Anatomy of a Contemporary Crisis*, Philip Jenkins had suggested that starting in the early 1980s, the media were "constructing a social reality" by focusing on cases of priests who were serial

---

showed fewer than thirty priests accused of abuse. The statistics are undoubtedly higher, but would remain considerably less than those of Boston reported above.

23. *See* 2006 John Jay Study, 7, fig. 1.2.

child molesters.[24] The construction of social reality involves certain facts which are then interpreted to constitute a social problem that threatens the public good. According to Jenkins, notorious cases such as those of James Porter and John Geoghan, who forcibly molested scores of small children over many years, afforded the basis for the construction of a social reality about the Catholic Church. Rather than viewing serial child abuse as a matter of individual pathology, the media focused on such cases as typical of "pedophile priests" and church authorities who protected them.[25] By the time it became full blown in the 2002 crisis, the social construction of reality implicated the doctrine, structure, and priesthood of Catholicism in the sexual abuse of minors. In particular, the celibacy requirement for Catholic priests was seen as a threat to the public good.[26]

According to Philip Jenkins, hostility generated by the clergy sexual abuse issue revived the anti-Catholicism of the nineteenth-century literature in the United States that linked priestly celibacy to sexual perversion.[27] One strain of the nineteenth-century literature portrayed Catholic priests as lecherous criminals who raped virgins and seduced married women even as they ruled their flocks with iron fists.[28] Another strain ascribed to Catholic clergy "authoritarianism, ostentatious wealth, theatricality, and all the flamboyant trappings of 'popery,'" that "implied effeminacy and secret homosexuality."[29] The alleged link between priestly celibacy and sexual perversion enjoys almost as long a history as the celibacy requirement itself, and was a standard feature of Reformation polemic.[30] Given the revival of the link in the twenty-first century, it is fair to ask whether it is supported by the factual evidence.

In this regard, Jenkins's theory needs to be qualified in several ways. First, Jenkins's 1996 study predated the John Jay studies. The studies demonstrate that there has been a serious problem of the sexual abuse of minors by Catholic priests in the United States from 1950 until 2004, the most recent year covered by the studies. It remains the proper role of the media in a democratic society to expose such a problem to public scrutiny. I do not understand Jenkins's theory to suggest otherwise. Second, I have presented here only a very brief

---

24. *See* JENKINS, PEDOPHILES AND PRIESTS: ANATOMY OF A CONTEMPORARY CRISIS, 4–10.

25. *See id.* at 46–48, which discusses the Porter case; and JENKINS, THE NEW ANTI-CATHOLICISM: THE LAST ACCEPTABLE PREJUDICE, 134–38.

26. *See* THOMAS P. DOYLE, A. W. R. SIPE, & PATRICK J. WALL, SEX, PRIESTS, AND SECRET CODES x–xi, 294 (Volt Press 2006).

27. *See* JENKINS, THE NEW ANTI-CATHOLICISM, 43–45, 150–51.

28. *See* MARK TWAIN, LETTERS FROM THE EARTH 53 (Bernard DeVoto ed., Harper Perennial Classics 1974).

29. *See* JENKINS, PEDOPHILES AND PRIESTS: ANATOMY OF A CONTEMPORARY CRISIS, 23.

30. *See id.* at 20–21.

summary of Jenkins's substantial research. Any fuller account of the so-called "social construction of reality" requires greater sophistication in theory and method than I have presented. Third, even if one rejects entirely Jenkins's account of the social construction of reality, one might nonetheless acknowledge that the 2002 sexual abuse crisis cast doubt in the popular imagination about the value of priestly celibacy. As discussed above, the statistical evidence does not necessarily support the aspersion cast on the canonical requirement of celibacy. Given the reality of the virulent anti-Catholicism in American history, there may be some truth to the claim that the sexual abuse crisis served to revive the malady.

However, it would be reductionistic of the complex social reality represented by the 2002 clergy sexual abuse crisis to attribute it entirely to anti-Catholicism. The question remains: In light of the statistical evidence that Catholic priests in the United States do not pose a unique threat to the public good as compared to groups of other religious ministers, public school teachers, and the population as a whole, what can account for the ferocious focus of the media on the priesthood and the reaction of certain government officials to investigate and punish the Catholic Church? Moreover, why did the crisis occur in 2002 when the evidence suggests that most of the sexual abuse cases were twenty to thirty years old and that the two decades prior to 2002 have a low incidence of sexual abuse cases among Catholic priests? Certainly, organized groups of victims of sexual abuse were correctly indicating that the sexual abuse of minors was a serious problem among Catholic priests. These organizations arose in part because individual victims all too often found their complaints to ecclesiastical authorities met with a combination of denial, incompetence, and arrogance. Starting in the early 1980s, individual victims and survivor groups began to receive support from professional psychological therapists in understanding the damage done by sexual abuse. At the least, individual victims and the professional therapists wanted the Catholic Church to pay for the costs of counseling. At the same time, it was also in the interests of plaintiffs' lawyers to facilitate the 2002 sexual abuse crisis. As a result of its hierarchical form of government, the organization of the Catholic Church entails a concentration of financial resources not in individual parishes alone but in the dioceses of which they are a part. The hierarchical form of government also meant that the diocese could be held liable for the torts of individual priests. With potential damages and settlements in the billions of dollars, plaintiffs' lawyers, who are traditionally entitled to one-third of payments, perceived the Catholic Church as a rich target. If the social construction of reality applies to the 2002 Catholic sexual abuse crisis, it seems to be a complex social reality which involved many factors and groups in contemporary American society.

II. CANON LAW AND THEOLOGY

A. Original Sin and the Limitation of Law

Although Catholic moral theology considers any offense by a cleric against the Sixth Commandment of the Decalogue to constitute objectively grave sinful matter, the *CIC-1983* expressly recognizes only four types of sexual sin to constitute crimes for which canonical penalties may be imposed. The four crimes include a sexual sin committed by a cleric with a minor, a sexual sin that involves force or threat of force, sexual sin committed in public, and continued open concubinage by a cleric with a woman after the cleric has been officially warned.[31] Canon law of course expresses an aspirational function when it urges all priests to live a life of chaste holiness.[32] At the same time, in limiting the kind of sexual sin that can be punished by canonical penalty, canon law reflects the anthropological reality of fallen human nature. The theological doctrine of original sin places inherent limitations on canon law's aspirations. Neither policy nor law, no matter how well designed, can eradicate sin from the fallen nature of the human situation. Like all other human beings, priests are going to act in sinful ways, sometimes gravely sinful. This has been the case from the beginnings of the church when the gospels recall that Peter, the first of the Apostles, denied Christ in his darkest hour.[33]

However, canon law's limitation does not excuse the injury caused by a priest to a victim of sexual abuse or by church authorities in covering up the crime. The unity between the theological doctrine of original sin and canon law does not mean that church authorities should not take all reasonable precautionary measures to prevent sexual abuse. On the contrary, the evidence suggests that clear policy and law assist in preventing sexual abuse by priests. Although the wave of media reports reached a crest at the beginning of the twenty-first century, the vast majority of cases of priest sexual abuse occurred several decades earlier during the second half of the twentieth century. Since the promulgation of the *CIC-1983* and the implementation of diocesan sexual abuse policies, there has been a marked decline in the number of incidents of sexual abuse reported. As previously discussed, the available evidence about sexual abuse suggests that for the last twenty years there may be a lower rate of sexual abusers among Catholic priests than the percentage of offenders in the general population of the United States, other groups of religious ministers, and public school teachers. The antinomian and legalistic approaches both overlook the unity between canon law and the theology of original sin. Antinomianism presumes that law is not necessary to check the fallen human situation, and legalism suggests that law has no limits in overcoming sin.

---

31. *See* Canon 1395, *CIC-1983*.
32. *See* Canon 276, *CIC-1983*.
33. John 18:15–17, 25–27.

B. Law and the Theology of Forgiveness

The ecclesiastical penal order depends primarily on "medicinal" sanctions.[34] Excommunication, interdict, and the suspension of a cleric constitute remedial penalties. The goal of such sanctions is to encourage the offender's change of mind and heart. Once conversion with repentance has occurred, the remedial penalty is lifted, and the offender is to be reintegrated into the full communion of the church. As an exception to the general principle, canon law provides for certain "expiatory" or "vindictive" penalties.[35] Such penalties obviously do not depend on the offender's change of heart, but are intended as a means of retributive justice. Few in number, they are imposed only for the most serious offenses, such as the sexual abuse of a minor by a cleric. The penalty's justification rests on the reality that the priest who sexually abuses a child has not only harmed the victim but the entire church. While the guilty priest may be forgiven his sin no matter how grave, a just ecclesial order may require that he can no longer function as a priest. Canon law's focus on medicinal penalties, with a small number of defined retributive exceptions for particularly grave crimes, thus reflects the unity of law and theology.

Neither antinomianism nor legalism enhances the unity between canon law and the theology of forgiveness. Antinomianism denies the need for penal sanctions in the church altogether, while legalism demands the imposition of penal sanctions without regard to mercy. The failure of rule of law in dealing with clergy sexual abuse disrupted the church's penal order with its deep roots in the development of the theology of forgiveness. One of the great issues to face the church of the first several centuries was the question of postbaptismal forgiveness of sin.[36] In the gospels, Jesus appears eating and drinking with sinners, and the *evangelium* (good news) is addressed not to the self- righteous but to those in need of redemption.[37] Questions arose concerning whether or not

---

34. *See* Velasio de Paolis, *Animadversiones ad schema documenti quo disciplina sanctionum seu peonarum in Ecclesia Latina denuo ordinatur*, 63 PERIODICA 37, 39 (1974); and Velasio de Paolis, *Il Libro VI del Codice di Diritto Canonico: Diritto Penale, Disciplina Penitenziale o Cammino Penitenziale?* 90 PERIODICA 85, 98–106 (2001).

35. *See* Canon 1312, *CIC-1983*. Penalties in the church are either medicinal or expiatory. Most of the penalties are remedial in nature in that they are to be lifted as soon as the offender demonstrates sincere repentance. A few penalties are expiatory in that they deprive the offender of some good permanently or a fixed period of time regardless of the offender's subsequent disposition.

36. *See* BERNHARD POSCHMAN, PENANCE AND THE ANOINTING OF THE SICK 34–61 (Francis Courtney trans., Herder and Herder 1964).

37. *See* JOACHIM JEREMIAS, NEW TESTAMENT THEOLOGY: THE PROCLAMATION OF JESUS 109 (John Bowden trans., Scribner 1971), which observes that Jesus brought the good news to sinners; and JOHN P. MEIER, A MARGINAL JEW, VOLUME III, COMPANIONS AND COMPETITORS 247 (Bantam Doubleday 2001), which states that Jesus "hobnobbed" with sinners.

there was forgiveness of sin after baptism, and if so, how often it might be repeated, what sins could be forgiven, and which sinners were worthy of penance. The questions admitted of stricter or milder answers. The second-century Christian writer, Hermas, endorsed the theory of "one penance" after baptism.[38] The early Tertullian (c.203) advocated full forgiveness for even the gravest sins, and to this end, described a rite of public penance.[39] In addition to public penance for postbaptismal sin, Origen (184–254) speaks of confessing one's sins to a priest who acts as a physician of souls.[40] Contrary to the Montanists and Novatians, who cast doubt about postbaptismal forgiveness, Canon 8 of the Council of Nicea (325) permitted even apostates to return to the church after penance.[41] Nonetheless, Constantine, who feared dying in the state of sin, postponed baptism until shortly before his death in 337, and when he died, he lay in state at Constantinople in the white robe of a neophyte.[42] Eventually, the forgiveness of sins through confession, contrition, and penance became a central feature of church doctrine and practice.[43]

Canon law recognizes a distinction between the internal and external fora in order to facilitate the forgiveness of sin.[44] The internal forum pertains to matters of conscience, and it involves confidentiality in both sacramental and nonsacramental communications. If it involves pastoral counseling, the therapy afforded priests accused of sexual abuse may sometimes fall within the parameters of the

---

38. *See* Jeremias, New Testament Theology, 37.

39. *See id.* at 39.

40. *See id.* at 70.

41. *See* Heinrich Denzinger, The Sources of Catholic Dogma 55 & 26 (Roy J. Deferrari trans., from the thirteenth edition of Enchiridion symbolorum, Loreto Publications 2001). Montanism was a second-century Christian movement that denied the possibility for the post-Baptismal forgiveness of sin. Tertullian converted to Montanism. Novatian was a Roman priest who in 251 AD opposed the election of Pope Cornelius. During the Emperor Decius's persecution of Christians in which many Christians went to their deaths for refusing to worship the Roman deities, Pope Cornelius favored Cyprian of Carthage's policy of readmitting the lapsed (those who had obeyed the imperial edict requiring the idolatry) to communion if they engaged in a period of penance.

42. *See* Henry Chadwick, The Early Church 136 (Penguin Books 1978).

43. In the thirteenth century, Thomas Aquinas afforded a sacramental analysis for the three parts of penance. *See* ST, III, 90, 2, which identifies contrition, confession, and satisfaction as the parts of penance.

44. Principle No 2 for the Revision of the *CIC-1983* had called for improved harmony between the internal and external fora especially with regard to the sacraments and ecclesiastical penalties. 1 Communicationes 77, 79 (1969). *See* Thomas J. Green, *The Future of Penal Law in the Church,* 35 Jurist 212, 220 (1975), which endorses the fundamental distinction in the *CIC-1917,* but notes that the confusion of fora also contributed to inefficacy which needed to be corrected in the proposed new Code.

nonsacramental internal forum.[45] In contrast, the external forum signifies an act of governance, which remains public and verifiable. For example, a status of person question, such as that of a cleric who has been suspended or dismissed from the clerical state for the sexual abuse of a minor, belongs to the external forum. Clearly, a credible accusation of the sexual abuse of a minor officially reported to an ecclesiastical authority belongs to the external forum. In dealing with clergy sexual abuse cases in the United States, the exclusive reliance on the psychological model tended to create the impression of secrecy and cover-up.

The distinction between the internal and external fora reflects a balance between the common good and the individual person's rights of privacy and good reputation.[46] When an act of governance is taken for the common good, such as dismissal from the clerical state, it concerns the public social relations among persons. Such an act must admit of external proof and verification. Alternatively, the vast majority of sins, including most mortal sins, are not crimes subject to the ecclesiastical penal order.[47] The distinction protects not just clerics but all of the vast mass of baptized persons who constitute the Body of Christ. In accord with theological anthropology, all are sinners, and all may benefit from the counsel and forgiveness available in the internal forum. The criticism of this traditional distinction on the ground that it enables a "clerical culture of secrecy" fails to appreciate the ancient wisdom of the church in protecting individual dignity and privacy. In dealing with cases of sexual abuse, the church's wisdom

---

45. The confession and forgiveness of sin belong to the sacramental internal forum, which absolutely safeguards the matter and identity of a penitent in the sacrament of Penance. In the sacramental forum, a priest-confessor can urge the penitent to disclose the sinful abuse to the ecclesiastical and public authorities, but the confessor remains always bound by the inviolable seal of the sacrament. *See* Canons 983, § 1 & 1388, § 1, *CIC-1983*. The nonsacramental internal forum refers to matters outside the sacrament, but which are not publicly known and best kept in confidence. Although not part of a sacramental confession, the matter revealed by an individual to a counselor, whether priest or layperson, constitutes a matter of conscience. Normally, the counselor bears the obligation of confidentiality. When the law of a civil jurisdiction requires a counselor in the nonsacramental internal forum to report child abuse, the counselor ordinarily may comply. *See* Raymond C. O'Brien, *Pedophilia: The Legal Predicament of the Clergy*, 4 J. Contemporary Health Law and Policy 91, 138–50 (1988). *See* also The Society of Jesus of New England v. Commonwealth, 442 Mass. 1049 (2004).

46. *See* Canon 220, *CIC-1983* ("No one may unlawfully harm the good reputation which a person enjoys, or violate the right of every person to protect his or her privacy.").

47. Some acts of governance, such as the lifting of nonpublic censures, may be exercised solely for an individual's own good and these acts remain in the internal forum. *See* Green, *The Future of Penal Law in the Church*, 220, which discusses the need for a clear distinction between the forum of law and the forum of conscience.

was not evident in a policy that focused on the therapeutic approach and neglected the external forum of the canonical penal sanctions.[48]

C. Priesthood as a State of Life

By the time of Augustine, Bishop of Hippo (395–430), it was well established that any sin, no matter how grave or frequent, might be forgiven as long as the sinner manifested repentance. The penance was public for notorious sins and secret for private ones.[49] The question of postbaptisimal forgiveness of sin was connected to another issue about the purity of the church. Particularly after the Constantinian establishment, "the impure" swelled the ranks of the pristine church of the martyrs. In fourth-century northern Africa, disagreement about the requisite level of purity to be a member of the church led to the Donatist schism. The Donatists wanted a church separate from the contamination of the world, one that was morally without fault, whose ritual counted as a sealed fountain of grace, a church whose clergy inherited the purity of the martyrs.[50] The Donatists pointed to the sins and corruption of Catholic deacons, priests, and bishops to justify the schism. They counted it as a triumph when they publicly exposed the sexual sins of the Catholic clergy. In the ensuing polemic, Catholics responded with revelations of the immoral and criminal behavior of the Donatist clergy.[51] Augustine himself remarked that one Donatist bishop had impregnated a thirteen-year-old virgin girl.[52] For Augustine, the rites of the church were holy because of the objective holiness of the church as the redeemed body of Christ. Neither the church's holiness nor the administration of her sacraments depended on the subjective qualities of the clergy. Rather, the sacraments, Augustine held, claimed an objective and permanent validity independent of the subjective experience of the individual deacons, priests, and bishops.[53]

---

48. Not all therapy necessarily falls within the internal forum. For example, therapists are sometimes compelled by law to reveal clients' secrets. Moreover, it is possible to conceive of a therapeutic approach in which close surveillance of an abuser involves regular reporting on the content of the therapy. Following the sexual abuse crisis, a report from the Congregation for Catholic Education at the conclusion of the Apostolic Visitation of seminaries in the United States stated that psychological counseling "may be confidential, but it is not internal forum." Congregatio De Institutione Catholica (*De Seminariis Atque Studiorum Institutis*) (Die 15 mensis dec. anno 2008), Prot No. 1009/2002.

49. *See* Henry Chadwick, The Early Church, at 67–68, which discusses Origen's position that even the gravest of sins may be forgiven.

50. *See* Peter Brown, Augustine of Hippo 213 (University of California Press 1969).

51. *See* Heid, Celibacy in the Early Church, The Beginnings of a Discipline of Obligatory Continence for Clerics in the East and West 204–06.

52. *See* Augustine of Hippo, *Epistola* 105, 2, 3f; 33 PL 396–97.

53. *See* Augustine of Hippo, *De Baptismo Contra Donatistas,* IV, 23, 30; 43 PL 170, 174.

The sexual abuse crisis has called into question canon law's recognition of the priesthood as an objective, permanent, and stable office in the church. *CIC-1983* recognizes several distinct states of life in the church.[54] The reference to states of life is not intended primarily as a manifestation of the church's hierarchical order. On the contrary, Canon 208 states that all the baptized enjoy "a genuine equality of dignity and action" in forming the "Body of Christ." Through Baptism, each member of the church participates in the priestly, prophetic, and kingly office of Christ.[55] Marriage, Holy Orders, and religious life are considered to be states of life which reflect the free choice of individuals. Canon 207 draws a fundamental distinction between clerics and laypersons, as well as recognizing the religious life.[56] Marriage is the most common state of life in the church. With language drawn from *Gaudium et spes*, Canon 1055 describes marriage as "the intimate partnership of life and love which constitutes the married state . . ."[57] Canon law treats marriage as a permanent state of life in the church. An act of adultery or even abuse, for example, does not dissolve a valid marriage. In such circumstances, canon law provides that one spouse might temporarily or permanently separate from the other, but canon law never grants an absolute divorce in the case of a valid and consummated sacramental marriage.[58]

---

54. *See* J. Hervada, *Commentary on Book II, in* Ottawa-1993, 185–86, which discusses the principles of radical equality and of variety as the two basic principles of Book II of the *CIC-1983*.

55. *See* Canon 208, *CIC-1983* ("Flowing from their rebirth in Christ, there is a genuine equality of dignity and action among all of Christ's faithful. Because of this equality they all contribute, each according to his or her own condition and office, to the building up of the body of Christ.").

56. *See* Canon 330, *CIC-1983* ("Just as, by the decree of the Lord, Saint Peter and the rest of the Apostles form one College, so for a like reason the Roman Pontiff, the successor of Peter, and the Bishops, the successors of the Apostles, are united together in one."). According to Catholic belief, Christ originally entrusted the faith to the Twelve Apostles with the mission to teach, sanctify, and govern. Canon 331, *CIC-1983*, focuses on the divine institution of the Petrine ministry as the head of the "College of Bishops, Vicar of Christ, and Pastor of the universal Church on earth." Canon 375, § 1, *CIC-1983* ("By divine institution, Bishops succeed the Apostles through the Holy Spirit who is given to them. They are constituted Pastors in the Church, to be teachers of doctrine, the priests of sacred worship and the ministers of governance."). *See Lumen Gentium*, 26–28, which teaches that the hierarchical offices of bishop and priest are ministerial examples of the self-emptying of Christ, which is the example for all Christians. *See* also St. Bonaventure, *Lignum Vitae*, 7, *in* 8 Doctoris Seraphici S. Bonaventurae opera omnia, edita studio et cura pp. Collegii a S. Bonaventura 72 (Collegium San Bonaventura 1882) ("So complete was his humility, that He who was perfect justice subjected himself to the Law.").

57. *Gaudium et spes*, 48.

58. *See* Canons 1151–1152, *CIC-1983*.

Likewise, the valid reception of the sacrament of Holy Orders means that the deacon, priest, or bishop has entered into a permanent state of life.[59] Theologically, the reception of Holy Orders is claimed to place an indelible character onto the recipient of the sacrament.[60] In medieval theology, this character was often described as an ontological change in the soul of the priest.[61] Canon 290, *CIC-1983* affirms the ancient tradition when it states that ordination once received never becomes invalid.[62] Permanent dismissal from the clerical state (laicization) does not mean that one is no longer a priest. Pursuant to Canon 292, *CIC-1983*, the laicized cleric loses the rights of the clerical state, and he may no longer be publicly acknowledged as a cleric. However, the imposition of the canonical penalty only renders the exercise of the priesthood unlawful in most circumstances. For example, a Mass celebrated by a priest who has been permanently removed from the clerical state may be a valid Mass even though the celebration is unlawful. In canonical terminology, validity of the sacrament perdures although the celebration by a laicized priest is illicit. Canon 976, *CIC-1983*, permits a laicized priest to hear the confession of, and grant absolution to, a person in danger of death. The danger of death provision is an example of the principle of the salvation of souls as the supreme law of the church.[63]

Contrary to the Augustinian sacramental theology *ex opere operato*, antinomian and legalistic approaches to canon law may reflect a desire for moral perfectionism in the church and the priesthood. Antinomianism espouses an idealistic image of the church whose priests and members have no faults that may need correction through the law. Legalism embraces a church whose priests and members are rendered morally perfect through law alone dislocated from the spiritual ends that underpin canon law.

III. ANTINOMIANISM, LEGALISM, AND THE NATURE OF CANON LAW

The antinomian and legalistic approaches to the sexual abuse of minors in the United States raise a broad jurisprudential question about the nature of canon law. Given the failure of canon law to render justice for victims, advance the

---

59. A religious who professes final vows has also entered into a permanent state of life in the church. However, permanent religious vows are not sacramental, and may be dispensed through the action of the Holy See.

60. *See* Sacrosanctum Concilium Oecumenicum Vaticanum II, Decretum De Presbyterorum Ministerio et Vita, *Presbyterorum Ordinis* (Die 7 mensis decembris anno 1965), 2, 58 AAS 991–92 (1966); and *Lumen Gentium*, 21.

61. *See* Council of Florence, November 22, 1439, *in* DENZINGER, THE SOURCES OF CATHOLIC DOGMA, 695; and Council of Trent, March 3, 1547, *in* DENZINGER, THE SOURCES OF CATHOLIC DOGMA, 852.

62. *See Lumen Gentium*, 21.

63. *See* Canon 1752, *CIC-1983*.

common good, and protect individual rights, does canon law count as law, properly speaking? Canon law purports to be normative in that it governs the behavior of persons and groups in the life of the Catholic Church. Canon law is, of course, not the most important normative domain in the church. Sacred scripture, tradition, moral theology, faith, and practical reason all serve as guides to the conduct of the baptized in the church. The question about the nature of canon law inquires into how it differs from these complementary normative domains and interacts with them.

Antinomianism raises the question as to whether coercive power remains an essential characteristic of law that distinguishes it from other normative claims. As reviewed at the outset of this chapter, canon law contains clearly established substantive and procedural provisions for the imposition of penalties on a priest who sexually abuses a minor. The antinomian approach to canon law meant that these canonical provisions were not employed for at least several decades by church authorities in the United States. From the perspective of Anglo-American legal theory, the early legal positivists such as Jeremy Bentham and John Austin argued that coercion counts as a constitutive component of law which separates it from other normative domains in a community. According to Austin's well-known "command theory," in order to count as law, each and every law of a society must be backed by threat of sanction.[64] Along similar lines, Hans Kelsen thought that law functioned to monopolize violence in a society and to impose its demands by violent means.[65] For both Austin and Kelsen, the ability of a subject and society to predict that punishment by the sovereign would follow upon detected disobedience to the law is essential to distinguishing law from other types of norms. If coercion is an essential characteristic of law, church authorities' antinomian approach to canon law in cases of priests who sexually abused minors calls into question the very nature of canon law as law.

Later legal positivists, such as H. L. A. Hart and Joseph Raz, have argued that the coercive element of law is more marginal than the pristine positivists thought. Responding to Austin, Hart objected "that the predictive interpretation obscures the fact that, where rules exist, deviations from them are not merely grounds for the prediction that hostile reactions will follow . . . but are also a reason or justification for such reaction and for applying the sanctions."[66] Likewise, Raz points out that many reasons for action might contain a threat of coercion,

---

64. *See* John Austin, The Province of Jurisprudence Determined 14 (W. E. Rumble ed., Cambridge University Press 1995).

65. *See* Hans Kelsen, Introduction to the Problems of Legal Theory 56–50 (B. L. Paulson & S. L. Paulson trans., Clarendon Press of Oxford University 1992).

66. H. L. A. Hart, The Concept of Law 82 (2nd ed. Clarendon Press of Oxford University 1997).

but do not necessarily constitute law.[67] For example, in the case of a terrorist who holds a gun to the hostage's head, the hostage may be able to predict the outcome should the hostage disobey the terrorist, but this threat of coercion does not dignify the terrorist's command by raising to the level of law. Hart and Raz both consider the command theory of law to reduce law to coercion while it ignores other important functions of law. I do not mean to conflate Austin's command theory of law with the view of law as coercion. An understanding of law as command may be ascribed to motives such as obedience to the rightful authority of the lawgiver while law as coercion may be understood simply as obedience out of fear of punishment. Nonetheless, in regard to Hart's terrorist example, command and coercion seem to be inadequate descriptions of law.

Consistent with the criticism of the command theory of law, it would be reductionistic to hold that canon law's sole function in the church is its coercive aspect with its related predictability. Rooted in its ancient historical tradition, canon law serves many other functions in the life of the Catholic Church besides mere coercion. Canon law fulfills aspirational and pedagogical purposes, embodies communal values, sets standards for desirable behavior, resolves coordination problems, and safeguards individual rights and the common good. Even if coercion is not the defining characteristic of canon law, does not coercion nonetheless fulfill an important function in the life of the church? Moreover, does not the coercive aspect of canon law reinforce the other functions that canon law fulfills in the life of the church and its members? To answer these complex theoretical questions, suffice it to recall the Boston victims' statement mentioned above that canon law was irrelevant. In *de facto* abrogating the coercive function of canon law in sexual abuse cases in favor of a psychological model, the antinomian approach called into question the normative nature of canon law itself.

Legalism also raises questions about the nature of canon law. In this regard, the work of another secular legal theorist, Ronald Dworkin, proves helpful. Rejecting the separation between fact and value drawn by the legal positivists, Dworkin maintains that the nature of a norm as law derives from an integration of facts and moral values. In Dworkin's words, "According to law as integrity, propositions of law are true if they figure in or follow from the principles of justice, fairness, and procedural due process that provide the best constructive interpretation of the community's legal practice."[68] The legalistic approach of church authorities following the 2002 sexual abuse crisis cast doubt on canon law's integrity. One such question was suggested by Julián Cardinal Herranz,

67. *See* Joseph Raz, The Authority of the Law: Essays on Law and Morality 242–44 (Clarendon Press of Oxford University 2002), which states that prudential reasons such as fear of punishment do not in themselves give law authority.

68. Ronald Dworkin, Law's Empire 225 (Belknap Press of Harvard University 2001).

who as Prefect of the Congregation for the Interpretation of Legislative texts, commented: "[I]t was absolutely essential that the norms reaffirm the principle, rooted in natural law and respected in legitimate legal systems throughout the world, that a person who is accused of an offense must be considered innocent prior to a determination of his guilt or innocence, either by means of a regular process in which the truth of the accusation could be ascertained and the alleged victim and the accused would both have the possibility of defending their positions, or by virtue of a confession."[69] Another question is evident in the appeal of the U.S. bishops described earlier in this chapter to establish a more relaxed standard of proof than that of canon law's moral certainty standard.

Perhaps, the most striking question of justice, fairness, and procedural due process is raised by the absolute rule that treats every instance of sexual abuse of a minor by a cleric as requiring the most severe canonical penalty of permanent removal from the clerical state. Although divine, natural, and canon law consider every instance of sexual abuse to be a grave wrong, all sexual abuse cases do not have identical facts. The cases range from the extremes of a priest who serially molested hundreds of young children over the course of several decades to that of a priest who committed a single offence with a seventeen-year-old over thirty years ago. In this second case, the priest has long since repented, and has given devoted service over the ensuing decades to several parish communities who hold him in high regard. Given the years of antinomianism that led to the 2002 crisis, the absolute rule of permanent dismissal may have been the only realistic option open to the U.S. bishops when they adopted the 2002 Dallas Charter. Even in the absence of the 2002 crisis, it may be true that the vast majority of cases of priests found guilty ought to result in the penal sanction of permanent removal. Nonetheless, each case remains fact-specific, and for this reason, the discretion to make exceptions to the absolute rule, even if rare, seems more reflective of the integrity of law as Dworkin describes it. Section 2 of Canon 1395, *CIC-1983*, permits this kind of discretion as an aspect of the integrity of canon law in promoting fundamental fairness and justice. In contrast, the 2002 Dallas Charter's absolute rule is more reflective of the rigidity that typifies legalism.

Canon law reflects the theological belief that bishops are successors to the Apostles, and as such are vested with sacred responsibility to teach, sanctify, and exercise a "ministry of governance."[70] The phrase "ministry of governance"

---

69. Interview with Archbishop Julián Herranz, ZENIT, November 4, 2002, *available at* http://www.zenit.org.

70. Canon 375, § 1, *CIC-1983*. This unitary ministry of governance is classified into legislative, executive, and judicial functions. *See* Thomas J. Green, *The Pastoral Governance Role of the Diocesan Bishop: Foundations, Scope, and Limitations*, 49 JURIST 472, 483–90 (1989), which discusses the unitary power of governance and its three distinct functions.

distinguishes the office of the bishop from some secular function.[71] Canon law considers the power of the bishop to be not worldly but sacred power. In fulfilling his ministry of governance, the words of canon law require the bishop to act in accord with "holiness, charity, humility and simplicity of life."[72] Although many bishops undoubtedly exemplify these characteristics, some bishops failed to convey the characteristics in addressing cases of clergy abuse. As just mentioned, each one of these cases is fact-specific. Canon law is designed to permit some flexibility and discretion in the way in which cases are resolved. The protection of individual rights as well as the common good depends on this kind of intelligent approach. Given the failure with regard to the rule of canon law, the bishops in the United States have now found it necessary to surrender their discretion for the zero tolerance rule. This absolutist approach may be necessary to restore confidence in the church, but it belies canon law's image of the bishop who exercises a wise discretion that flows from integrity, compassion, and holiness.

The discussion of canon law from the perspective of certain secular legal theorists is not intended to overlook what distinguishes canon law from modern secular legal systems. In contrast to the fact/value debate which plays such an important role in secular legal theory, canon law has no hesitation about its connection to moral value. The question of the law's authority, or what gives canon law its power to bind, has a strong answer in divine and natural law. These sources are normative in the Catholic community on the basis of the integration of faith and practical reason. Even without canon law, the sexual abuse of a minor remains a grave violation of divine and natural law. Although the normativity of canon law interfaces with divine and natural law, canon law nonetheless enjoys

---

71. *See Lumen Gentium*, 2. As envisioned in the 1983 Code, the role of the bishop reflects the ecclesiology of *Lumen Gentium*. The narrative of *Lumen Gentium's* ecclesiology starts with the radical economy of love in the absolute self-gift among each of the three persons in the one God. The relational and donative characteristics of trinitarian love have implications for membership in the College of Bishops. *See id.* at No. 20, 371–72. (Since "that divine mission, which was committed by Christ to the Apostles, is destined to last until the end of the world, . . . the Apostles took care to appoint successors in this hierarchically structured society."). It means that the bishop is among his people in humble service and kenotic love at the head of the one Body of Christ. *See id.* at No. 18, 370 (Article 18 of *Lumen Gentium* states that the church was hierarchically ordered by Christ in the selection of the Twelve Apostles because: "He willed that their successors, namely the bishops, should be the shepherds of the Church until the end of world."). For a discussion of the historical evidence for this theological truth, *see* generally FRANCIS J. SULLIVAN, S.J., FROM APOSTLES TO BISHOPS, THE DEVELOPMENT OF THE EPISCOPACY IN THE EARLY CHURCH (Newman Press 2001).

72. *See* Canon 343, § 1, *CIC-1983*, stating in part that "[i]n exercising his pastoral office, the diocesan bishop is to be solicitous for all Christ's faithful entrusted to his care, whatever their age . . ." and Canon 387, which envisions that the bishop will be "[m]indful that he is bound to give an example of holiness, charity, humility and simplicity of life . . . seeking in every way to promote the holiness of the Christian faithful . . ."

a certain level of autonomy. The restoration of confidence in the rule of canon law will require that the bishop implement the new policy in a just manner. Canon law functions to fulfill certain essential purposes in the life of the ecclesiastical community that only law, in distinction from other sources of normativity, can fulfill. The consideration of certain aspects of secular legal theory assists in revealing the negative impact of antinomianism and legalism on canon law as proper law. By diminishing the rule of law in the life of the church, antinomianism and legalism cause injury to the rights of individuals and communities, and thus call the nature and effectiveness of canon law into question.

4. CHURCH PROPERTY

A Comparison of the Theories of Property in Canon Law and Liberal Theory

In Chapters 4 and 5, I discuss the ownership of property in the Catholic Church. Chapter 4 lays the theoretical foundation for the discussion through a comparison of several seminal elements in the understanding of property in canon law and the liberal political theory. The idea of property—its justifications, functions, and limitations—plays an important role in both canon law and liberal theory. Property is in essence the relationship between an individual, group, community, or state and a tangible or intangible thing. It includes not just real property, such as land and edifices constructed upon it, but also intangible acquisitions, as—to mention but a few examples—copyrights, trademarks, stocks, bonds, promissory notes, air rights, options for purchase, franchises, and government licenses for broadcasting. The concept of property admits of various other distinctions. Property may be public or private, movable and immovable, fungible or personal, productive or consumptive. It may be owned in a plenary sense of permanent control or partially in the sense of entitlement to its usufruct. The focus here is on private property and its fruitful ownership.

In the teaching of the Catholic Church, private property is understood as a way of assigning common resources. It is not absolute. Section 1 of Canon 1254, *CIC-1983*, states: "The Catholic Church, in order to pursue its proper objectives, has the inherent right, independent of any secular power, to acquire, retain, administer, and alienate temporal goods." The phrase "independent of any secular power" indicates both the basis of the property right, which in the teaching of the church may be traced to the nature of the human person and therefore is not dependent on the state. The phrase also reflects the long experience of the church with governments hostile to the church's property rights. However, according to the church's teaching, the state regulates private property for the common good. Consistent with state regulation, the church controls its own property for its mission, which transcends the common good.

I. ELEMENTS IN CANON LAW'S APPROACH TO PROPERTY

Here, I shall identify five elements that have influenced canon law's approach to property including: (1) the anthropological basis of private property based on reason, freedom, and the social nature of the human person; (2) the position of the fathers of the church, who considered private property to be a consequence of original sin and therefore not part of the original state of nature; (3) property ownership in the early church; (4) medieval approaches to property, especially the theory of Thomas Aquinas; and (5) the social teaching of the church about property.

A. Anthropological Basis for Private Property

The anthropology, or understanding of the human person, that underpins canon law offers a positive justification for the institution of private property as necessary to the good of the human person and society. First, without the use of material things, the person would be unable to survive, to care for family, to develop potentiality, to fulfill his or her ultimate end. The right to the use of material things flows from the reality of the human person as an embodied spirit. The fundamental right to the use of material things would prove nugatory without the right of the human person to acquire and possess material things. The institution of private property is the necessary extension of the primordial principle of use and the correlative rights of the person to acquire and possess material things. As the philosopher Simon Weil expressed it:

> Private property is a vital need of the soul. The soul feels isolated, lost, if it is not surrounded by objects which seem to it like an extension of the bodily members. All men have an invincible inclination to appropriate in their own minds anything which over a long, uninterrupted period they have used for their work, pleasure, or the necessities of life. But where the feeling of appropriation doesn't coincide with any legally recognized proprietorship, men are continually exposed to extremely painful spiritual wrenches.[1]

From Weil's perspective, private property then is a legal recognition of the nature of the human person and what the person needs for the body and soul to flourish.

Second, the human person's capacity for reason and freedom require the recognition of private property. If one was unable to exclude others from the use of his or her property, an ordered and virtuous life would prove next to impossible. One would be unable to advance a plan for life by procuring the property necessary for the activity which implements and perfects one's life plan. One would be unable to direct one's work to the goods of consumption and production. The human person's rational nature, and the acquisition of material goods in accord with that nature, presents opportunities for virtue through which the person shapes the self. The freedom of the human person as a unique being who participates in the creation of self through reason and will depends on the exclusive use of material things. The facts that the person wears certain clothes, the scholar acquires books, the sculpture needs a piece of marble, and the musician an instrument with which to practice and to play all express the link between private

---

1. Simon Weil, The Need for Roots: Prelude to a Declaration of Duties towards Mankind 34–35 (Arthur Wills trans., Routledge Classics 2002).

property and individual creativity. For this reason Margaret Jane Radin observes "most people posses certain objects they feel are almost part of themselves."[2] Private property may be "personal" as opposed to "fungible" in the meaning that it holds for an individual human person. Private property then encourages both virtue and creativity in the human person.

Third, private property is also indispensable given the social nature of the human person. Private property is a legal institution that enables the coordination of the use and distribution of material resources in a way that promotes societal harmony and peace. Moreover, participation and cooperation in complex and far-reaching enterprises makes possible progress in civilization. Such enterprises depend on the fact that some persons possess more property than is necessary for their maintenance and are able to invest their surplus wealth into the financing of the enterprises. Public works such as hospitals, roads, libraries, tunnels, performance centers, canals, and stadiums all require government taxation on surplus wealth and/or private investment. The role of private wealth in developing industry for the manufacture, sale, distribution, and maintenance of goods further demonstrates that private property is a powerful factor in the advance of civilization. Private property is necessary not only in order to set the economic conditions in which the human person may survive and flourish, but it also betters the progress of the arts and sciences. Public and private investment in an artistic production or scientific research serves the good of individuals and society.

Fourth, although the anthropology points to the necessity of private property, it also suggests that exclusive use of material goods cannot be unfettered lest it disrupt a just economic and social order. Material goods are meant to be useful to all persons, and no one should take unjust advantage of others by an acquisition of private property that results in material deprivation. Each human person needs more than just those material things which are necessary to survival, but no human person needs so much surplus wealth as to result in a disproportionate distribution of material goods. Profit pursued without limit is devoid of the social responsibility that the human person bears on account of his or her social nature. Not only does the anthropology call for a just distribution of goods, but it also suggests a certain generosity of spirit on behalf of those who have ample wealth toward those who are in need. An aspect of the anthropology holds that human freedom depends on acts of sacrifice so that one can more readily participate in solidarity with others.

Fifth, the fourth aspect of the anthropological justification of private property leads to a theological qualification. Based on the example of the poor Christ, Christians throughout the centuries have voluntarily relinquished the right to

---

2. *See* Margaret Jane Radin, *Property and Personhood*, 34 Stanford L. Rev. 957, 959 (1982).

private property. This voluntary act of self-sacrifice is understood to increase human freedom. Unfettered from material concerns, the human person may more fully devote himself or herself to the love of God and the love of others. This qualification need not be theological. It is also possible that a person might renounce the ownership of material goods for philosophical reasons not necessarily related to theological ones. The possibility of renouncing the ownership of private property suggests that the human person has the freedom to constitute the self in favor of the higher human capacities of the intellect and will over the needs of the body. Whether for theological or philosophical reasons or a combination thereof, the desire for some level of detachment from material wealth seems characteristic of human flourishing. Weil's description of private property as "a vital need of the soul" needs to be understood in the light of the human desire to gain greater freedom through detachment from material goods.

B. The Fall and Private Property

Complementary to the positive anthropological justification of private property, the biblical anthropology offers a negative justification for private property. Patristic authorities such as Irenaeus, Ambrose, and John Chrysostom thought that private property was a result of original sin.[3] The fathers hypothesized that there was no need for private property prior to the Fall, original sin, and disorder of the human situation.[4] Focusing on original sin, Augustine acknowledged the existence of two approaches to property in a Christian society reflecting the

---

3. *See* Irenaeus, *Adversus Haereses Libri Quinque*, 4, 30, 1; 7 PG 1065 ("All of us receive a greater or smaller number of possessions from the mammon of injustice. Whence comes the house in which we dwell, the clothes we wear, the vessels we use, and everything else that serves us in our daily lives if not from that which we gained either through avarice while we were yet pagans or through inheritance of what was unjustly acquired by pagan parents, relatives, and friends?"); Ambrose, *In Psalmum CXVIII Expositio*, 8, 22; 15 PL 1372 ("God our Lord wanted the earth to be the common possession of all men and to offer its fruits to all; but greed has fragmented the right of ownership."); John Chrysostom, *Homiliae XVIII in Epistolorum primam ad Timotheum*, 12, 4; 4 PG 562–63. ("Tell me where you got your wealth? You owe it to another. And this other, to whom does he owe it? . . . Will you be able now, following the tree of genealogy, to give proof that this possession was acquired justly? You cannot. On the contrary, its beginning, its root, must lie in injustice. Why? Because God did not in the beginning create one man rich and another poor . . . but gave to all men the same earth as their possession."); *cited in* Hans Urs von Balthasar, The Christian State of Life 116–17 (Sister Mary Frances McCarthy trans., Ignatius Press 1983).

4. Genesis 1:27–30. *See* Ambrose, *Expositionis in Evangelium secundum Lucam Libri X*, 7, 124; 15 PL 1819. ("Consider the birds of the air! They rejoice in the abundance of nourishing food available to them without toil only because they have nothing of the presumption that would lay claim by a kind of private ownership to what is proffered as the common food of all.").

heavenly and earthly cities.[5] Augustine thought that the heavenly treasury had its own rules of property in which one gave up private wealth for the sake of the heavenly city to the *dominium* of God. For Augustine, to endow God in this world meant to endow the church.[6] In contrast, secular rulers of the earthly city made human laws by which "a man says 'this is my villa, this is my house, this is my slave.'"[7] Augustine held that neither the state nor private ownership, even of slaves, was evil, arguing on the basis of Christ's command to respect political authority.[8] He was adamant, however, that all earthly goods belong to God, and that one possesses private property only by human law.[9] In the patristic view, original sin and its consequence of human selfishness make private property necessary as an institution which enables the imperfect justice of the earthly city.

C. The Early Church

The gospels express a preference for poverty and common ownership of property as marks of discipleship.[10] This theological characteristic is evident in the Acts of the Apostles, which records that the members of the early Christian community:

> were of one heart and soul, and no one said that any of the things which he possessed was his own, but they held everything in common. . . . There was not a needy person among them, for as many were possessors of lands or houses sold them, and brought the proceeds of what was sold and laid it at the apostles' feet; and distribution was made to each as any had need.[11]

The theological ideal of the gospel existed in tension with the church's institutional need for secure structures to enhance its mission.

During the first several centuries of its existence, Christianity developed in a social context marked by governmental suspicion and intermittent persecution. The Eucharist was often celebrated secretly in private homes and the catacombs of the early martyrs. Christianity was illegal, and the church could not own property. By the year 251, the church in Rome had, nonetheless, accumulated sufficient resources to support "not only the bishop, 48 presbyters, 7 deacons, 7 subdeacons,

---

5. *See* David Ganz, *The Ideology of Sharing: Apostolic Community and Ecclesiastical Property in the Early Middle Ages*, *in* PROPERTY AND POWER IN THE EARLY MIDDLE AGES 18–20 (Wendy Davies & Paul Fouracre eds., Cambridge University Press 1995).

6. *See* Augustine of Hippo, *Enarrationes in Psalmos*, 38, 12; 38 PL 327.

7. Augustine of Hippo, *In Ioannis Evangelium Tractatus CXXIV*, 6, 2518–2026; 35 PL 1437.

8. *See* Augustine, *De Moribus Ecclesiae Catholicae, et De Moribus Manichaeorum Libri II*, I, 35; 32 PL 1342–44.

9. *See* Augustine of Hippo, *In Ioannis Evangelium Tractatus CXXIV*, 6, 25; 35 PL 1437.

10. Mark 10:21.

11. Acts 4:32.

42 acolytes, and 52 exorcists, readers and doorkeepers, but also more than 1,500 widows and needy persons . . ."[12] In 260, the Roman emperor Gallineus issued an edict granting toleration of Christianity. In response to petitions from bishops, the emperor restored churches and property which had been previously confiscated by the Roman government.[13] Starting after the year 312, the benefactions of Constantine to the church were on a large scale and included land, buildings, and a generous fixed proportion of provincial revenues for the support of the church's charitable activity. Government recognition of Christianity permitted the church to acquire property. Roman law distinguished between *possessio* and *dominium*. *Possessio* was a question of fact, while *dominium* meant that one had an enforceable legal title and ultimate right to the land. *Possessio* could be terminated through a legal process by one who had *dominium*.[14]

Some of the Constantinian era donations to the church were secured through a document known as *The Donation of Constantine*. Like many such early property documents, it is spurious, probably having been forged in the eighth century. Forgeries of this type were common during late antiquity and the early middle ages and represented attempts to secure legal title to property based on accumulated oral tradition, legend, and the desire for a larger justice. In the words of one scholar:

> The forgeries, which are a conspicuous feature of the age, provided documentary proofs for claims which, in the minds of those who made them, scarcely needed to be justified. The pen corrected the corruptions of nature and restored the gross imperfections and injustices of the world to a primitive excellence. The falsehoods in these documents did indeed raise moral problems of which contemporaries were not unaware, but the authors believed that they enforced truths which could not be abandoned without grave danger to their souls. Forgeries . . . brought order into the confusions and deficiencies of the present. Such, among very many other documents, was the *Donation of Constantine*.[15]

Despite the apostolic ideal of poverty, ecclesiastical authorities drafted such documents in order to secure property through *dominium* of which they clearly had *possessio*. The "not of this world" needed to be reconciled to the "mission to the world."[16] Sacred worship, Christian education, and charitable causes such as care for widows, orphans, and the sick were enhanced by the ownership of

---

12. Henry Chadwick, The Early Church 57–58 (Penguin Books 1978).

13. *See id.* at 120.

14. *See* W. W. Buckland, A Text-Book of Roman Law From Augustus to Justinian 186–99 (3rd ed. rev. by Peter Stein, University of Cambridge Press 1966).

15. R. W. Southern, Western Society and the Church in the Middle Ages 93 (Penguin Books 1977).

16. Balthasar, The Christian State of Life, 115.

property. The endowments of the church were retained to sustain a community, and the ownership of property within the ecclesiastical community was held in tension with the apostolic ideal of poverty and common ownership.

John Cassian explained how the pristine perfection of the apostolic church waned soon after Pentecost. In his view, even as the lukewarm and tepid joined the church, the original apostolic ideal was kept alive by early Christian monks.[17] In the sixth century, the Christian Emperor Justinian legislated that the private property of those who entered monastic communities passed to the monastery.[18] Justinian also enacted laws that prohibited the alienation of church property but permitted churches to exchange property with one another without either of them incurring liability. Such an exchange required the approval of the ecclesiastical authority, who acted as "steward" of the property.[19] The legislation identified church property as including "churches, hospitals, monasteries, orphan asylums, old men's homes, foundling hospitals, insane asylums or any other establishment of this kind."[20] Justinian also legislated to protect the will of a person who wished to bequeath his estate, or a part thereof, to the church. In such instances the church beneficiary enjoyed the right to retain or sell the bequeathed property with the approval of the bishop and clergy.[21]

Various theories and textual proofs have been offered to explain the juridical status of ecclesiastical property in the Roman Empire, but they seem to raise more questions than answers. Was the property vested in the church (*ecclesia catholica*) as a whole? Was God himself viewed as the owner of ecclesiastical property? Was each separate local church recognized as an institution with proprietary rights? Were the patron saints of churches considered to be successors to the Roman gods such as Jupiter and Diana who owned *res sacra* such that

---

17. *See* John Cassian, *De Coenobiorum Institutis*, 2, 5; 49 PL 84–86.

18. *See* JUSTINIAN, CODEX, 1, 13, *in* 12 THE CIVIL LAW INCLUDING THE TWELVE TABLETS, THE INSTITUTES OF GAIUS, THE RULES OF ULPIAN, THE OPINIONS OF PAULUS, THE ENACTMENTS OF JUSTINIAN, AND THE CONSTITUTIONS 19 (S. P. Scott ed., Central Trust Co. 1932); NOVELLAE, 5, 5, *in* 16 THE CIVIL LAW INCLUDING THE TWELVE TABLETS, THE INSTITUTES OF GAIUS, THE RULES OF ULPIAN, THE OPINIONS OF PAULUS, THE ENACTMENTS OF JUSTINIAN, AND THE CONSTITUTIONS 27–28; and NOVELLAE, 123, 38, *in* 17 THE CIVIL LAW INCLUDING THE TWELVE TABLETS, THE INSTITUTES OF GAIUS, THE RULES OF ULPIAN, THE OPINIONS OF PAULUS, THE ENACTMENTS OF JUSTINIAN, AND THE CONSTITUTIONS 101.

19. *See* Justinian, CODEX, 1, 14, *in* 12 THE CIVIL LAW INCLUDING THE TWELVE TABLETS, THE INSTITUTES OF GAIUS, THE RULES OF ULPIAN, THE OPINIONS OF PAULUS, THE ENACTMENTS OF JUSTINIAN, AND THE CONSTITUTIONS OF LEO, 19 & 25.

20. *See id.* at 1, 18, *in* 12 THE CIVIL LAW INCLUDING THE TWELVE TABLETS, THE INSTITUTES OF GAIUS, THE RULES OF ULPIAN, THE OPINIONS OF PAULUS, THE ENACTMENTS OF JUSTINIAN, AND THE CONSTITUTIONS OF LEO, 27.

21. *See id.* at 1, 14, 1, *in* 12 THE CIVIL LAW INCLUDING THE TWELVE TABLETS, THE INSTITUTES OF GAIUS, THE RULES OF ULPIAN, THE OPINIONS OF PAULUS, THE ENACTMENTS OF JUSTINIAN, AND THE CONSTITUTIONS OF LEO, 19.

Saint Agnes and Saint Peter were regarded as the proprietors of what belonged to the churches dedicated to them? Was ecclesiastical property owned by the bishop, who in some way "incarnated" it? It may well be the case that the jurists of the early centuries held no clear conception of the precise nature of ecclesiastical property rights. In his study of the early church prior to the law of Justinian, Jean Gaudemet concludes that ecclesiastical goods were considered the property of local churches under the authority of the bishop.[22]

D. Medieval Theory

With the flourishing of monastic communities in the early Middle Ages, the tension between the theological ideal and institutional necessity expressed itself in the idea of common property owned by the monastic community and governed by its communal authority.[23] The tension was reinforced by rediscovery of the sixth-century Justinian *Digest*, a rediscovery that coincided with the renaissance in legal studies and law schools during the third quarter of the eleventh century. Scholars at the new centers would discover in the *Digest* the assumption that natural law (*ius naturale*) contained no provision for private ownership. The Emperor Justinian's great compilation reinforced the view held from the earliest days of Christianity that private ownership was a provision of the law of nations (*ius gentium*), that part of human legal systems which is widely shared because its rationality is apparent.[24] Indeed, the medieval canonist Gratian identified the common possession of all things as an example of natural law.[25]

Likewise, Thomas Aquinas observed that worldly goods considered per se belong no more to one person than to another.[26] Although he borrowed the terminology of the Roman jurists, he changed its meaning.[27] For Thomas, God alone has *dominium* over created things. Property is "merely a power of stewardship over what belongs to God, who intends material goods to be for the benefit of all men."[28] *Possessio* embraces both collective and private ownership; it means the

22. *See* JEAN GAUDEMET, L'EGLISE DANS L'EMPIRE ROMAIN: IVE–VE SIÈCLES 299–315 (Sirey 1990).

23. *See* David Ganz, *The Ideology of Sharing: Apostolic Community and Ecclesiastical Property in the Early Middle Ages, in* PROPERTY AND POWER IN THE EARLY MIDDLE AGES 17–30 (Wendy Davies & Paul Fourace eds., Cambridge University Press 1995).

24. *See* Justinian, DIGEST, 41, 1, 1–13, *in* 9 THE CIVIL LAW INCLUDING THE TWELVE TABLETS, THE INSTITUTES OF GAIUS, THE RULES OF ULPIAN, THE OPINIONS OF PAULUS, THE ENACTMENTS OF JUSTINIAN, AND THE CONSTITUTIONS OF LEO, 154–55.

25. D. 1, c.7, 3.

26. *See* ST, II-II, 57, 3 ("For if a particular piece of land be considered absolutely, it contains no reason why it should belong to one man more than to another . . .").

27. DROSTAN MACLAREN, PRIVATE PROPERTY AND NATURAL LAW, AQUINAS PAPERS, no. 8 at 15 (Blackfriars 1948).

28. *See id.* at 18.

thing owned either by everyone or by some specific person.[29] Thomas recognized private property (*proprietas*) as the "ownership of possessions . . . not contrary to natural law, but an addition thereto devised by human reason."[30] *Proprietas* is the right to private property. It is a legal right established by positive law.[31] In terms of positive law, Thomas described the *ius gentium* and the *ius civile* as being derived from the *ius naturale* in two ways. First, the *ius gentium*, as the law common to all nations, means generally applicable conclusions draw from the basic principles of *ius naturale*. Second, the *ius civile* represents the specification (*determinationes*) of these conclusions in the law of particular states.[32] In Thomas's description, the *ius gentium* is a bridge between the *ius naturale* and *ius civile*. Although he did not deny that private property is a natural right, as far as I am aware, Thomas did not expressly identify it as such.

Thomas justified private property rights on the grounds that they are necessary to avoid quarreling, to provide an incentive for work, and to ensure that property is cared for by the owner.[33] He required that private property be possessed in such a way that it is always in readiness for the community.[34] Based upon the Thomistic analysis, the right to private property in the Catholic tradition is a qualified, and not absolute, right. The Thomistic theory of property affirms the legal right to private property while balancing the right against the common good and requirements of distributive justice.[35] Commenting on Thomas's theory, John Finnis observes:

> (1) *everything* one has is 'held as common (or in common)' in the sense that it is morally available, as a matter of right and justice, to *anyone* who needs it to survive; (2) one's *superflua* are all 'held as common,' in the sense that one has a duty *of justice* to dispose of them for the benefit of the poor.[36]

---

29. *See* ST, II-II, 66, 2, 2 ("A rich man does not act unlawfully if he anticipates someone in taking possession of something which at first was common property, and gives others a share: but he sins if he excludes others indiscriminately from using it.").

30. *See id.* at II-II, 66, 2 ("Hence the ownership of possessions is not contrary to natural law, but an addition thereto devised by human reason.").

31. *See id.* at II-II, 57, 3.

32. *See id.* at I-II, 95, 2.

33. *See id.*

34. *See id.* at II-II, 66, 2 ("In this respect man ought to possess external things, not as his own, but as common, so that, to wit, he is ready to communicate them to others in their need.").

35. *See* Dennis P. McCann, *The Common Good in Catholic Social Teaching, in* In Search of the Common Good 121–46 (Patrick D. Miller & Dennis P. McCann eds., T & T Clark 2005).

36. John Finnis, Aquinas: Moral, Political, and Legal Theory 191 (Oxford University Press 1998).

Thomas argues that for persons in extreme necessity all resources become common resources to the extent that the life-threatening condition requires.[37] Moreover, a person who is aware of another's extreme necessity has a duty to relieve it not just from *superflua* but through contributing resources up to the extent that the contribution does not reduce the donor and dependents themselves to extreme necessity.[38] Absent extreme necessity, the right of owners to keep property extends only so far as necessary to maintain oneself and dependents in a reasonable condition of life. All further resources are held in common, and are to be given to the poor.[39] These obligations, Finnis notes, were not simply from charity, but strict obligations in justice necessary to the common good.[40]

Hans Urs von Balthasar argues that the Thomistic theory of private property reflected a change in the understanding of the natural law itself.[41] Up to Thomistic theory, von Balthasar contends, the *ius naturale* represented the law of the human person in the state of nature prior to the Fall. According to von Balthasar, Thomas's approach represented a new way of thinking in which the *ius naturale* came to represent the law of human nature without regard to history, in other words, absent any notion of the Fall. Von Balthasar thus sees the shift in the approach to the state of nature from the historical (focus on human nature prior to and after the Fall) to the unequivocal (without reference to history). The sharp distinction drawn by von Balthasar between the historical and ahistorical may be overstating the case. The general theory understands natural law as not confined to prelapsarian paradise but more or less a universal law of reason. Thomas had predecessors in this view, not the least of whom was Gratian, who ascribed to the theory that natural law was available to all persons through the use of reason.

While recognizing that the Thomistic approach to property remained rooted in the "evangelical ethic," von Balthasar sees Thomas's adoption of Aristotle's unequivocal concept of nature in favor of the historical concept as "laying the foundation for the canonization of private ownership."[42] Von Balthasar's use of the term *canonization* seems to mean not the legitimate recognition of the right to private property but a legal approach that displaces the essential theological meaning. Again, von Balthasar may also be overstating the case. As already mentioned, Thomas justifies the division and legal regulation of property with the reservation that property remains fundamentally available to the community. For this reason, von Balthasar acknowledges that "the evangelical ethic was thus preserved" in the Thomistic theory of property rights.[43]

---

37. *See* ST, II-II, 32, 7, 3; and II-II, 187, 4c.
38. *See id.* at II, 32, 5c.
39. *See id.* at II-II, 87, 1, 4; and II-II, 66, 7c.
40. *See* FINNIS, AQUINAS, 192.
41. *See* BALTHASAR, THE CHRISTIAN STATE OF LIFE, 115–19.
42. *Id.* at 115.
43. *Id.* at 117.

Even as the Dominican Thomas Aquinas developed his influential theory of property rights, an already existing dispute among the Franciscans reflected the continuing power of the theological ideal. Based upon his reading of the gospels and profound religious experience, Saint Francis of Assisi embraced a radical poverty forsaking ownership of material possessions.[44] From the time of Francis of Assisi, his followers fell into dispute about the meaning of poverty in the Franciscan Order.[45] In particular, the spiritualist wing of Franciscans repudiated the need for any material goods and property.[46] This was consistent in general with the spiritualists' antinomian approach to the Franciscan Order and the institutional church.[47] In 1230, Pope Gregory IX attempted to resolve the dispute over Franciscan poverty with the decree *Quo elongati*.[48] The decree permitted the Franciscan Order to possess and enjoy the use of property while the Holy See held title to the property. The attempted papal resolution thus recognized the need for institutional structure and property while granting pontifical approval to the Franciscan desire to live the gospel ideal.[49] A contemporary of Thomas Aquinas in the faculty of theology at Paris, Bonaventure, who was elected General of the Franciscan Order, remained an apologist for evangelical poverty while checking the antinomianism of his spiritualist brethren.[50] The expression *usus pauper* (use as a poor person) gained currency among the spiritualist Franciscans, who held that renunciation of ownership was insufficient. They argued that gospel poverty required restricting possession within the church to the barest minimum.[51] Neither Pope Gregory's decree nor Bonaventure's governance quelled the dispute over Franciscan poverty, which continued to weaken the unity of the Order and trouble the life of the church well into the fourteenth century.[52]

---

44. *Legenda maior*, 3, 3, *in* 8 S. BONAVENTURA OPERA OMNIA, EDITA STUDIO ET CURA PP. COLLEGII A S. BONAVENTURA 504, 510 (Quaracchi: Collegium S. Bonaventura 1882). *See also* LAWRENCE D. CUNNINGHAM, FRANCIS OF ASSISI, PERFORMING THE GOSPEL LIFE 25 (Eerdmans Publishing 2004).

45. *See* C. H. LAWRENCE, THE FRIARS: THE IMPACT OF THE EARLY MENDICANT MOVEMENT ON WESTERN SOCIETY 39–42 (Longman 1994).

46. *See* DAVID BURR, THE SPIRITUAL FRANCISCANS: FROM PROTEST TO PERSECUTION IN THE CENTURY AFTER SAINT FRANCIS 2–41 (Pennsylvania State University Press 2001).

47. For a discussion of the antinomian effects of the theology of Joachim of Fiore on the Franciscan spiritualist, *see* JOSEPH RATZINGER, THE THEOLOGY OF HISTORY IN ST. BONAVENTURE 48–55 (Zachary Hayes trans., Franciscan Herald Press 1971).

48. *See* JOHN MOORMAN, A HISTORY OF THE FRANCISCAN ORDER 89–91 (Clarendon Press of Oxford University 1968).

49. *See* ROSALIND B. BROOKE, EARLY FRANCISCAN GOVERNMENT, ELIAS TO BONAVENTURE 74 (Cambridge University Press 1959).

50. *See* LAWRENCE, THE FRIARS, 57–60.

51. *See* DAVID BURR, OLIVI AND FRANCISCAN POVERTY: THE ORIGINS OF THE USUS PAUPER CONTROVERSY 111 (University of Pennsylvania Press 1989).

52. *See id.* at 60–64; and MOORMAN, A HISTORY OF THE FRANCISCAN ORDER, 307–19.

E. The Social Teaching of the Church

The Thomistic synthesis, of course, has a general applicability to society, and it is not limited to the question of the ownership of property within the Catholic Church. Starting with Pope Leo XIII's 1891 encyclical, *Rerum Novarum*, Catholic social teaching would recognize the right to private property based upon the Thomistic theory.[53] According to the social teaching, the right to private property is not based on "indiscriminate ownership" and must "serve the common interest of all" even as the compensation for individual labor justifies private property as "clearly in accord with nature."[54] Pope Pius X articulated two principles for the regulation of private property: (1) "unlike the beast, man has on earth not only the right to use, but a permanent right of ownership; and this is true not only of those things which are consumed in their use, but also of those which are consumed by their use"; and (2) "private property is under all circumstances, be it the fruit of labor or acquired by conveyance or donation, *a natural right*, and everybody may make such reasonable disposable of it as he thinks fit."[55] On the fortieth anniversary of Pope Leo's *Rerum Novarum*, Pius XI issued the encyclical, *Quadragesimo anno*, which reiterated the natural right to private property while emphasizing the correct proportions of the right in terms of the human person and the social order.[56]

In this regard, Pope John XXIII's *Mater et Magister* states: "private property, including that of productive good, is a *natural right* possessed by all, which the State may by no means suppress. However, as there is from nature a social aspect to private property, he who uses his right in this regard must take into account not merely his own welfare but that of others as well."[57] Recall that Thomas Aquinas had no doubt that the human person has a natural right to the use of

---

53. Leo Pp. XIII, Litterae Encyclicae *Rerum Novarum* (Dei 15 mensis maii anno 1891), 10–17, *in* 11 Leonis XIII P.M. Acta 97-144 (Editrice Vaticana 1892).

54. *Id.* at 14–15.

55. Pius Pp. X, Motu Proprio, *Arduum sane munus* (Die 18 mensis decembris anno 1903); 37 ASS 549–51 (1903–1904) (emphasis added).

56. *See* Pius Pp. XI, Litterae Encyclicae, *Quadragesimo anno* (Die 15 mensis maii anno 1931), 44–48; 23 AAS 171–228 (1931). In No. 45 Pope Pius XI states: "let it be considered as certain and established that neither Leo nor those theologians who have taught under the guidance and authority of the Church have ever denied or questioned the twofold character of ownership, called usually individual or social according as it regards either separate persons or the common good. For they have always unanimously maintained that *nature, rather the Creator Himself, has given man the right of private ownership* not only that individuals may be able to provide for themselves and their families but also that the goods which the Creator destined for the entire family of mankind may through this institution truly serve this purpose. All this can be achieved in no wise except through the maintenance of a certain and definite order." (emphasis added).

57. Ioannes Pp. XXIII, Litterae Encyclicae, *Mater et Magister* (Die 15 mensis iulii anno 1961), 19; 53 AAS 401–64 (1961) (emphasis added).

material things, but he understood the property right as part of the *ius gentium*. For Aquinas, it is quite certain that property is a relative and not absolute right. The Thomistic theory agrees with the patristic theory that understood private property as not necessary in the original state of nature but as a consequence of original sin. The twentieth-century papal pronouncements that private property is a "natural right" must be interpreted with this tradition in mind as well as the historical circumstances in existence at the time of these pronouncements. The twentieth-century identifications of private property as a natural right were a response to the challenges of unbridled capitalism and Marxist collectivism. On the one hand, the unregulated free market of certain capitalist approaches could indicate the acquisitive instinct of the human person was free from moral restraint. On the other hand, state ownership and control of all property and means of production defiled individual dignity, freedom, and creativity.

Vatican II's *Gaudium et Spes* affirmed that social principle that the goods of this world are originally meant for all and stated that the necessity of private property does not nullify this principle.[58] This teaching was reinforced by Pope John Paul II in *Soliticitudo Rei Socialis,* in which the pontiff criticized communism for its collective ownership for the means of all production and liberal capitalism for its inequitable distribution of material resources.[59] In John Paul II's words: "Private property, in fact, is under a 'social mortgage,' which means that it has an intrinsically social function, based upon and justified precisely by the principle of the universal destination of goods."[60] On the one hundredth anniversary of *Rerum Novarum*, Pope John Paul II in *Centesimus Annus*, extolled the right to private property which must be understood in light of the principle of the "universal destination of the earth's goods."[61] In fidelity to the Thomistic tradition, Catholic social teaching affirms the human reality of need for private property but calls for proper state regulation to ensure a just economic and social order.

II. PROPERTY IN LIBERAL POLITICAL THEORY

What follows is by no means a comprehensive treatment of property rights in liberal political theory. Rather, I present several seminal elements of the theory in order to facilitate the comparison with the understanding of property in canon law. The philosophical justification for the law of private property rights in liberal theory traces its roots to theorists such as Thomas Hobbes, John Locke,

58. *See Gaudium et Spes*, 69.

59. *See* Ioannes Paulus Pp. II, Litterae Encyclicae, *Sollicitudo Rei Socialis* (Die 30 mensis decembris anno 1987), 20, 21, 41, and 42; 80 AAS 513–86 (1988).

60. *Id.* at 42.

61. Ioannes Paulus Pp. II, Litterae Encyclicae, *Centesimus Annus* (Die 15 m. maii a. 1991) 6.2; 83 AAS 793–887 (1991).

and David Hume. Writing in seventeenth-century England, Hobbes rejected the idea that ownership of property derived from nature. He envisioned nature as a state in which property belonged to no one, and competition among persons to acquire property produced a "war of all against all."[62] The desire of self-preservation led the individual to surrender self-governance to the state. Prior to the state, there was no society, only warring individuals. Private property is the invention of the state to protect the owner from encroachments from other individuals.[63] In contrast to Hobbes, Locke depicted the state of nature not as one of constant strife, but of freedom and equality. In Locke's view, the self-sufficient individual in the state of nature consents to enter society in order to obtain certain advantages.[64] These advantages include, *inter alia*, increased personal security, the right to private property and the state's protection of it, the specialization of work, availability of capital, the market economy, and opportunities to maximize individual wealth. For Locke, the supreme responsibility of the state is to set the rules that protect the individual's right to own private property.

Hobbes and Locke shared the underlying assumption that the individual agrees to forego the state of nature in order to gain the benefit of private property, which is protected by the state. This "contractarian individualism" focuses on the human being as autonomous, ceding the minimum amount of autonomy to the state in order to gain these advantages. Private property plays a critical role both in protecting individual autonomy and maximizing wealth. Freedom is defined as the absence of government constraint on the individual. The economic goal of the individual is to acquire as much private property as possible in accord with the minimal constraints placed on individual freedom by the government. Writing in the eighteenth century, Hume thought of private property as a mere convention that people respected because it set the conditions for general economic prosperity. Viewing the human person as filled with various gradations of vices and virtues, Hume thought that the individual owned private property in an individual and exclusive way. He stated: "'tis certain, that rights, and obligation, and property, admit of no such insensible gradation, but that a man either has a full and perfect property, or none at all."[65] Consistent with these elements of liberal political theory, the "fee simple absolute" is the most unrestricted form of holding real property known to Anglo-American law.

---

62. *See* Thomas Hobbes, De Cive, 6–7, *in* De Cive: the English version (Howard Warrender ed., Clarendon Press of Oxford University 1983).

63. *See* Thomas Hobbes, Leviathan, 2, 21, at 165 (J. C. A. Gaskin ed., Oxford University Press 1998).

64. *See* John Locke, Second Essay Concerning Civil Government, §§ 15, 21, 87, 95, *in* Locke, Two Treatises of Government 278, 282, 324, 330–31 (Peter Laslet ed., Cambridge University Press 1988).

65. David Hume, A Treatise on Human Nature 3.2.6, 339 (David Fate Norton & Mary Jane Norton eds., Oxford University Press 2001).

As with chattel, which may also be owned absolutely, it is of infinite duration and permits the titleholder to use the property in accord with subjective preferences with few restrictions. It testifies to the sovereignty of individual autonomy in Anglo-American property law.

An early U.S. Supreme Court case, *Johnson v. M'Intosh*,[66] has been termed "the unofficial beginning of American property law."[67] The 1823 case turned on a title dispute to real property. The plaintiff Johnson had first possession in the land originally purchased from Native Americans. The defendant M'Intosh had acquired a later title to the same land in a chain of ownership that could be traced to the grant of the English Crown. Chief Justice John Marshall reasoned that, although the plaintiff's title was first in time as to its origin, it did not come through the U.S. government, and therefore could not be recognized by the Court.[68] Marshall based the Supreme Court's decision on the 1783 Treaty of Paris, which brought an end to the Revolutionary War. Pursuant to the treaty, any rights in land that the English sovereign had granted prior to the Revolution were to be respected and enforced. The defendant's right to the disputed property fell clearly within the terms of the treaty. In Marshall's view, the plaintiff's title was based on rights in property which, although they may have possessed some validity among Indian nations, could not be recognized by a court of the United States. The Court therefore held for the defendant.

The Chief Justice attempted to bolster the Supreme Court's ruling in *Johnson v. M'Intosh* with additional arguments. First, Marshall argued that the law of discovery entitled the nation which discovered a particular territory first to occupy and control the property, subject to limited rights of occupancy in the aboriginals. He analogized the law of discovery to the law of conquest in which the spoils of war belong to the victor. Second, Marshall seemed to believe that the law of discovery applied only to the nations of Europe on account of the "superior genius" that they contributed to aboriginals.[69] Marshall's line of argument has, of course, been the subject of a much deserved critique not the least of which considers the reasoning to be racist.[70] The problems of Marshall's reasoning notwithstanding, *Johnson v. M'Intosh* affirmed the understanding of private property held by the liberal theorists that the individual has an absolute right to property to the extent that the title to the property is recognized by the government. The idea of property in Anglo-American law has gone through many

---

66. 21 U.S. 543, 8 Wheat, 543 (1823).

67. Note, *The Myth of Johnson v. M'Intosh*, 52 UCLA L. Rev. 289, 290 (2004).

68. *See* 21 U.S. at 572.

69. *Id.* at 573.

70. *See, e.g.*, Robert A. Williams, Jr., The American Indian in Western Legal Thought: The Discourses of Conquest 317 (Oxford University Press 1990); and Richard A. Epstein, *Property Rights Claims of Indigenous Populations: The View from the Common Law*, 31 U. Tol. L. Rev. 1 (1999).

developments in the course of its history, not the least of which have been the development of the modern corporation, financial markets, income taxation, the rise of the welfare state, entitlements, the regulatory state, and environmental protection. While many of these developments have tended to weaken property rights, the idea that an individual enjoys the right to private property contingent on state approval has perdured as characteristic of liberal theory.

III. COMPARISON OF CATHOLIC AND LIBERAL THEORIES OF PROPERTY

What conclusions might be drawn from the comparison of the seminal elements of canon law and liberal theory in their respective approaches to property? First, both canon law and liberal theory recognize the right to private property. Both understand the right as essential to human flourishing for somewhat different reasons. Liberal theorists would not necessarily dispute Thomas Aquinas's three justifications for private property, which are applicable to religious and secular societies alike. According to Thomas, the right to private property serves to offer incentives for human productivity, care of property, and the avoidance of property disputes. However, there is a difference between canon law and liberal theory about the source of the right. The anthropological foundation for private property in canon law suggests that the right reflects the nature of the human person. The location of the right in the reason, freedom, and social nature of the human person justifies the conclusion that private property is a natural right. At the same time, this conclusion must be understood in light of Christian theology. According to the theological understanding private property is a consequence of human nature after the Fall, but not part of human nature as it was originally created by God. Form the a-historical perspective, one may speak of a natural right to private property, but less so from the historical perspective. The balance between the historical and a-historical approaches to private property means that the right must not be understood as absolute. The right of private property in canon law is limited by the theological concerns about evangelical poverty and common ownership. Liberal political theory developed in separation from divine revelation, and consequently, the political theory was not concerned with the theological ideals. For the early liberal theorists, it is in the interests of the individual to leave the state of nature and enter the social contract. Although Hobbes and Locke endorsed a certain view of natural law, they did not understand a right of private property to exist prior to the social contract. In liberal theory, the state creates the right in order to set the conditions which are most advantageous to the greatest number of individuals. The right to private property may be more absolute in liberal theory than it is in canon law. Pristine liberal theory does not endorse the Catholic view that private property be possessed in such a way that it is always in readiness for the community. Nonetheless, this theoretical difference may not be so great in practice. Property law rooted in liberal theory has developed in order to permit the state to act against individual interests for the common good. As the law of eminent domain illustrates, the state may use its power to take private property from individuals who receive compensation for the taking if the state's action is justified by the common good.[71]

Second, the juxtaposition of the fundamental approaches to property in canon law and liberal theory reflects different anthropological conceptions. Canon law assumes an understanding of the human person as one who is essentially social in nature and who discovers fulfillment through participation and solidarity with others.[72] This anthropological understanding differs from the image of contractarian individualism in the pristine version of liberal theory. According to Locke's articulation of the pristine version, the individual cedes a degree of autonomy to enter the social contract in order to optimize the opportunities to acquire material wealth in accord with subjective choices. In a more recent version of the liberal tradition, John Rawls described society as a cooperative venture of individual citizens based upon a theory of justice.[73] For Rawls, justice depends on the distribution of societal goods to each individual in accord with legitimate need. Although not antithetical to Rawls's theory of distributive justice, Catholic tradition considers justice in human society to be more than that of the Rawlsian description.[74] With the focus on individual need, Rawls's account may undervalue communities that are distinct from political society, such as family, church, and nonpolitical associations. From the Catholic perspective, these communities naturally constitute the person as a social being, and foster the conditions for participation and solidarity. If these communities are to prosper, Catholic social theory holds that it is not sufficient for the government to simply secure the protection of individual property rights, a market economy, and an ever-increasing subjective consumerism. The tax-exempt status of churches and other not-for-profit organizations is an indication that the secular state recognizes the

71. *See* Kelo v. City of New London, 545 U.S. 469 (2009) (holding that pursuant to eminent domain, the city could take private property owned by an individual and transfer the property to a private developer on the ground that the general benefits a community gained from economic growth qualified the redevelopment plans by the private developer as a permissible "public use" under the Takings Clause of the Fifth Amendment). *See also* Nicole Stelle Garnett, *The Neglected Political Economy of Eminent Domain,* 105 Mich. L. Rev. 101, 142-147 (suggesting that high compensation to individuals by the government for the taking of property may not always advance the common good as the high compensation may undermine political opposition to the project and may result in non-instrumental harms to individuals and communities).

72. *See Lumen Gentium*, 18–29.

73. *See* John Rawls, A Theory of Justice 515–20 (Harvard University Belknap Press 1971).

74. *See* Jean Porter, *The Common Good in Thomas Aquinas, in* In Search of the Common Good 106–20 (Patrick D. Miller & Dennis P. McCann eds., T & T Clark 2005).

value that religious and other communities afford to the individual and the common good.

Third, the comparison of the approaches to property in canon law and liberal theory points to diverse definitions of freedom. The theological element in canon law includes the gospel preference for poverty. Canon law reflects the theological view that the intentional renunciation of property may facilitate human freedom. According to the theological view, the more one is detached from material possessions, the more one experiences inner freedom. Not endowed with the theological meaning, liberal theory maintains a close nexus between the right to own private property and individual freedom. The state functions to ensure that each individual is afforded an equal opportunity to acquire a fair share of property, defined broadly as any right, benefit, or entitlement that enhances individual well-being. Liberal theory has no interest in propagating the theological view that true freedom depends on detachment form material goods.

Finally, canon law exhibits trust in ecclesiastical authority to direct the use of the church property so that the property serves the mission of the church. Liberal theory, of course, neither shares the church's mission nor recognizes an ecclesiastical office vested by divine authority to discern how best to implement that mission. A central feature of liberal theory values a minimal level of government regulation on the individual's right to private property. While canon law reflects trust in ecclesiastical authority with regard to the regulation of ecclesiastical property in accord with the church's mission, liberal theory holds to a rule of suspicion of the exercise of government power lest it infringe on the freedom of the individual to employ the property right.

5. CHURCH PROPERTY CONTINUED
The Diocese and Parish; Canon Law and State Law

Given the theoretical differences discussed in the previous chapter, it would be an ill fit simply to superimpose the liberal theory of property onto canon law. The imposition would disturb the careful balance canon law attempts to attain between the theological ideal, which values common ownership and apostolic poverty, and the legal reality, which recognizes that private property arises from legitimate human need as well as the institutional stability and continuity of the church. Approaching the question of the ownership of property in the Catholic Church from the perspective of liberal theory alone fosters legalism. Legalism overlooks the proper role played by theology in affording the inner meaning or *intellectus* of canon law. The legalistic approach obscures the fact that ecclesiastical property always serves the mission of church. Absent this *intellectus*, canon law fails to function as a life-giving force in the church.

A legalistic approach to church property in the United States was advocated by John J. McGrath. In the years immediately following Vatican II, McGrath argued that a great deal of ecclesiastical property in the United States was not in fact ecclesiastical property subject to the provisions of canon law.[1] He based his argument on the historical assumption that many institutions such as colleges, universities, and hospitals, which were originally founded by Catholic religious communities and dioceses, were intended to fulfill a primarily secular purpose, and therefore ought not to be regarded as ecclesiastical property. Other canonists, including Adam Maida and Nicholas Cafardi, have questioned the historical assumption that underpins the McGrath thesis. They argue that there can be no doubt that such institutions, even if they may have also served secular purposes, were originally intended as primarily religious in nature and a direct manifestation of the church's apostolic activity.[2] Pursuant to the McGrath thesis, the theological

1. *See* John J. McGrath, Catholic Institutions in the United States: Canonical and Civil Law Status (Catholic University Press 1968). *See also* Robert T. Kennedy, *McGrath, Maida, Michiels: Introduction to a Study of the Canonical and Civil Law Status of Church Related Institutions in the United States,* 50 Jurist 351–401 (1990).

2. *See* Adam J. Maida, *Canonical and Legal Fallacies of the McGrath Thesis on the Reorganization of Church Entities,* 19 The Catholic Lawyer 275–86 (1973); Adam J. Maida & Nicolas P. Cafardi, Church Property, Church Finances, and Church-Related Corporations 271 (Catholic Health Association of the United States 1984). *See also* James A. Coriden & Frederick R. McManus, *in* Church and Campus: Legal Issues in Religiously Affiliated Higher Education 145–46 (University of Notre Dame Press 1979).

element of canon law remains obscure or irrelevant in the determination of the ownership of many institutions founded under church auspices.

In this chapter, I address several specific issues in light of the theories of property discussed in Chapter 4. First, I examine the theological and canonical relationship between the diocese and the parish in terms of the ownership of property. Second, I recount the nineteenth-century struggle of the Catholic Church to secure its parish property in accord with the hierarchical structure required by canon law in opposition to the congregational model embraced by many Protestant churches. Third, I discuss the relationship between canon law and state law with regard to ecclesiastical property and in particular the ways in which state law permits the Catholic Church to hold its property in accord with canon law. Finally, I consider antinomian and legalistic approaches to church property and their impact on the rule of law from the perspective of the secularization of Catholic institutions.

I. THE DIOCESE AND THE PARISH

In the wake of plaintiffs' lawsuits against dioceses as a result of clerical sexual abuse, the decisions of several dioceses to enter into bankruptcy proceedings under U.S. federal law have called into question the relationship between diocese and parish.[3] Specifically, the dioceses have asserted that parish property is not to

---

3. By a conservative estimate, the cost of settlements of sexual abuse cases to dioceses and religious communities in the United States has thus far easily been several billion dollars. *See* The Nature and Scope of the Problem of Sexual Abuse of Minors by Catholic Priests and Deacons in the United States, A Research Study Conducted by the John Jay College of Criminal Justice, 6.1.1, 105 (2004), which states that the total costs paid by diocese and religious communities for compensation to victims, treatment of offenders, and attorneys fees was $572,507,095; *see also* 2004 Annual Report on the Implementation of the Charter for the Protection of Children and Young People, United States Conference of Catholic Bishops, 3, 9 (United States Conference of Catholic Bishops 2005), which states that in the year 2004, the total costs paid by diocese and religious communities for compensation to victims, treatment of offenders, and attorneys fees was $157,802,811. These two reports placed the cost of the sexual abuse cases from 1950 to 2004 for the Catholic Church in the United States at $730,309,906. However, another 2005 account stated that the total amount of settlements has exceeded one billion dollars. *See* N.Y. Times, June 12, 2005, at 1, 33. In reality by 2007, the amount may have been in excess of three billion dollars. *See* Stephen M. Bainbridge & Aaron H. Cole, *The Bishop's Alter Ego: Enterprise Liability and the Catholic Priest Sex Abuse Scandal*, 46 Journal of Catholic Legal Studies 65–106 (2007). At the time of writing this chapter, at least seven Roman Catholic dioceses had filed for bankruptcy protection. They are: the Archdiocese of Portland, Oregon, *see* N.Y. Times, July 7, 2004, at A12; the Diocese of Tuscon, Arizona, *see* N.Y. Times, Sept. 21, 2004, at A18; the Diocese of Spokane, Washington, *see* N.Y. Times, Dec. 7, 2004, at A24; the Diocese of Davenport, *see* N.Y. Times, Oct. 11, 2006, A, 22;

be counted as part of the assets of a diocese in a federal bankruptcy proceeding.[4] This assertion has a certain technical validity in light of the fact that under the *CIC-1983*, the parish is a distinct juridic person with the right to own ecclesiastical property.[5] As convenient as the assertion may be for the diocese at this time, however, I do not believe that it fully reflects the correct relationship between the diocese and its parishes with regard to the ownership, administration, regulation, and alienation of parish assets.[6] The assertion carries multifaceted consequences that transcend the significance of the diocese attempting to shield parish assets when the diocese files for bankruptcy relief in a federal court. The assertion may well prove detrimental to the interest of a diocese in a different kind of case in the secular courts where control of parish assets is contested. It certainly will not serve diocesan interests in a financing endeavor backed by diocesan assets as the security. More importantly from an ecclesiastical perspective, the assertion dislocates canon law from the theology of the particular church expressed in the documents of Vatican II.

A. The Unity of Law and Theology

A correct analysis of the relationship between the diocese and the parish reflects the unity of law and theology. The theology of the particular church articulated at Vatican II is indispensable to the analysis of the canonical relationship. The documents of Vatican II use the term "particular church" in a variety of ways. First, it means the autonomous churches of the East in union with Rome.[7] The term also refers to patriarchal and major archiepiscopal churches as well as to the church that comprises a certain cultural and/or geographic region.[8] Canon 368

---

the Diocese of San Diego, California, *see* N.Y. Times, Feb. 28, 2007, at A16; the Diocese of Fairbanks, Alaska, *see* N.Y. Times, Feb. 16, 2008, at A12; and the Diocese of Wilmington, Delaware, *see* N.Y. Times, October 20, 2009, at A14. *See also* In re The Catholic Bishop of Spokane, United States Bankruptcy Court, Eastern District of Washington (Aug. 26, 2005), which held that the parish property belongs to the diocese for the purposes of a bankruptcy proceeding.

4. *See, e.g.*, Statement of Archbishop John Vlazny of Portland, Oregon, *Archdiocese Files for Bankruptcy Protection*, 34 Origins 113, 113–15 (July 15, 2004) ("Under canon law, parish assets belong to the parish.").

5. *See* Canons 516, § 3 and 1256, *CIC-1983*.

6. Please permit me to clarify that when I refer to parish property, I am addressing all the assets including but not limited to real property. Furthermore, I have in mind the normal relationship between the diocese and parish. In the long history of the Catholic Church, there are, of course, exceptions in which a religious order or some other canonically recognized entity owns specific property related to a parish ministry. Instead, I have in mind the more normative relation between the diocese and parish in which the parish property is under the authority of the bishop. *See* Canons 515, § 1 & 381, § 1, *CIC-1983*.

7. *See generally Orientalium Ecclesiarum*, 441.

8. *Lumen Gentium*, 13. *See also* Canon 55, *CCEO*, which recognizes the ancient tradition of the Patriarchal Church; and Gianfranco Ghirlanda, S.J., Il diritto nella

of the *CIC-1983* incorporates a third meaning derived from Vatican II in which the particular church includes the diocese and similar juridical structures such as territorial prelature, territorial abbacy, apostolic vicariate, apostolic prefecture, and an apostolic administration which has been erected on a stable basis.[9] All of these meanings share the sense of the autonomy of the particular church. The particular church is not a mere administrative unit of the Roman church.

According to *Lumen Gentium,* the universal church, in its concrete and historical manifestation, exists "in and from" the particular churches.[10] An influential theologian at Vatican II, Henri De Lubac explains that each particular church is considered to constitute the Body of Christ and contains within itself all that is necessary for salvation.[11] At the same time, the *communio* of the particular churches with the Successor to Saint Peter at its head is viewed as more than a federation. Rather, in words of De Lubac, the *communio* is "organic and mystical."[12] De Lubac explains that the relationship between the universal church and the particular churches is one of "mutual interiority."[13] The universal church, according to *Lumen Gentium,* remains always a reality ontologically prior, from which the particular churches take their origin.[14] In the words of Eugenio Correco, "the particular church cannot exist except in so far as she is a concrete realization of the universal Church."[15] The ecclesial *communio* of all of the particular churches united in the universal church coincides with the hierarchical *communio* of the college of bishops with the Roman Pontiff at its head. As the title "Roman Pontiff" indicates, the pope who is the Bishop of Rome serves as a "bridge" among all the particular churches which are headed by his brother bishops. The delicate relationship between the Roman Pontiff and the bishops responsible for the particular churches is at the same time collegial and

---

Chiesa mistero di Comunione 42 (Editrice Paoline e Roma: Editrice Pontificia Università Gregoriana 1990).

9. *See CIC-1983,* Canon 368. There was no parallel definition in the *CIC-1917.* The *CCEO,* Canon 177, § 1 identifies the eparchy as a particular church.

10. *Lumen Gentium,* 23 ("*in quibus et ex quibus*").

11. *See* Henri De Lubac, *Particular Churches in the Universal Church, in* The Motherhood of the Church 191–211 (Sergia Englund trans., Ignatius Press 1982).

12. *See* De Lubac, *Particular Churches in the Universal Church,* 191–211. *See also* Joseph Ratzinger, *The Pastoral Implications of Episcopal Collegiality,* 1 Concillium 37–38 (1975).

13. De Lubac, *Particular Churches in the Universal Church, in* The Motherhood of the Church, 201, citing Yves Congar, *La collégialité de l'épiscopat,* I: "*Avant le milieu du IV*e *siècle.*"

14. *Lumen Gentium,* 26. *See also* Wilhelm Bertrams, S.J., *De analogia quod structuram hierarchicam inter Ecclesiam universalem ac Ecclesiam particularem,* 56 Periodica 267–308 (1967).

15. Eugenio Corecco, Canon Law and Communio, Writings on the Constitutional Law of the Church (Graziano Borgonovo and Arturo Cattaneo, eds., Liberia Editice Vaticana 1999), 74.

hierarchical. Out of respect for the collegiality among the bishops and the autonomy of the individual churches, the Roman Pontiff does not generally interfere in the governance of the particular churches.

The diocese is the most common canonical manifestation of the particular church.[16] A definition of the diocese may be found in *Christus Dominus*: "A diocese is a section of the people of God entrusted to a Bishop to be guided by him with the assistance of his clergy so that, loyal to its pastor and formed by him into one community in the Holy Spirit through the Gospel and the Eucharist, it constitutes one particular Church in which the One, Holy, Catholic and Apostolic Church of Christ is truly present and active."[17] In no sense is the diocesan bishop an employee of the pope. The existence of a hierarchical relationship between parties does not automatically give rise to an employee-employer relationship. While it is often the case that the Roman Pontiff appoints the diocesan bishop, the diocesan bishop teaches, sanctifies, and governs as a successor to the Apostles. The diocese then is an autonomous church in ecclesial communion with the universal church.

In contrast, the parish does not constitute an autonomous church.[18] Section 1 of Canon 515 of the *CIC-1983* describes the parish as "a certain community of Christ's faithful stably established within a particular church, whose pastoral care is entrusted to a priest as its proper pastor under the authority of the diocesan bishop." For the purpose of this discussion, this description contains three significant elements. First, the parish is a *community of the Christian faithful*. The element of the description reflects a return to the ancient understanding of the term "parish," which finds its etymological roots in the Greek word *paroikia* (παροικία), meaning a pilgrim people.[19] It is perhaps at the local level that the *communio* of the church may be experienced in its most intimate form. In the words of *Lumen Gentium*: "In these communities, though frequently small and poor, or living far from any other, Christ is present."[20] Second, the parish is *established within a particular church*. Defining the parish in relation to the diocese,

---

16. As the particular church is more than a mere administrative unit, one must be careful that the canonical word "diocese" means more than the idea evoked by the ancient diocese of the Roman Empire. *See* De Lubac, *Particular Churches in the Universal Church*, 200–01.

17. *Christus Dominus*, 11, Canon 369 of the *CIC-1983* contains a similar definition of the diocese.

18. *See* Louis Boyer, L'Église de Dieu 488 (Cerf 1970).

19. *See* Ludwig F. von Hertling, Communio: Church and Papacy in Early Christianity 102 (Jared Wicks, S.J. trans., Loyola University Press 1972).

20. "In his communitatibus, licet saepe exiguis et pauperibus, vel in dispersione degentibus, praesens est Christus . . ." *Lumen Gentium*, 26. *See* Francesco Coccopalmerio, De Paroecia 8 (Editrice Pontificia Università Gregoriana 1991).

Christus Dominus states that the parish is a part of the diocese.[21] It is only by analogy to the *communio* of the particular churches that one may speak of *communio* as the relationship between the diocese and the parishes that comprise it.[22] Third, the care of the parish is *entrusted to a priest under the authority of the diocesan bishop*. The parish is the communion of the baptized presided over by the priest who is appointed by and collaborates in the pastoral ministry of the bishop.[23] Not only is the priest appointed pastor by the bishop, canon law establishes the diocesan bishop's right to remove or transfer him under certain conditions and procedural safeguards.[24] Although the bishops form one college with the Roman Pontiff at its head, the pastor of a parish is in a hierarchical relation to the diocesan bishop. The parish is of its nature dependent on the bishop as head of the diocese. Section 2 of Canon 529 requires the priest to foster among the faithful an authentic sense of communion with the diocesan bishop and the Roman Pontiff.

As with the hierarchical relationship between the Roman Pontiff and the bishop, canon law does not view the parish priest as an employee of the diocesan bishop. The hierarchical relationship between the diocesan bishop and the pastor of the parish reflects the theological belief that the bishop is a successor to the Apostles and that the priest cooperates in this apostolic ministry.[25] In accord with the apostolic tradition, the governing role exercised by the diocesan bishop remains primarily pastoral. Canon 383 of the *CIC-1983* urges that the diocesan bishop is: to "function as a pastor"; "show concern for all"; "extend an apostolic spirit"; "provide for spiritual needs"; "act with humanity and charity"; and "shine the charity of Christ as a witness before all people." The governing power of the bishop is exercised as the spiritual father of the priest and parish. Likewise, the priest who is pastor of the parish is the minister of the Word, the minister of the Sacraments, and the minister of pastoral charity to the portion of the people of God entrusted to his care.[26]

---

21. Sacrosanctum Concilium Oecumenicum Vaticanum II, Decretum De Pastorali Episcoporum Munere In Ecclesia, *Christus Dominus* (Die 28 mensis octobris anno 1965), 30,1; 58 AAS 673–96 (1966). *See* John A. Renken, *Parishes and Pastors in* CLSA-2000, 676 ("The parish is part of the particular church, not an autonomous entity."). *See also* James A. Coriden, The Parish in Catholic Tradition, History, Theology, and Canon Law 101–03 (Paulist Press 1997), which discusses the parish as part of the diocese.

22. *See* Congregatio pro Doctrina Fidei, *Litterae ad Catholicae Ecclesiae Episcopos de aliquibus aspectibus Ecclesiae prout est Communio* (Die 28 mensis maii anno 1992), 85 AAS 838–50 (1993), which explicates the dogmatic implications of *communio*.

23. *See* Francesco Coccopalmerio, *Il concetto di parrocchia nel Vaticano II*, 106 La Scuola Cattolica 123–42 (1978).

24. *See* Canons 1732–1752, *CIC-1983*.

25. *See* Canon 375, § 1, *CIC-1983*.

26. *See* Canons 528, §§ 1 & 2; and Canon 529, *CIC-1983*.

This theological justification for the careful and consultative nature of the bishop's ministry is reenforced by the natural law principle of subsidiarity. Pope Pius XI formulated a description of the principle as an integral aspect of the church's social teaching: "it is an injustice . . . to transfer to the larger and higher collectively functions which can be performed and provided for by the lesser and subordinate bodies."[27] Consistent with the principle of subsidiarity, the parish structure enables a local congregation of the faithful to engage in activities that foster a community of faith among the members. Just as the specific traditions and customs of the particular church do not detract but enhance the universal church, the local parish churches also enjoy a legitimate right to develop special practices as long as they express the unity of the one faith of the universal church. However, Pius XI's philosophical description of subsidiarity was formulated in response to societal developments in the industrialized world. It would be a methodological error to apply it as a general sociological device to structures in the church.[28] The natural law principle of subsidiarity is not intended to detract from the hierarchical relation between the diocesan bishop and the parish. In the exercise of his pastoral leadership, the bishop is always to be respectful of the life of the local community. This in no way abrogates the bishop's responsibility and right to exercise pastoral governance over his diocese and the parishes which are part of it.

In defining the relationship between the diocese and the parish, the *CIC-1983* holds in tension the principle of hierarchy and the principle of equality. Canon 330 reflects the ecclesiological claim that Christ instituted the church as a hierarchical communion of the Apostles and their successors with Saint Peter and his successors at the head of the College of Bishops. At the same time, Canon 208 recognizes the fundamental equality of all the baptized as members of the People of God. These canons are based upon the idea that the church is at once a communion in which holiness is equally available to all, and one in which the members of the College of Bishops function with hierarchical office. The theological understanding of the church as *communio* is at odds with competition between individual baptized persons or groups to acquire exclusive property rights over the church's temporal goods. An approach to canon law that neglects to take account of this theological claim amounts to legalism. It approaches the law as separate from the theology of the church.

---

27. Pius Pp. XI, Litterae Encylicae, *Quadragesimo Anno* (Die 15 mensis maii anno 1931), 79–80, 23 AAS 35 (1931). English translation in SEVEN GREAT ENCYCLICALS 147 (William J. Gibbons ed., Paulist Press 1963).

28. *See* CORECCO, CANON LAW AND COMMUNIO, WRITINGS ON THE CONSTITUTIONAL LAW OF THE CHURCH, 375.

B. Parish Property in Canon Law

In their respective commentaries on church property, Francis G. Morrisey and Robert T. Kennedy concur that "property legitimately acquired by a parish . . . is owned by the parish, not by the diocese."[29] Morrisey describes the parish ownership as "exclusive."[30] He explicates his opinion by stating that a diocese that seeks to appropriate parish property must purchase or lease the property from the parish in question.[31] The justification for this opinion may be found in Section 3 of Canon 515 of the 1983 Code of Canon Law, which recognizes the parish as a juridic person. Kennedy provides a description of a juridic person as "an artificial person, distinct from all natural persons or material goods, constituted by competent ecclesiastical authority for an apostolic purpose, with a capacity for continuous existence and canonical rights and duties like those of a natural person . . ."[32] Canon 1256 establishes that "[u]nder the supreme authority of the Roman Pontiff, ownership of goods belongs to that juridic person which has legitimately acquired them." It follows that the parish owns the property which it has legitimately acquired. To end the inquiry at this point of the analysis, however, would be incomplete. In regard to the ownership of parish property, several other specific provisions of the canon law need to be considered. These canonical provisions reflect the theological concerns about the hierarchical relation between the diocese and the parish, the dedication of ecclesiastical property to the mission of the church, and the gospel ideal of common ownership and poverty. The juridic person of the parish in canon law is different from the corporation in secular legal theory on account of these theological concerns.

First, the recognition of an entity as a juridic person in canon law does not abrogate the principle of hierarchy. Although the parish is a separate juridic person with the right to private property (*dominium* or *proprietas*), it remains part of the diocese and subject to the authority (*imperium*) of the diocesan bishop.[33] Section 1 of Canon 1276 requires that the "Ordinaries must carefully supervise the administration of all the goods which belong to the public juridic persons subject to them . . ." As the Ordinary of the diocese, the bishop incurs the obligation to supervise the administration of all the assets of the parishes and other juridic persons under his authority. Consistent with Vatican II's theology of the particular

---

29. Robert T. Kennedy, *Book V, The Temporal Goods of the Church, in* CLSA-2000, 1457; *see also* Francis G. Morrisey, *Book V, The Temporal Goods of the Church, in* CLSGB & Ireland, 709.

30. Morrisey, *Book V, The Temporal Goods of the Church,* 709.

31. *See id.*

32. Kennedy, *Book V, The Temporal Goods of the Church,* 155.

33. The *CIC-1983* uses the terms *dominium* (Canon 1256) and *proprietas* (Canon 1284, § 2, 2°) interchangeably to signify the ownership of property. The interchangeable use of the terms in the *CIC-1983* means that they are different in meaning from the ancient Roman jurists' use of *dominium,* which signified an undivided and absolute ownership. *See* Kennedy, *Book V, The Temporal Goods of the Church,* 1458.

church, the juridic personality of the parish does not constitute it as an autonomous unit which may acquire, administer, or alienate its property without regard to the authority of the diocesan bishop. The parish is a part of the diocese, and the bishop has both the responsibility and right to exercise the power of governance over it. Section 1 of Canon 381 recognizes that the bishop exercises ordinary, proper, and immediate power with the jurisdiction of his diocese. This includes power over any of the temporal goods that belong to the parish.

Several additional canonical provisions are helpful in clarifying the hierarchical relation between the diocese and parish with regard to the ownership of parish property. Canon 532 establishes that the parish priest acts in the name of the parish as a juridic person. Section 1 of Canon 1279 vests the administration of ecclesiastical goods in one who "exercises the direct power of governance" over the juridic person. Pursuant to Canon 531, the parish priest exercises the direct power of governance over the parish. However, within his diocese the bishop sets the limits for ordinary and extraordinary administration. A priest who is pastor of a parish has the right to engage in the ordinary administration of the parish, which includes, *inter alia*, control of its temporal goods. Beyond what the bishop has declared for ordinary administration in his diocese, any act of extraordinary administration by a pastor in the absence of the bishop's permission would constitute an invalid alienation of ecclesiastical property. Canon 1291 sets the requirement for valid alienation, and Canon 1296 deals with an invalid alienation under canon law which might be valid under civil law.

The hierarchical principle is also evident in Section 2 of Canon 515 establishing that only the diocesan bishop may erect, suppress, or alter parishes. When a parish is entirely suppressed, Canon 123 requires that the property of the now extinct juridic person be distributed in accord with the suppressed parish's statutes. Presumably, the parish statutes and bylaws have been drawn in such a way as to ensure that the property passes to the diocese.[34] In the case that the parish statutes do not make provision for the distribution of its property upon extinction, Canon 123 provides that the property reverts to the diocese. The merging of two or more parishes into one presents a different case. Canon 122 states that "the first obligation is to observe the wishes of the founders and benefactors, the demands of acquired rights, and in accord with the approved statutes." Generally speaking, when the juridic person of one parish is to be altered by combining it with the juridic person of another parish, the property of the first parish is transferred

34. Canon 117, *CIC-1983*, requires that the statutes of the juridic person be approved by the competent ecclesiastical authority. In the case of the approval of the statutes of the parish, the competent ecclesiastical authority would be the bishop. In this regard, the civil law for tax exemption requires a provision for distribution to other tax-exempt organizations upon dissolution.

to the remaining juridic person with which it is combined.[35] This is accomplished through the canonical authority of the diocesan bishop. Such a transfer is also consistent with the exercise of the bishop's pastoral care for the members of the parish. In light of the canonical aspects of the hierarchical relation between the diocese and the parish, it is misleading to state that the parish exercises an "exclusive right of control" over its own property.

Finally, the ecclesiastical property of a juridic person remains an integral part of the mission of the church. All ecclesiastical property is dedicated to the mission of the church, and serves communities by advancing the mission under the supervision of the appropriate hierarchical figure.[36] Any given piece of church property must always be available to serve the common good in light of the gospel ideals of common ownership, apostolic mission, and poverty. Parish property is part of the mission of the diocese as the particular church within the universal church. The ultimate authority in the diocese with regard to the church's mission is vested in the diocesan bishop. Based on Vatican II's theology of the particular church, the diocesan bishop retains the right to direct the property under his canonical jurisdiction in accord with what he discerns best advances the mission of the church. It would be an error about canon law if a pastor, parishioner, or group of persons concluded that the diocesan bishop lacked the authority to direct parish property in accord with the church's mission. Such an error would deny the theological element that forms the *intellectus* of canon law, yielding legalism rather than the unity of law and theology. In the words of von Balthasar, it would result in a "canonization of private ownership" as an absolute right distinct from the particular and universal church.[37]

II. CONGREGATIONALIST V. HIERARCHICAL FORMS OF CHURCH GOVERNANCE

The nineteenth-century historical experience of the United States Catholic bishops attempting to organize parish property in accord with church teaching demonstrates the importance of the unity of law and theology. During the eighteenth century, the United States had emerged as a Protestant nation. While the various denominations maintained their independence, a commonality of habits, customs, and mores resulted in a *de facto* Protestant establishment. Only those who shared Protestant culture could claim to be authentically American. Starting in the 1820s, the dominant Protestant ethos would be challenged by massive waves of Catholic immigrants from Ireland and Germany. By 1850, Roman Catholics

---

35. *See* Dario Cardinal Castrillon, *Letter to United States Bishops Concerning the Assets of Merged Parishes, in* 36 ORIGINS 190 (Aug. 31, 2006).

36. *See* Canon 1254, §§ 1 & 2, *CIC-1983*.

37. BALTHASAR, THE CHRISTIAN STATE OF LIFE, 115.

constituted the single largest Christian denomination in the United States. The arrival of new immigrants who did not share in the ethos of the dominant religious culture posed a threat not only to the *de facto* establishment but to the self-identity of the United States as a Protestant nation. Due to their numbers, Catholics could not be ignored, and opposition to their religion soon produced a virulent anti-Catholicism.[38]

According to Philip Hamburger, the anti-Catholicism could be attributed in no small part to the growth of the liberal Protestant emphasis on individual freedom. Consistent with attitudes formed in post–Reformation and Enlightenment Europe, nineteenth-century American liberalism saw Catholicism's adherence to a unified creed enforced by a central ecclesial governance as a threat to the primacy of individual conscience.[39] John T. McGreevy states that throughout the nineteenth century the American "focus on individual autonomy . . . continued to nurture a concomitant anti-Catholicism."[40] Anti-Catholic hostility was embodied by the Know Nothings of the 1850s. Philip Jenkins has examined how this hostility was inflamed in anti-Catholic literature by unfavorable depictions of Catholic priests and by antagonism to hierarchical forms of church governance. One strain of the literature portrayed Catholic priests as lecherous criminals who raped virgins and seduced married woman even as they ruled their flocks with iron fists.[41] Another strain ascribed "authoritarianism, ostentatious wealth, theatricality, and all the flamboyant trappings of 'popery,'" that "implied effeminacy and secret homosexuality" to the Catholic clergy.[42] Jenkins suggests that the nineteenth-century literature presented Catholicism as an "emotional, irrational, effeminate" religion in contrast to the "virile" nature of liberal Protestantism with emphasis on individual autonomy.

Given the hostility toward Catholicism during the nineteenth century, it is not surprising that the Catholic bishops' efforts to organize ecclesiastical property conflicted with widely held notions about church property in the United States.[43] In nineteenth-century America, the accepted approach to church property was Protestant. It focused on local democratic control by laymen. Church property was viewed as belonging to a trustee corporation through which the elected lay

---

38. *See* Thomas J. Curry, Farewell to Christendom, The Future of Church and State in America 18, 53–56 (Oxford University Press 2001).

39. *See* Philip Hamburger, Separation of Church and State 194–202 (Harvard University Press 2002).

40. John T. McGreevy, Catholicism and American Freedom 94–95 (Norton 2003).

41. *See* Mark Twain, Letters from the Earth 53 (Bernard DeVoto ed., HarperCollins Perennial Press 1974).

42. *See* Philip Jenkins, Pedophiles and Priests 23 (Oxford University Press 1996).

43. *See* Patrick J. Dignan, A History of the Legal In-Corporation of Catholic Church Property in the United States (1784–1932) 51 (Catholic University of America 1933).

trustees exercised physical control over it.[44] Legislators, judges, and other public servants were largely Protestant and tended to view the Catholic Church's claim that its temporal goods were under the control of its hierarchy as nothing less than an attempt to impose government by a foreign sovereignty.[45] Eager to adapt to the American way of life, some Catholics were also attracted to the concept of local democratic control of church property by the laity.[46]

The lay trustee controversy presented a significant challenge to the Catholic Church's understanding of itself and regulation of its temporal goods in the United States. During the nineteenth century, some states, such as Pennsylvania, adopted statutes that required control of church property be vested in the lay members of the various congregations.[47] This kind of statute set the stage for bitter disputes between lay members of Catholic parishes and their bishops over title to parish property. During these disputes, the laity sometimes also sought to exercise control over the hiring and discharge of the pastor and all other significant administration of the parish. In certain instances, bishops were left with no alternative but to resort to strong canonical penalties against the laity.

On occasion these conflicts over lay trustees in Catholic parishes were litigated in the courts. The verdicts of various state courts during this time period must be described as mixed and fact specific. No clear pattern in favor of either side can be said to have carried the day. In a Pennsylvania case, for example, the highest court of the state held that canon law could not predominate over civil law and that the state simply did not recognize any temporal power of the bishop.[48] While in states such as Missouri, precedent was established that recognized the hierarchical nature of the Catholic Church and vested control over church property in the diocesan bishop.[49]

In response to this confusion, the Catholic bishops asserted the church's rights pursuant to canon law in a series of provincial and plenary councils at Baltimore. As early as 1829, while assembled for the First Provincial Council of Baltimore, the American bishops expressed their position that:

> Since lay trustees have frequently abused the right given to them by the civil power to the great detriment of religion and not without scandal to the faithful, we most earnestly [*maxime optamus*] desire that in the future no

---

44. *See* Note, *Judicial Intervention in Disputes over Church Property*, 75 Harv. L. Rev. 1142, 1149–54 (1962).

45. *See* Paul G. Kauper & Stephen C. Ellis, *Religious Corporations and the Law*, 71 Mich. L. Rev. 1499, 1521 (1973).

46. *See* Dignan, A History of the Legal In-Corporation of Catholic Church Property in the United States, 72.

47. *See* 2 Pa. Digest of Laws (1860) (12th ed. 1895), as amended, Pa. Stat. Ann. tit. 10, § 81 (1965).

48. *See* Krauczunas v. Hoban, 70 A. 740 (1908).

49. *See* Klix v. Polish Roman Catholic St. Stanislaus Parish, 137 Mo. App. 347 (1909).

> church shall be erected or consecrated, unless it shall be assigned by written instrument to the Bishop in whose diocese it is to be erected, wherever this can be done . . .[50]

The aversion of the American bishops to utilizing state statutory provisions that regarded church property as held by lay trustees was again evident at the Fourth Provincial Council of Baltimore of 1840. When necessary to secure ecclesiastical property, movable and immovable, the Council decreed that the property was to be held in the bishop's name and passed to his successor through the provisions of civil law, such as wills and testaments.[51] In 1843, the First Decree of the Fifth Provincial Council required that the diocesan bishop, within three months of his taking possession of the diocese, execute a written will securing ecclesiastical property in accord with state law.[52] The Seventh Decree of the same council admonished that no church property was to be alienated (sold, mortgaged, or leased) without the bishop's approval.[53] The First and Second Plenary Councils of Baltimore affirmed the necessity of holding title to property in accord with the canon law of the church and whatever appropriate provisions of the civil law insured that the rights of the bishop were respected.[54] In 1866, the Third Plenary Council permitted the bishop to hold title under three different legal theories: as corporation sole, as trustee for the diocese, or as an individual with title in fee simple absolute.[55]

---

50. CONCILIA PROVINCIALIA BALTIMORI HABITA AB ANNO 1829 USQUE AD ANNUM 1849, at 5, 74 (Joannem Murphy et Socium 1851). The above translation of the quoted portion of the Fifth Decree of the First Provincial Council of Baltimore appears in DIGNAN, A HISTORY OF THE LEGAL IN-CORPORATION OF CATHOLIC CHURCH PROPERTY IN THE UNITED STATES, 145.

51. *See* CONCILIA PROVINCIALIA BALTIMORI HABITA AB ANNO 1829 USQUE AD ANNUM 1849, at 8, 172. This portion of the Eighth Decree of the Fourth Provincial Council of Baltimore is quoted in DIGNAN, A HISTORY OF THE LEGAL IN-CORPORATION OF CATHOLIC CHURCH PROPERTY IN THE UNITED STATES, 162 ("We advise all prelates sedulously to look after the security of ecclesiastical goods by every means in their power; therefore they are to seek the protection of the laws or of the civil authority, wherever it can be had, the safety of the rights of the bishop, however, being guaranteed."); PETER GUILDAY, A HISTORY OF THE COUNCILS OF BALTIMORE, 1791–1884, at 138 (Arno Press 1969).

52. CONCILIA PROVINCIALIA BALTIMORI HABITA AB ANNO 1829 USQUE AD ANNUM 1849, at 1, 216. See GUILDAY, A HISTORY OF THE COUNCILS OF BALTIMORE 138, which states that the will was to be deposited with the archbishop or, in the case of the archbishop's will, with the senior suffragan bishop.

53. CONCILIA PROVINCIALIA BALTIMORI HABITA AB ANNO 1829 USQUE AD ANNUM 1849, at 7, 217. *See* GUILDAY, A HISTORY OF THE COUNCILS OF BALTIMORE, 139.

54. *See* DIGNAN, A HISTORY OF THE LEGAL IN-CORPORATION OF CATHOLIC CHURCH PROPERTY IN THE UNITED STATES, 189, 210–11.

55. *See* ACTA ET DECRETA CONCILII PLENARII BALTIMORENSIS TERTII, 153–54, 267–69 (Joannis Murphy et Sociorum 1886). English translation in JOHN D. M. BARRETT,

A notorious case in 1888 involving the Archbishop of Cincinnati, John Baptist Purcell, exposed the dangers of allowing bishops to hold title to diocesan property in fee simple.[56] The Vicar General of the Archdiocese, who was the brother of the archbishop, had been accepting deposits of money from individual Catholics and then lending to others at interest. The archbishop had guaranteed to insure the deposits with his personally owned property, which included all the diocesan property that he held in fee simple. When the credit scheme failed, an assignee of the original investors sued the archbishop and the archdiocese for recovery. In *Mannix v. Purcell*, the Ohio courts denied the requested relief, holding that the bishop had no power under canon law to bind church property for his personal debts. [57] This holding was significant in that it deferred to the provisions of canon law. Although the archdiocese was saved by the civil courts from financial ruin, the American bishops and the Holy See were deeply concerned that an individual bishop, who held ecclesiastical property in fee simple, might be able to jeopardize or even pillage church property.[58] In 1911, the Sacred Congregation for the Council issued a decree that required the bishop to hold title to church property either through the method of religious corporation or corporation sole. The Sacred Congregation also decreed that "[t]he method which is called *in Fee Simple* is totally to be abolished."[59] In situations where the civil law did not permit the religious corporation or corporation sole, canonical commentators at the time suggested that the bishop was permitted to hold the property as a trustee but not in his own name in fee simple.[60]

Starting at the end of the Civil War and continuing through the first half of the twentieth century, the hostility of civil law jurisdictions in the United States to the Catholic hierarchy's claims about church property gradually subsided. A variety of state arrangements emerged under which the rights of the church were recognized.[61] A prototypical statute was adopted in New York State at the end of the nineteenth century that allowed the acts of incorporation to be drawn so that the control of church personal and real property was left in the hands of

---

A COMPARATIVE STUDY OF THE COUNCILS OF BALTIMORE AND THE CODE OF CANON LAW 186–87 (The Catholic University of America 1932).

56. *See* DIGNAN, A HISTORY OF THE LEGAL IN-CORPORATION OF CATHOLIC CHURCH PROPERTY IN THE UNITED STATES, 219–22.

57. *See* Mannix v. Purcell, 24 N.E. 595 (1888).

58. *See* DIGNAN, A HISTORY OF THE LEGAL IN-CORPORATION OF CATHOLIC CHURCH PROPERTY IN THE UNITED STATES, 235.

59. An English translation of the decree appeared in 45 AMERICAN ECCLESIASTICAL REV. 585–86 (1911). *See also* A HISTORY OF THE LEGAL IN-CORPORATION OF CATHOLIC CHURCH PROPERTY IN THE UNITED STATES, 239–40.

60. *See* DIGNAN, A HISTORY OF THE LEGAL IN-CORPORATION OF CATHOLIC CHURCH PROPERTY IN THE UNITED STATES, 266–68.

61. *See id.* at 214–44.

the bishop.[62] In the statute, each parish corporation is composed of the bishop, the vicar general, and two other trustees who serve at the bishop's will.[63] The New York law functioned as the basis for the Congregation of the Council's 1911 decree.[64] That decree expressed a preference for the parish corporation over the corporation sole.[65] As a result of the changes to civil law during the twentieth century, dioceses throughout the United States were able to secure title to diocesan property, including that of the parishes. The history of the long, difficult, and ultimately successful effort of the Catholic bishops in the United States to obtain state law recognition of the hierarchical nature of parish property should not be overlooked in the discussion of the contemporary issue about the ownership of parish property raised in the bankruptcy claims noted at the outset of this chapter.

III. CANON LAW AND STATE LAW

This section of Chapter 5 continues to draw upon the specific example of how the Catholic Church in the United States is able to secure its property in a way that reflects a harmony of canon law and state law. I use the phrase "state law" to refer in general to the concept of the civil law of the state as distinct from the canon law of the church. Depending on the context, I hope it will be clear when I employ the same phrase in reference to the law of the fifty states that comprise the United States. As a global institution, the Roman Catholic Church encounters many different forms of state law with regard to property. These various forms range from nations with which the Holy See has a formal concordat that protects the property rights of the church to nations which curtail the church's religious freedom and property rights. The United States represents a modern democracy that respects religious freedom while purporting to maintain neutrality about religion. This section of the chapter first discusses the various ways in which state law in the fifty states permits the Catholic Church to hold its property in accord with canon law. In light of the harmony between canon law and state law,

---

62. *See Act Supplementary to the Act entitled An Act to Provide for the Incorporation of Religious Societies, passed April 5, 1813*, in *Laws of New York State Passed at the Eighty-Sixth Session of the Legislature* (Albany 1863).

63. *See* GEN. LAWS OF N.Y., I, 499 (1895).

64. *See* 45 AMERICAN ECCLESIASTICAL REV. 585–86 (1911), which translates 1° of the Sacred Congregation's 1911 decree as: "Of the methods which now exist in the United States, for possessing and administering the possessions of the Church, that is to be preferred, which is popularly called the *Parish Corporation*, with however, those conditions and precautions, which are in use in the State of New York.".

65. *See id.*

this section of the chapter then treats the specific question of the hierarchical relationship between the diocese and parish.

A. The Harmony of State and Canon Law

Canon 1290, *CIC-1983*, establishes the importance of securing the rights of the church through respect for, and use of, the provision of state law. Canon 22, *CIC-1983*, provides that canon law yields to state law in certain instances. As mentioned in Chapter 1, this is known as the "canonization" of the state law. To mention but one example, Section 1 of Canon 1282, *CIC-1983*, requires that state statutes of labor law and policy be meticulously observed together with the church's own social teaching in the church's employment policies. The church employer is thus bound by canon law to follow the state legislation that might for example establish a minimum wage or social security. Of course, it could be the case that the social teaching of the church requires even greater benefits than the state law requires. Canon law does not yield to state law in general, but only in certain matters defined by the canon law itself. Canon 22 requires that the effects of state law be observed in canon law with the same effects, and in this sense, the effects of the state law are canonized. In other words, the effects of the specific state law become part of the canon law.

Sixteen states now provide special corporate forms for specific religious denominations, and nine of those states expressly identify the Catholic Church.[66] Many states also generally permit the establishment of some type of a religious corporation for other religious denominations.[67] At least seventeen states and

---

66. They are: Connecticut, CONN. GEN. STAT. ANN. §§ 33-265 to -281a (West 1997); Delaware, DEL. CODE ANN. tit. 27, §§ 114–18 (2004); Illinois, 805 ILL. COMP. STAT. ANN. 110/50 (West 2004); Louisiana, LA. REV. STAT. ANN. §§ 12:481–:483 (West 2004); Maine, ME. REV. STAT. ANN. tit. 13, § 2986 (West 2003); Maryland, MD. CODE ANN., CORPS. & ASS'NS § 5-314 to -338 (2004); Massachusetts, MASS. GEN. LAWS ANN. ch. 67, §§ 39–46, 55 (West 2001); Michigan, MICH. COMP. LAWS ANN. §§ 458.1–.535 (West 2002); New Hampshire, N.H. REV. STAT. ANN. §§ 292:15–:17 (2004); New Jersey, N.J. STAT. ANN. §§ 16:2-1 to :20-7 (West 2004); New York, N.Y. RELIG. CORP. LAW §§ 40–455 (McKinney 2003); Vermont, VT. STAT. ANN. tit. 27 §§ 861–66 (2003); and Wisconsin, WIS. STAT. ANN. §§ 187.04, .10–.11, .15, .17–.19 (West 2004). The state statutes of Connecticut, Delaware, Massachusetts, Michigan, New Jersey, New York, and Wisconsin—specifically mention the Roman Catholic Church. It should also be noted that the state constitutions of Virginia and West Virginia expressly forbid the granting of a charter of incorporation to any church or religious entity. *See* VA. CONST. art. IV, § 14; W. VA. CONST. art. VI, § 47. At least one court, however has found such a provision unconstitutional under the free exercise clause of the First and Fourteenth Amendments of the United States Constitution. *See* Falwell v. Miller, 203 F. Supp. 2d 624 (W.D. Va. 2002).

67. They are: Alabama, ALA CODE § 10-4-20, -4-40 (2003); Colorado, COLO. REV. STAT. ANN. § 7-51-113 (West 1998); Connecticut, CONN GEN. STAT. ANN. § 33-264a (West 1997); Delaware, DEL. CODE ANN. tit. 27, § 101 (2004); Washington, D.C., D.C. CODE ANN. § 29-801 to -806 (2004); Georgia, GA. CODE ANN. §§ 14-5-43 to -51 (2004); Kansas, KAN.

the District of Columbia permit the corporation sole, which, as its name implies, is a one-person incorporation.[68] In hierarchical churches such as the Catholic Church, the office holder of this corporate form is the diocesan bishop. All of the states have some form of statutory recognition of nonprofit incorporations, which include not only religious organizations but also other kinds of educational, social, and charitable organizations. Twenty-one states plus Washington, D.C., have statutes that recognize unincorporated voluntary religious associations, and two other states unincorporated voluntary associations without specification of whether or not these associations are religious.[69] Numerous states allow a church to elect one or more of the above types of organization.

STAT. ANN. § 17-1701 (2003); Illinois, 805 ILL. COMP. STAT. ANN. 110/35 (West 2004); Maine, ME. REV. STAT. ANN. tit. 13, §§ 2861 (West 2003); Maryland, MD. CODE ANN., CORPS. & ASS'NS § 5-301 to -313 (2004); Massachusetts, MASS. GEN. LAWS ANN. ch. 67, §§ 21–23, 47–54 (West. 2001); Minnesota, MINN. STAT. ANN. §§ 315.01–.51 (West 2004); New Jersey, N.J. STAT. ANN. § 16:1-1 to -39 (West 2004); Ohio, OHIO REV. CODE ANN. §§ 1715.01-.22 (West 2005); Vermont, VT. STAT. ANN. tit. 27 §§ 701–706 (2003); and Wisconsin, WIS. STAT. ANN. § 187.01 (West 2004).

68. They are: Alabama, ALA. CODE § 10-4-1 (2003); Alaska, ALASKA STAT. §§ 10.40.010-.150 (Michie 2003); Arizona, ARIZ. REV. STAT. ANN §§ 10-11901 to -11908 (West 2004); California, CAL. CORP. CODE §§ 10000–15 (West 2004); Colorado, COLO. REV. STAT. ANN. §§ 7-52-101 to -106 (West 1998); Hawaii, HAWAII REV. STAT. §§ 419-1 to -9 (2002); Indiana, IND. CODE ANN. § 23-17-2-12 (West 2005); Mississippi, MISS. CODE ANN. §§ 79-11-127 (2004); Montana, MONT. CODE ANN. §§ 35-3-101 to -103 (2003); Nebraska, NEB. REV. STAT. § 21-1914 (2004); Nevada, NEV. REV. STAT. 84.002–.150 (2003); Oregon, OR. REV. STAT. § 65.067 (2003); South Carolina, S.C. CODE ANN. § 33-31-140 (Law. Co-op. 2004); Utah, UTAH CODE ANN. §§ 16-7-1 to -16 (2004) (but note that according to § 16-7-16 a corporation sole cannot be formed in Utah after May 3, 2004); Washington, WASH. REV. CODE ANN. §§ 24.12.010–.060 (West 2004); and Wyoming, WYO. STAT. ANN. §§ 17-8-101 to -117 (Michie 2004).

69. They are: Alaska, ALASKA STAT. § 10.40.120 (Michie 2003); Arkansas, ARK. CODE. ANN. §§ 18-11-201 to -202 (Michie 2002); Connecticut, CONN. GEN. STAT. ANN. § 33-264a (West 1997); Washington, D.C., D.C. CODE ANN. § 29-701 to -712 (2004); Florida, FLA. STAT. ANN. §§ 617.2004–2005 (West 2001); Kansas, KAN. STAT. ANN. §§ 17-1711 to -1758 (2003); Kentucky, KY. REV. STAT. ANN. §§ 273.090–.140 (Banks-Baldwin 2003); Massachusetts, MASS. GEN. LAWS ANN. ch. 67, § 2 (West 2001); Mississippi, MISS. CODE ANN. §§ 79-11-31 to -47 (2004); Nebraska, NEB. REV. STAT. §§ 21-2801 to -2803 (2004); New Hampshire, N.H. REV. STAT. ANN. §§ 306:1–:12 (2004); New Jersey, N.J. STAT. ANN. § 16:1-39 (West 2004); North Carolina, N.C. GEN. STAT. §§ 61-1 to -6 (2004); Oklahoma, OKLA. STAT. ANN. tit. 18, § 562 (West 1998); Pennsylvania, PA. STAT. ANN. tit. 10, §§ 21, 81 (West 1998); Tennessee, TENN. CODE. ANN. §§ 66-2-201 to -203 (2003); Utah, UTAH CODE ANN. §§ 16-7-10 (2003); Vermont, VT. STAT. ANN. tit. 27, §§ 781–944 (2003); Virginia, VA. CODE. ANN. §§ 57-1 to -17 (Michie 2003); West Virginia, W. VA. CODE ANN. §§35-1-1 to -13 (Michie 2004); Wisconsin, WIS. STAT. ANN. § 187.07 (West 2002); and Wyoming, WYO. STAT. ANN. § 1-32-121 (Michie 2004). While not specifically religious, New Mexico and Texas do allow for unincorporated associations formed for nonprofit reasons, and thus

B. The Relationship between Diocese and Parish in State Law

The structures of organization that a particular diocese adopts to secure its temporal goods in state law should reflect the hierarchical relationship between the diocese and parish. In many instances, parishes are separately incorporated from the diocese in state law. Other dioceses elect to form religious associations under a particular state's statutory scheme. Alternatively, the bishop may be recognized under state law as a corporation sole with the power over the property of the diocese and all its parishes. The separate incorporation of parishes should not be understood as meaning that the bishop intends to forsake his hierarchical authority in favor of self-rule by the parish corporation. As discussed in the previous section, the separate incorporation of Catholic parishes in the United States is not a new phenomenon. During the nineteenth century, the United States Catholic bishops engaged in an arduous battle to secure state law recognition of their church's hierarchical form of government. From the perspective of the Catholic Church, the preferential organizational form for the diocese pursuant to state law remains separate parish incorporations. Typically, the bylaws for each of the parish corporations establish the bishop as the sole member with power to appoint and remove directors at will. They also identify the bishop as one of the directors. Characteristic bylaws require that all actions of the board of directors must have approval of the bishop. The bishop may exercise control over the parish corporation through his veto power and his power to appoint the vicar general and pastor as directors. The state's corporation law thus provides a legal method for the Catholic bishop to fulfill his responsibility under canon law to govern the diocese and its parishes. In canon law, the canonization of state law is intended to secure the right of the Catholic Church to own property in accord with the church's communal and hierarchical characteristics that are intended to foster certain religious and charitable objectives.

Whether or not separate incorporation of diocesan units such as parishes, hospitals, and schools will shield them from liability in a child abuse case against the diocese is open to debate. The secular legal doctrines of piercing the corporate veil and enterprise liability apply when a court concludes that the separate incorporation must yield to a functional unity between it and some other legal or real person on account of ownership and/or control. The idea that the separate incorporations function as the "alter ego" of the bishop remains critical to piercing the corporate veil, a finding of enterprise liability, or some other legal means for reaching the assets of the separate corporations. Stephen M. Bainbridge and Aaron H. Cole argue that the alter ego principle does not apply to the diocesan-parish relationship.[70] An entity such as a parish corporation is considered

---

include religious associations. N.M. STAT. ANN. §§ 53-10-1 to -7 (Michie 2004); TEX. CORPS. & ASS'NS CODE ANN. §§ 252.001–.017 (Vernon 2004).

70. *See* Bainbridge & Cole, *The Bishop's Alter Ego: Enterprise Liability and the Catholic Priest Sex Abuse Scandal*, 65–106.

to be the alter ego of another person or entity such as a bishop or diocese when two requirements are met. First, one entity exercises such a high degree of control over the other that the entities have lost a separate existence. As evident from the relationship between diocese and parish as discussed in this chapter, the parish enjoys a significant amount of autonomy although the bishop has ultimate responsibility for its governance and continued existence. Second, the control of one entity over the other must involve an abuse of the power of control. In evaluating the second requirement, courts may take into account the ability of an innocent party to fulfill its legitimate corporate ends. In a lawsuit against the diocese for clergy sexual abuse, the parish which has no connection to the sexual abuse and which is separately incorporated from the diocese may claim that a finding that it is liable for the abuse that occurred in another place would unfairly penalize its ability to pursue its corporate ends.

IV. ANTINOMIAN AND LEGALISTIC APPROACHES TO CHURCH PROPERTY

Up to this point in this chapter, I have been primarily concerned with the proper relationship between the diocese and parish with regard to property. The theory of property, with its unity of law and theology, which I discussed in the previous chapter, is not limited to the relationship between the diocese and the parish, but pertains to ecclesiastical property in general. Prior to leaving the subject of church property, I therefore wish to make several brief observations on the ways in which legalistic and antinomian approaches to church property can defeat the unity of law and theology. Again, my focus is on the recent experience of the Catholic Church in the United States, but the specific examples raise broader issues in canon law. Antinomian and legalistic tendencies pose threats to the proper canonical order for the ownership of ecclesiastical property.

First, legalism has been evident in the secularization of church property associated with institutions such as hospitals, universities, and colleges during the second half of the twentieth century in the United States. These kinds of institutions were often started by religious communities in the United States to serve both religious and secular purposes. In canon law, it is possible that the Catholic institution itself has been recognized as a juridical person directed "to a purpose befitting the Church's mission" and which "concerns of piety, of the apostolate, or of charity, whether spiritual or temporal."[71] When a Catholic institution is a juridical person under canon law, it enjoys the right to own its own property. More likely, the Catholic institution has been considered part of the juridical person of the religious community that founded it. The juridical person of the religious community seeks "the perfection of charity in the service of

71. Canon 114, §§ 1 & 2, *CIC-1983*.

God's Kingdom, for the honor of God, the building up of the Church, and the salvation of the world."[72] In this case, the religious community as the juridical person owns the property of the Catholic institution according to canon law. Pursuant to state law, the Catholic institution may be recognized as a religious not-for-profit entity either in a corporate or noncorporate form. The law of the state requires that the purposes for the institution's existence, articulated in the articles of incorporation or other relevant documents, be fulfilled. The secularization of Catholic institutions in the United States represents a legalism in which the religious mission of the institution and its property is diminished while the secular purposes of the property are exaggerated. The secularization is contrary to both canon law and state law, which share the expectation that the institution will fulfill its religious mission.

Second, during the last five decades in the United States, it has been increasingly common that the control over such Catholic institutions and their property has been given to a board of trustees, whose membership consists principally or entirely of laypersons. As far as canon law is concerned, it ultimately makes little difference whether a Catholic institution is directed by priests, religious, laypersons, or any combination of these. Canon law envisions that whoever has responsibility for the governance of a Catholic institution will exercise vigilance to ensure that the religious purpose of the institution is being fulfilled.[73] From a theological perspective, this responsibility pertains to all the baptized no matter what their status in the church. On the basis of natural law and the requirements of justice, the responsibility is not limited to members of the church, but it pertains to any human person who accepts the responsibility to participate in the governance of the Catholic institution. To give but one example, the president of a Catholic hospital who happens to be Jewish has just as much responsibility for the religious mission of the institution as a Catholic bishop who is a member of the board of directors. This is not to diminish the fact that the bishop who is a director brings a grace of office, which any person of intelligence and goodwill would recognize and value. Likewise, the state law also anticipates that the directors of a religious entity, recognized by the state, will fulfill their fiduciary duties in ensuring that the institution satisfies its religious purpose. Contrary to these theological and natural expectations, the shift in control of many Catholic institutions to a lay board of directors often leads to a reduction or even abrogation of the institution's religious mission and reason for existence.

Third, the process of the secularization of Catholic institutions has often also meant the *de facto* alienation of church property.[74] The governance of the Catholic institution may have been transferred from the religious community to a lay

72. Canon 573, § 1, *CIC-1983*.

73. *See* Canons 114, §§ 1 & 2; and Canon 118, *CIC-1983*.

74. *See* Adam J. Maida, *Canonical and Legal Fallacies of the McGrath Thesis on the Reorganization of Church Entities*, 275–86.

board of trustees. The creation of a board of trustees does not automatically result in the alienation of ecclesiastical property according to canon law. Such a valid alienation would require official canonical permission. While canon law recognizes the validity of state law provisions that secure the right of the church to acquire and sell private property, canon law stipulates its own requirements for the valid alienation of ecclesiastical property.[75] For example, the religious community that sponsors a Catholic healthcare or educational institution holds title to the property of the institution in a way that is protected pursuant to the state law as well as recognized as valid in canon law. In some instances, the title to such property may have been transferred pursuant to state law, but without the requisite permission required from the competent ecclesiastical authority as required by canon law for the valid alienation of ecclesiastical property. Under canon law, the property of the Catholic institution has never been licitly alienated, and therefore, the property still belongs to the religious community. My concern in this example is to illustrate the *de facto* but invalid alienation of church property. There are, of course, other possibilities. First, a less absolute *de facto* alienation of church property might occur when control of the institution has been secularized but the title to its property remains with the religious community under both state and canon law. Second, title could be passed in a way that is valid in both state and canon law. In canon law, this would be an alienation of the property *de facto* and *de iure*. A third, perhaps less likely, possibility could occur when the property has been validly alienated in canon law but not so under state law. In any event, ignoring the requirements of canon law for the valid alienation of property represents an antinomianism. Like the legalism that separates the theological purpose from the question of legal ownership, this antinomianism threatens the rule of law in the church.

Finally, as the secularization process and the invalid alienation of the property of Catholic institutions has been occurring in the church in the United States for the last five decades, there often seems to be no intervention on the part of church authorities. One aspect of this problem is to know who has responsibility to intervene. Canon law is not always totally clear on this point. Canon law also fails to provide an immediate and effective way for the diocesan bishop to intervene in a situation where the religious community or the juridical person in question is situated in his diocese, but is not under his direct hierarchical authority. This situation is different from the relationship between the diocesan bishop and a parish which, as discussed, does fall directly under his canonical authority. With exempt religious communities and juridical persons that report directly to

---

75. *See CIC-1983*: Canon 1291 (valid alienation of church property requires the proper process and permission from the competent hierarchical superior); Canons 1292–1298 (general rules for the alienation of church property); Canon 1254; Canons 634 §§ 1 & 2, and 741 (alienation of the property of religious institutes and societies of apostolic life); and Canon 1190 (alienation of relics and sacred images).

the Holy See, it may be the case that the geographic distance involved makes it difficult for the Holy See to have the necessary knowledge upon which to take affirmative action to check against the problems associated with the secularization of Catholic institutions. It may also be the case that the Holy See elects not to intervene directly in a local situation in accord with the understanding of the universal as a *communio* of the particular churches. Another aspect of the problem is that the diocesan bishop, who is more likely to have knowledge of the situation, neglects to exercise his responsibility as the "coordinator" of all apostolic activity in his diocese and to conduct the required "apostolic visitation" of the Catholic institutions within his diocese.[76]

Another disquieting aspect of the apparent lack of intervention on the part of church authorities in the process of the secularization of Catholic institutions concerns the relation between the religious community that founded and sponsors the Catholic institution and the members of the board of directors of the Catholic institution. As mentioned, the laypersons who are members of the board have just as much responsibility for the Catholic character and mission of the institution as the members of the religious community. However, it may also be the case that the lay trustees through no fault of their own have little understanding of the Catholic mission of the institution. In such a case, it would seem to be the responsibility of the superiors in the religious community to make provisions for faithful ongoing education about the Catholic character and mission of the institution. An aspect of this education would offer a deeper understanding of the institution's expression of its Catholic character and mission in the local and universal church.[77]

The present confusion over the ownership of parish property is illustrative of a misunderstanding of the proper function of canon law. It is true that canon law establishes the parish as a juridical person with the right to own property (*dominium*). However, when a bishop repudiates canonical authority (*imperium*) over parish property, it fosters a congregationalist approach in which the parish owns property irrespective of the Church's communal and hierarchical nature. An equally, and perhaps even more, troubling question concerns the status of Catholic institutions and their property which do not fall under the direct hierarchical authority of the diocesan bishop. The on-going secularization of Catholic institutions and their property reflects antinomianism and legalism. Legalism diminishes the theological emphasis on the religious mission, common ownership, and apostolic property in canon law. By severing the unity of law and

---

76. *See* Canons 294, §§ 1 & 2; and Canon 397, §§ 1 & 2, *CIC-1983*.

77. For an analysis of the importance of the relation of Catholic Universities and the bishop according to Ex Corde Ecclesiae, see James Conn, S.J., L'Applicatione della 'Ex Corde Ecclesiae' negli Stati Uniti: Analisi e Valutazione delle 'Ordinationes,' in PAROLA DI DIO E MISSIONE DELLA CHIESA, A cura di Davide Cito e Ferando Puig 193–214 (Giuffrè 2009).

theology, legalism diminishes the function of any given piece of ecclesiastical property to serve the apostolic mission of the Church. Antinomianism rejects the function of canon law in regulating church property, and fosters misunderstanding about the hierarchical nature of the Catholic Church. Both types of confusion disrupt the careful balance between theological and legal elements in canon law's approach to ecclesiastical property.

6. INDETERMINACY IN CANON LAW

The Refusal of Holy Communion to Catholic Public Officials: Canon 915: "A Central Case"

In Chapters 6 and 7, I raise the indeterminacy claim with regard to canon law. Specifically, I consider the indeterminacy claim from the perspective of the refusal of Holy Communion to Catholic public officials pursuant to Canon 915 of the *CIC-1983.*[1] My purpose here is not to offer an argument about whether or not Catholic public officials ought to be excluded from Holy Communion. Rather, I am examining the application of a particular canonical provision and the disagreement among the bishops over its application in an attempt to gain a deeper understanding of the way in which canon law functions. Chapter 6 consists of three major sections. First, I describe the controversy about the application of Canon 915 during the 2004 U.S. electoral campaign and discuss this controversy in reference to the indeterminacy claim. Second, I rely on two prominent features of H. L. A. Hart's legal theory—the rule of recognition and internal aspect of the law—to explore whether the application of Canon 915 to public officials is valid in the legal system of canon law. I also discuss indeterminacy and Canon 915 in light of another feature of Hart's theory—the law's open texture. Third, I ask whether the application of Canon 915 is a "central case" in light of traditional aspects of Catholic doctrine such as objective truth, individual conscience, and cooperation in evil.

While I believe that certain features of H. L. A. Hart's legal theory assist in understanding the legal aspects of the controversy over the application of Canon 915, several preliminary qualifications are in order. First, I do not mean the reliance as an endorsement of Hart's legal positivism. Pristine legal positivism denies any connection between law and morality. It has been criticized as legalstic and amoral.[2] Hart's so-called "soft positivism" acknowledges an overlap between law and morality as well as a kind of minimum content that can be

1. *See also* Canon 712, *CEEO.*

2. *See* John Finnis, *On the Incoherence of Legal Positivism,* 75 NOTRE DAME L. REV. 1597, 1598 (2000); and Ronald Dworkin, TAKING RIGHTS SERIOUSLY 17–80 (Harvard University Press 1978). See also Brian Leiter, *Legal Realism and Hard Positivism, in* HART'S POSTSCRIPT: ESSAYS ON THE POSTSCRIPT TO THE CONCEPT OF LAW 355–70 (Jules Coleman ed., Oxford University Press 2001), which distinguishes between hard positivism, which requires a complete separation of law and moral principles, and soft positivism, which acknowledges that if officials decide legal questions by reference to morality, then morality is a criterion of validity in that legal system.

derived from natural law.[3] In his 1958 debate with Lon Fuller, Hart argued that legal positivism was more likely than natural law to afford a clear moral evaluation of law as a result of the separation of the question "what is law" from the question "what is moral."[4] Nonetheless, canon law is a system of a religious law ultimately based upon a thick natural law theory as well as claims rooted in revealed truth. Irrespective of one's position on the Hart-Fuller debate, I believe, for reasons that I hope will be evident in this chapter, that Hart's positivism is particularly helpful as an analytical tool in understanding the controversy about Canon 915.

Second, Hart's theory represents a legal positivist's rendition of what counts as law. Typical of the legal positivists, Hart thought that a proper law contained its own authority and carried the power to bind. If Canon 915 satisfies Hart's requirements for proper law, a positivist approach to the law would call for its intelligent enforcement as part of the rule of law. Canon law shares the concern about the rule of law but claims to transcend legal positivism, asserting a metaphysical basis for its authority. For one who accepts the validity of canon law on its own terms, such as a Catholic bishop, canon law would seem to offer a more profound justification of law than that of legal positivism. Apart from the metaphysical claim, assuming that Canon 915 satisfies Hart's requirements for proper law, the reticence of many Catholic bishops to enforce Canon 915 may reveal something about the indeterminate nature of this provision in canon law. Whether from a positivist or metaphysical perspective on the authority of law, this indeterminacy weakens the rule of law in the life of the Catholic Church.

Third, in relying on Hart's theory, I am aware that it has been the subject of much criticism. In addition to Fuller, theorists such as Ronald Dworkin, John Finnis, and Joseph Raz have raised significant questions about Hart's approach to law.[5] To the extent that they prove helpful in exploring Canon 915, these questions are mentioned in this chapter. In the *Postscript* to *The Concept of Law*, Hart conceded that some of the criticism held merit.[6] Despite the criticism, Hart's theory has remained influential especially in the English-speaking legal world. The theory has proved particularly useful in examining the nature of law. With these qualifications in mind, I rely on Hart's theory to explore the nature of canon law in light of the controversy raised by the application of Canon 915.

---

3. *See* H. L. A. HART, THE CONCEPT OF LAW 195–200 (Penelope A. Bulloch & Joseph Raz eds., 2nd ed. with *Postscript*, Oxford University Press 1997).

4. *See* H. L. A. Hart, *Positivism and the Separation of Law and Morals*, 71 HARV. L. REV. 593, 621–42 (1958); *cf.* Lon L. Fuller, *Positivism and Fidelity to Law—A Reply to Professor Hart*, 71 HARV. L. REV. 630 (1958).

5. For a collection of essays discussing Hart's legal theory, *see* HART'S POSTSCRIPT: ESSAYS ON THE POSTSCRIPT TO THE CONCEPT OF LAW (Jules Coleman ed., Oxford University Press 2001).

6. *See* HART, THE CONCEPT OF LAW, 238–76.

I. CANON 915 AND INDETERMINACY

During the 2004 U.S. presidential campaign, Archbishop Raymond L. Burke of Saint Louis and several other bishops announced their intention to enforce Canon 915 against certain Catholic political officials.[7] Canon 915 of the 1983 Code of Canon Law states:

> Those upon whom the penalty of excommunication or interdict has been imposed or declared, and *others who obstinately persist in manifest grave sin, are not to be admitted to Holy Communion.* (italics added for emphasis).[8]

Specifically, the bishops indicated that the words "obstinately persist in manifest grave sin" applied to Catholic public officials who had clear records in support of legalized abortion (hereafter "the application of Canon 915"). The position and voting record of the Democratic candidate for president, Senator John Kerry, a Catholic, seemed to place him within the stricture of Canon 915. Other U.S. bishops objected to Burke's interpretation, and public controversy soon ensued. Some political commentators opined that the refusal of Holy Communion to Catholic political officials transgressed the acceptable parameters of church involvement in the political process. In a hotly contested and close presidential race, the commentators worried that the Burke position could tip the balance of the electorate's vote.[9] Other commentators praised Burke and his fellow bishops

7. On November 23, 2003, the Most Reverend Raymond L. Burke, then the Bishop of La Crosse, issued a pastoral letter to his diocese, about the dignity of human life and civic responsibility. *See* Raymond L. Burke, Pastoral Letter to Christ's Faithful of the Diocese of La Crosse, On the Dignity of Human Life and Civic Responsibility (2003). Months before, Bishop Burke had initiated communications with Catholic political officials who were members of the diocese and who had taken public pro-abortion stances. The bishop urged the Catholic political officials to consider the truth of the church's teaching about the value of every human life and to change their public positions. Only after certain public officials remained unpersuaded did Bishop Burke bar them from receiving Holy Communion. Pursuant to the bishop's policy, the individuals were to be excluded from reception of the sacrament until such time as they might publicly modify their position in accord with the teaching of the church. On January 26, 2004, Most Reverend Raymond L. Burke was installed as the archbishop of St. Louis. In response to inquiries from members of the press during the heated presidential campaign of 2004, Archbishop Burke indicated his intention to continue his pastoral initiative in his new Metropolitan See. *See* Raymond L. Burke, *Prophecy for Justice: Catholic Politicians and Bishops*, 190 America 11–15 (June 21–28, 2004).

8. In Catholic theology, the terms *Eucharist* and *Holy Communion* refer to the reception of sacramental bread and sometimes also wine, which Catholics believe are transformed into the Body and Blood of Christ at Mass. Eucharist and Holy Communion are used interchangeably in this chapter to represent the action of receiving the sacrament.

9. *See* David D. Kirkpatrick & Laurie Goodstein, *Group of Bishops Using Influence to Oppose Kerry*, N.Y. Times, Oct. 12, 2004, A1; Kenneth L. Woodward, *A Political Sacrament*, op. ed., N.Y. Times, May 28, 2004, A21.

for courageously fulfilling their responsibilities as pastors in the church. They viewed the application of Canon 915 as a matter of internal church discipline, which remained independent of the secular political process.[10]

A bishops' task force was formed to consider the application of Canon 915. Some forty-eight Catholic members of Congress wrote to the bishops' task force and stated that while they are personally opposed to abortion, they favor legalized abortion as a matter of public policy.[11] The head of the bishops' task force, Theodore Cardinal McCarrick, then the Archbishop of Washington, emphasized that every bishop must judge "not whether denial of communion is possible, but whether it is pastorally wise and prudent."[12] The Congregation for the Doctrine of the Faith (CDF) circulated an unofficial protocol that essentially affirmed Archbishop Burke's approach to Canon 915.[13] In the brief statement issued after the June 2004 meeting in Colorado, the U.S. bishops declined to adopt a general policy with regard to Canon 915. The bishops explained:

> The question has been raised as to whether the denial of Holy Communion to some Catholics in political life is necessary because of their public support for abortion on demand. Given the wide range of circumstances involved in arriving at a prudential judgment on a matter of this seriousness, we recognize that such decisions rest with the individual bishop in accord with established canonical and pastoral principles. Bishops can legitimately make different judgments on the most prudent course of pastoral action.[14]

Subsequent to the U.S. 2004 elections, a synod of bishops from around the world meeting at the Vatican advised that the application of Canon 915 should be left to the determination of the individual bishop in his diocese.[15] At a June 2006 meeting of the U.S. bishops, Cardinal McCarrick made the final report of the bishops' task force reaching the same conclusion.[16]

Although certain bishops apparently thought that the law permitted only one correct interpretation, a large majority of the bishops in the United States were

---

10. *See* Richard John Neuhaus, *Bishops at a Turning Point*, First Things 78–81 (October 2004).

11. This was essentially the position taken by Mario Cuomo several decades ago in a well-known speech at the University of Notre Dame. Critics of the Cuomo position argue that one cannot logically profess to believe on a personal level that abortion or euthanasia is the killing of innocent human life while speaking and acting in public as if the crime constituted some kind of good. *See* 34 Origins 35–36 (June 3, 2004).

12. 34 Origins 107–09 (July 1, 2004).

13. The protocol was published in the U.S. *See* Congregation for the Doctrine of the Faith, *Vatican, U.S. Bishops: On Catholics in Political Life (Statement of Six Principles for the Application of Canon 915)*, 34 Origins 133 (July 1, 2004).

14. *Id.* at 99.

15. *See Overview of the Synod's Propositions*, 35 Origins 348 (Nov. 3, 2005).

16. *See Final Report: Bishops and Catholic Politicians*, 36 Origins 97–100 (June 29, 2006).

unwilling to apply Canon 915 to public officials who had public records in favor of permissive abortion laws. The disagreement among the bishops raises the indeterminacy claim. The indeterminacy claim holds "that legal questions do not have correct answers, or at least not unique correct answers."[17] The indeterminacy claim is based on the vague nature of language, exceptions to the rules, the application of law to specific cases, contradictions between particular statutes, gaps in the law (*lacunae legis*), inconsistencies between legal precedents, incommensurability, the subjective nature of interpretation, cultural differences, and the need for resort to extra-legal materials and sources in order to interpret the law.[18]

One formulation of the indeterminacy claim stresses law's instrumental possibilities over it normative content. Starting with the thought of Oliver Wendell Holmes, Jr., American legal realism advanced the indeterminacy claim against what it considered to be formal and legalistic reasoning. Legal realism focused on the "open-textured vague" meaning of the law rather than its "precision" or "certainty."[19] During the last decades of the twentieth century, the realist approach to law was adopted and intensified by the critical legal studies movement. Critical theorists ascribe radical indeterminacy to the law.[20] From this perspective, law is simply a cover for ideological interests that attempt to use the power of law to achieve their own political ends.[21] Building on the realist belief in the manipulability of law, the critical theorists reject the idea that law reflects neutral principles designed to guarantee fundamental fairness. Duncan Kennedy, for example, argues that, from a phenomenological perspective, indeterminacy is not the result of legal texts but rather the interaction between legal texts and interpreters who advance ideological interests by blurring the meaning of the law.[22]

Another formulation of the indeterminacy claim is that the law per se does not provide correct answers to legal claims. This formulation suggests that certain legal questions have correct answers only when extra-legal materials are considered to supplement the legal texts. The possibilities for the extra-legal materials may range from economic factors to sociological evidence to religious

17. *See* Brian H. Bix, A Dictionary of Legal Theory 97 (Oxford University Press 2004).

18. *See* Timothy A. O. Endicott, Vagueness in Law 31–55 (Oxford University Press 2000).

19. *See* Stephen L. Pepper, *The Lawyer's Amoral Ethical Role: A Defense, a Problem, and Some Possibilities*, American Bar Foundation Research Journal 613, 624 (1986).

20. *See* Joseph Singer, *The Player and the Cards: Nihilism and Legal Theory*, 94 Yale L. J. 1, 13 (1984).

21. *See* David Kairys, *Introduction*, *in* The Politics of Law 5–6 (Pantheon Books 1982).

22. See Duncan Kennedy, A Critique of Adjudication *{fin de siècle}* 316–19 (Harvard University Press 1997), which discusses how judges interpret the language of rights, as an example of legal rules in general, on the basis of ideological considerations.

claims.[23] The introduction of extra-legal materials such as moral principles is obviously problematic for the pure legal positivists and other theorists who advocate law's autonomy from extra-legal sources. As we shall see in this chapter, the application of Canon 915 raises a series of theological, pastoral, and political issues which are related to canon law and are indispensable from the perspective of the unity of canon law and theology. In this regard, the unity of canon law and theology distinguishes canon law from secular legal theories that depend on the strict separation of law from morality.

Still another formulation of the indeterminacy claim concerns linguistic indeterminacy. Timothy Endicott acknowledges that the vague nature of law may render its application in specific cases indeterminate.[24] However, Endicott notes that from a linguistic perspective every rule involves the interpretation of language, and in this sense, the indeterminacy claim is vast and typical. Nonetheless, Endicott points to the meaning of a stop sign to indicate that linguistic indeterminacy may be overstated. The interpretation of the stop sign is not indeterminate. The correct interpretation is to stop. Not to stop is an infraction of the rule signified by the stop sign.[25] Endicott's example points to cross-cultural indeterminacy in law. With respect to canon law, it is appropriate to recall that it consists of rules for a church with a global presence. Anyone who has driven an automobile in Italy or certain countries in Latin America understands that the meaning of a stop sign may be interpreted in a different way than it is in Anglo-American culture. The cross-cultural application of canon law seems to fuel the indeterminacy claim. As with linguistic indeterminacy, cultural indeterminacy may also be overblown. Since at least the third quarter of the eleventh century, canonists have applied the rules across cultural, racial, and national lines. While the application of canonical provisions has not always been successful in transcending such categories, there has obviously been sufficient success over time to permit canon law to develop and flourish.

It may be impossible to prove or refute the indeterminacy claim. In response to the claim, Ronald Dworkin suggests that nearly all legal questions have correct answers. Dworkin advances numerous arguments in favor of his "right answers thesis."[26] One of his main arguments is that judges believe there are correct or at least best answers to legal cases, and that some answers are better

---

23. *See, e.g.*, Richard A. Posner, Overcoming Law 471–72 (Harvard University Press 1995).

24. *See* Endicott, Vagueness in Law, 7–29.

25. *See id.* at12–13, 159–83.

26. *See* Ronald Dworkin, *A Reply by Ronald Dworkin, in* Ronald Dworkin and Contemporary Jurisprudence 275–78 (M. Chen ed., Duckworth 1984). *Cf.* E. Philip Soper, *Legal Theory and the Obligation of a Judge: The Hart/Dworkin Dispute*, 75 Mich. L. Rev. 473 (1977).

than others from the perspective of reason in light of past legal precedents.[27] If the indeterminacy of law is vast, then this has negative implications for the rule of law. It means that the rule of law is based upon vague meanings and subjective interpretations rather than fundamental concepts of justice and fairness.[28] In this chapter, I shall suggest that the arguments for the indeterminacy of Canon 915 are in each case met by detached normative statements based on the interdependence of canon law, theology, and practical reasonableness. At the same time, the confusion among the bishops about the correct application of Canon 915 suggests that the indeterminacy claim may have at least some merit with regard to canon law.

II. THE RULE OF RECOGNITION AND THE INTERNAL ASPECT OF LAW

In applying Hart's theory of law to the question of refusing Holy Communion to Catholic public officials, pursuant to Canon 915, a preliminary issue must be considered. Is the application of Canon 915 a valid law? Hart identified the rule of recognition as that rule or rules by which a legal system identifies what is valid law.[29] In Hart's conception, the rule of recognition is a secondary or power-conferring rule which identifies the primary rules of the legal system.[30] It posits the existence of "conventional criteria, agreed upon by officials, for determining which rules are, and which are not, part of the legal system."[31] In other words, my question here is whether the refusal of Holy Communion to Catholic public officials is a valid rule of canon law.

---

27. *See* Ronald Dworkin, *Pragmatism, Right Answers, and True Banality*, *in* PRAGMATISM IN LAW AND SOCIETY 360 (P. Amselek & N. MacCormick eds., Westview Press 1991).

28. *See* ENDICOTT, VAGUENESS IN LAW, 185–203. One of the early theorists of the rule of law in a modern democratic society, F. A. Hayek, argued, in a book first published in 1944, that the rule of law could guarantee procedural justice through the principle of equality before the law but not substantive equality such as that called for by the principle of distributive justice. *See* F. A. HAYEK, THE ROAD TO SERFDOM 87–88 (Chicago University Press 1994).

29. *See* JOSEPH RAZ, THE AUTHORITY OF THE LAW: ESSAYS ON LAW AND MORALITY 95–97 (Oxford University Press 2002). Raz suggests that a legal system may have more than one rule of recognition which sets up the criteria for the validity of law. *Id.*

30. *See* HART, THE CONCEPT OF LAW, 91–92.

31. BRIAN BIX, JURISPRUDENCE: THEORY AND CONTENT 39 (3rd ed. Carolina Academic Press 2004). *See* HART, THE CONCEPT OF LAW, 94–110. This aspect of the theory comports with the separation of law from morality. It permits the separation of statements about what the law is from statements about what the law ought to be. *See* Hart, *The Separation of Law and Morality*, 600–06.

A. The Rule of Recognition and Canon 915

In light of the rule of recognition, the question may be raised as to whether or not the application of Canon 915 constitutes valid law within the context of the system of canon law. One aspect of the rule of recognition in canon law is the promulgation of law through the appropriate hierarchical authority. There can be no question that the relevant words of Canon 915 are part of the *CIC-1983*. At their November 2006 meeting, the U.S. bishops voted to issue a document that affirms the significance of the relevant words of Canon 915.[32]

A more interesting aspect of the rule of recognition in canon law involves continuity with a vast history of doctrine, law, rules, interpretation, tradition, custom, and jurisprudence in the Catholic Church. Requirements for participation in, and the reception of, the Eucharist are not new in the history of the church. In his First Letter to the Corinthians, Saint Paul admonished:

> Whoever, therefore, eats the bread or drinks the cup of the Lord in an unworthy manner will be guilty of profaning the body and blood of the Lord. Let a man examine himself , and so eat of the bread and drink of the cup. For any one who eats and drinks without discerning the body, eats and drinks judgment upon himself.[33]

Over the course of many centuries, a system of canon law emerged in the church with specific provisions for the reception of Holy Communion. Canonical provisions indicate that ecclesiastical authorities have a long history of barring persons guilty of certain types of behavior from the reception of Holy Communion. In the third century, Cyprian, Bishop of Carthage, denied communion to the so-called "lapsed," who had offered sacrifice to Roman deities, until the lapsed repented of their idolatry.[34] The medieval law of the *Corpus Iuris Canonici* mentions blasphemers, *historines* (operators of brothels), and public usurers, who were *ipso facto* not permitted to receive Holy Communion.[35]

The first edition of the *Roman Ritual* published in 1614 provided the following illustrative list of public and notorious sinners who were to be barred from reception of Holy Communion: usurers, sorcerers, prostitutes, persons living in concubinage, and blasphemers.[36] During the eighteenth century, Pope Benedict XIV affirmed the ancient tradition that public and notorious sinners must not be

---

32. *See* 36 ORIGINS 389, 393 (Nov. 30, 2006).

33. 1 Corinthians 11:27–29. *See also* Augustine of Hippo, *Sermo 227, In die Paschae, IV, Ad Infantes, de Sacramentis*; 38 PL 1101.

34. *See* Cyprian of Carthage, *Epistolae* 5–10, & 19; 4 PL 235–46, 259–81.

35. *See, e.g.*, X 5. 19. 3. 5. *See also* C. 24, 86; C. 11, 9, 3; C. 24, 20, 3; D. 2, 95, *de cons.*

36. *See* Tit. IV, c.1, *De sanctissimo Eucharistiae*, n. 8, *in* 7 CODICIS IURIS CANONICI FONTES 143, n. 4598 (Typis Polyglottis Vaticanis 1933–1962); *see also* RITUALE ROMANUM, EDITIO PRINCEPS (Malino Sodi & Juan Javier Flores Arcas eds., Vaticano, Liberia Editrice Vaticana 2004) (1614).

admitted to Holy Communion, whether they request the sacrament publicly or secretly.[37] On August 1, 1855, the Holy Office ordered that notorious and public members of the Freemasons be refused Holy Communion.[38] In a 1930 Instruction, the Sacred Congregation of the Council forbade the ministration of the Eucharist to immodestly dressed women.[39] Although some of these examples seem curious and dated to contemporary sensibilities, the Roman Curia continues to define what conduct might be a ground for the refusal of Holy Communion. As recently as 2000, the Pontifical Council for Legislative Texts affirmed a 1994 declaration from the CDF that the minister of Holy Communion must refuse it to divorced and civilly remarried Catholics who have not obtained a church annulment.[40] In 2002, Pope John Paul II issued the Encyclical Letter, *Ecclesia de Eucharistia*, which affirms the application of Canon 915 to those who remain obstinate in manifest grave sin.[41]

In June 2004, Cardinal Joseph Ratzinger, then Prefect at CDF, issued a Statement of Six Principles concerning the application of Canon 915 to the Catholic political official. Principles 2 and 3 state that abortion and euthanasia have a greater moral weight than other serious moral issues including ones that involve the taking of human life, such as the death penalty and the application of just war theory. Principle 5 affirmed the applicability of Canon 915 to Catholic political officials with clear public records in support of abortion and/or euthanasia. Regarding the specific situation of the Catholic political official, the CDF principles address only the issues of abortion and euthanasia. However, the document does not expressly limit the application of Canon 915 to these two cases. It is doubtful that the CDF principles enjoy force of law in the church. These principles were originally communicated by Cardinal Ratzinger in a private manner to the U.S. bishops. Although they were eventually published in *Origins*, the principles were not published as an authoritative decree of the Holy See.[42] For this

---

37. *See* Benedictus Pp. XIV, *Ex omnibus* (Die 16 mensis oct. anno 1756), § 3f, *in* 2 Codicis Iuris Canonici Fontes, 536, n. 441.

38. *See* Coll. Propaganda Fide, n. 1116, *see also* 8 Codicis Iuris Canonici Fontes, 546, n. 6426.

39. *See* S. C. C., instr. (Die 12 mensis dec. anno 1930), IX; 22 AAS 26 (1930).

40. *See* Pontifical Council for Legislative Texts, Declaration, II, *Concerning the Admission to Holy Communion of the Faithful Who Are Divorced and Remarried*, June 24, 2000, *available at* http://www.vatican.va/roman_curia/pontifical_councils/intprtxt/documtnts/rc_pc_20000706_declaration_en.html; and Congregatio Pro Doctrina Fidie, *Epistola ad Catholicae Ecclesiae Episcopos De Receptione Communionis Eucharisticae a Fidelibus Qui Post Divortium Novas Inierunt Nuptias* (Die 14 mensis septembris anno 1994); 86 AAS 974–79 (1994).

41. *See* Ioannes Paulus Pp. II, Litterae Encyclicae, *Ecclesia de Eucharistia* (Die 17 mensis aprilis anno 2003), 37; 95 AAS 433–75 (2003).

42. *See* Congregation for the Doctrine of the Faith, *Vatican, U.S. Bishops: On Catholics in Political Life (Statement of Six Principles for the Application of Canon 915)*, 133–34.

reason, the CDF principles remain private and in comparison to a decree that has been officially promulgated, they enjoy only a limited authority. This, of course, does not necessarily render the principles any less correct as an interpretation of the law. They are from an authoritative source even though they were not officially promulgated.

Three observations may be made on the basis of the rule of recognition. First, ecclesiastical authorities have long been concerned with protecting the ecclesial order of the Eucharist by positing rules that prohibit participation by those who persist in public behavior deemed to be gravely sinful. Starting with sacred scripture and the ancient church, through the medieval and Tridentine periods, and continuing to the present time, ecclesiastical authorities have set forth rules for the reception of Holy Communion. This historical continuity indicates that such rules are not simply the product of a particular lawgiver's will. Rather, they are an aspect of well-established canonical tradition and law.

Second, the provisions indicate that the question of what constitutes the kind of public grave sin, which requires denial of Holy Communion, has been answered differently throughout the church's history. Presumably, even within a given time frame and a particular place, there may have been disagreement among ecclesiastical authorities regarding what behavior triggered the canonical stricture. This suggests that any particular provision of church law on this subject such as Canon 915 is positive law rather than divine or natural law. In contrast to legal positivism, canon law recognizes divine and natural law as immutable sources of law. The positive provisions of canon law regulating reception of Holy Communion have changed over the course of time and in response to the social context of the ecclesiastical community in a particular place. Canon 915 may be described as the positive law of the church which reflects the legislative intent to design positive law on the foundation of natural and divine law. The designation of Canon 915 as a positive law does not diminish its significance as an aspect of the rule of law in the Roman Catholic Church.

Third, notwithstanding the historical continuity of canonical provisions about the reception of Holy Communion, if a majority of bishops refuse to apply Canon 915, one must ask if they have internalized law. Hart's rule of recognition stands in contrast to Austin's so-called command theory of law in which law is a manifestation of will backed by coercive force. Hart observed that there are many persons who obey the law not on the basis of threat but because they have internalized the rules as reason for acting in a certain way and for censuring others when they do not act as the rule requires. Otherwise, Hart noted, one could not distinguish law from the threat of a gunmen.[43] A hostage to a terrorist may obey

43. Hart objected to the command theory as inconsistent with modern systems of government with checks and balances, as unable to explain the continuity of law when a sovereign is replaced by a new sovereign who has no history of receiving habitual obedience

the terrorist's demands no matter how unreasonable, but that does not make the demands law.

Commenting on Hart's rule of recognition, Raz notes that "the behavior of the population is not part of the conditions for the existence of the rule of recognition." Rather, "its existence consists in the behavior of the 'officials' of the system, by which Hart presumably means law-applying officials."[44] With regard to the application of Canon 915, it is the understanding of the bishops as the law applying officials, and not that of the Catholic public officials as the subjects of the law, which is crucial to the rule of recognition. For example, the pro-choice Catholic public official may claim to object on jurisprudential or moral grounds to the U.S. Supreme Court's decision in *Roe v. Wade*, which recognized a constitutional right to abortion. At the same time, this Catholic layperson recognizes the constitutional right as a legal fact. This official decides that the constitutional right is established, whether rightly or wrongly, as a legal matter until *Roe* may be overruled. Such a Catholic public official may see the application of Canon 915 to his or her case as merely a command of the church to be obeyed under threat of deprivation of Holy Communion. Assuming *arguendo* that the position of this public official has some validity, it has no bearing on the rule of recognition and the validity of Canon 915. If the bishops as the law applying officials in the system of canon law have internalized the perspective of the public official just described, it might create doubt as to whether or not the application of Canon 915 represents a valid law under the rule of recognition. This leads to Hart's point about the internal aspect of law.

B. The Internal Aspect of Law and the Application of Canon 915

Hart rejected the position of early legal positivists who "claimed that the only method of representation of the law to figure in a modern rational science of law was one which shared the structure and logic of statements of empirical science."[45] Hart found the scientific method, which relies solely on objective data, to be inadequate for understanding law. According to Hart, law is a human and social process unlike scientific method, which requires an objective description of processes such as photosynthesis or atomic fusion. In Hart's legal theory, whatever insight the external point of view of scientific method offers, it fails to account adequately for the perspective of the participant in the legal system. Hart postulated that the internal aspect of law remains indispensable to a proper understanding of the law's nature, function, and purpose. In Hart's own words, "the methodology of the empirical sciences is useless; what is needed is

---

from subjects, and as an incomplete description of law which is a richer concept than that of commands backed by threats. *See* Hart, *The Separation of Law From Morality*, 603.

44. Raz, The Authority of the Law, 92.

45. H. L. A. Hart, Essays in Jurisprudence and Philosophy 30 (Clarendon Press of Oxford University 1983).

a 'hermeneutic' method which involves portraying rule-governed behavior as it appears to its participants."[46] Hart wanted the legal theorist to act both as an external observer and as one who endeavors to understand the "internal aspect" of the legal system. He sought a legal theory that would be free from moral judgments and based on an objective description of the internal point of view of an actual participant in a given legal system.[47]

In any legal system, there are, of course, many different participants, and not all of them share the same point of view about the rules of the system. In adopting the internal perspective of a participant, how does the legal theorist choose among the various participants' perspectives? A student of Hart's, Joseph Raz, offers some helpful examples in response to this question. Raz notes that someone who is not a vegetarian is nonetheless able to advise a vegetarian friend in a restaurant "given your beliefs you should not order that dish."[48] Likewise, Raz observes that a Catholic who is an expert in orthodox Judaism may be able to make correct statements about faithful observance of rabbinical law even though the Catholic is not committed to that normative system of religious law.[49] According to Raz, these are examples of "detached normative statements."[50] A detached normative statement permits one to make a factual statement about what there is reason to do from the perspective of a normative system of which one is not an adherent.

Raz suggests that such detached normative statements represent a middle ground between two other approaches to the question about participant perspectives. Another student of Hart's, John Finnis, posits that the perspective chosen should be that of the participant who relies on practical reasonableness to recognize binding moral obligations established by law.[51] In contrast, Ronald Dworkin argues that the perspective must be that of a participant in the legal system who offers an interpretation of the law on the basis of the morally soundest of past governmental actions.[52] When it comes to canon law, Raz's detached normative statement and Finnis's practical reasonableness may amount to unequivocal approaches. It is a correct detached normative statement to observe that the practical reasonableness of natural law theory is a prominent feature of canon law.

---

46. *Id.* at 13

47. *See* HART, THE CONCEPT OF LAW, 56–58; 88–91.

48. JOSEPH RAZ, PRACTICAL REASON AND NORMS 175–76 (2nd ed. Princeton University Press 1990).

49. *See* RAZ, THE AUTHORITY OF LAW, 156–57.

50. *Id.* at 153.

51. *See* JOHN FINNIS, NATURAL LAW AND NATURAL RIGHTS 3–18 (Clarendon Press of Oxford University 1986).

52. *See* RONALD DWORKIN, LAW'S EMPIRE 46–48, 225–28, 245–58 (Belknap Press of Harvard University 1986).

Hart's internal aspect of the law proves helpful in understanding the disagreement among the bishops about the application of Canon 915. From an internal perspective, it is possible to identify at least four different approaches among the U.S. bishops. First, a bishop could conclude that the applicability of Canon 915 constitutes a clear case and enforce it after a consideration of all the circumstances in the particular case following dialogue with the Catholic public official. Second, a bishop could conclude that the applicability of Canon 915 is uncertain and therefore elect not to apply it after a consideration of a number of theological, canonical, political, and pastoral issues which seem to render the applicability of the canon indeterminate. Third, a bishop could refuse to apply Canon 915 in complete antinomian deference to the individual conscience of the Catholic public official who is pro-choice and decides to receive Holy Communion. Fourth, a bishop might adopt a legalistic interpretation that considers the question about reception of the Eucharist to be a confidential matter belonging strictly to the internal forum. Legalism would also be evident in an application of Canon 915 without consideration of the various circumstances involved in an individual case or in a rigid manner that precludes dialogue between the bishop and the Catholic public official.

III. THE OPEN TEXTURE OF LAW: A CENTRAL CASE

Hart thought that the application of law included "central cases," in which the application of law is clear, and a "penumbra of doubt," in which the application of the law is uncertain.[53] The first possibility then is the central, certain, and clear case, and the second possibility is the doubtful, difficult, and hard case. Hart's example of the distinction involved the rule "No vehicles in the park." The rule was intended to ban automobiles, but Hart queried, did the rule also apply to bicycles, roller skates, or baby carriages?[54] Hart attributed two possibilities to account for the "open texture" of law. First, the legislative intent could be incomplete, as the legislator did not consider all of the possibilities. Second, the language of the rule could be imprecise as in what the term vehicle means.[55] Hart's analysis suggests that the fundamental disagreement among the bishops about the application of Canon 915 concerns whether the application is a clear or hard case. To the extent that the application of Canon 915 amounts to a hard case, it favors the indeterminacy claim. The bishops who consider the application of Canon 915 to constitute a clear or central case may support their interpretation on the (1) plain meaning of the words of the canon, (2) theological and

53. Hart, The Concept of Law, 123.
54. *Id.* at 126–27.
55. *See id.* at 126–30.

canonical justifications that underpin the canon, and (3) limited effects of application of the words of the canon.

A. The Plain Meaning

The pertinent words of Canon 915 state that those "who obstinately persist in manifest grave sin are not to be admitted to Holy Communion."[56] This phrase consists of three subphrases, which are considered here in reverse order.

1. "Are Not to Be Admitted" The Latin phrase of the authoritative text is "*ne admittantur,*" which constitutes the subjunctive imperative. The equivalent provision of the 1917 Code, Canon 855, Section 1, employed the Latin passive periphrastic form "*arcendi sunt*" with the same imperative meaning that the "publicly unworthy" must be barred from the Eucharist. Indeed, the Latin word "*arceo*" carries the meaning of to be "prevented from approaching" or "kept at a distance." Canon 712 of the 1990 Eastern Code of Canon Law also employs the Latin form "*arcendi sunt.*" The imperative meaning of all three of these provisions' terms leads to the conclusion that the application of Canon 915 is not optional.

2. "Manifest Grave Sin" It would be a detached normative statement to observe that the Roman Catholic Church considers abortion and euthanasia to constitute gravely sinful matter ("*gravi peccati*"). Speaking of the "deplorable crime" of abortion in *Evangelium Vitae,* Pope John Paul II taught:

> Therefore, by the authority which Christ conferred upon Peter and his Successors, in communion with the Bishops of the Catholic Church . . . I declare that direct abortion . . . constitutes a grave moral disorder, since it is the deliberate killing of an innocent human being.[57]

This rare formulary invocation of the apostolic authority vested in the Petrine ministry attests to the level of gravity that the church attributes to the taking of innocent human life. A Catholic's public support of abortion or euthanasia would thus differ from many other issues that do not involve the taking of innocent human life, but which nonetheless might give rise to a discontinuity between church teaching and civil law.

---

56. The Latin original of Canon 915, *CIC-1983,* reads as follows: "Ad sacram communionem ne admittantur excommunicati et interdicti post irrogantionem vel declarationem poenae aliique in manifesto gravi peccato obstinate perseverantes."

57. Ioannes Paulus Pp. II, Litterae Encyclicae, *Evangelium Vitae* (Die 25 mensis martii anno 1995), 57; 87 AAS 401, 464–66 (1995). English translation from *Evangelium Vitae, in* THE ENCYCLICALS OF JOHN PAUL II 682, 739 (J. Michael Miller, C.S.B. ed., Our Sunday Visitor Press 2001). In No. 56, John Paul stated: "Therefore, by the authority which Christ conferred upon Peter and his Successors, and in communion with the Bishops of the Catholic Church, *I confirm that the direct and voluntary killing of an innocent human being is always gravely immoral.*" (emphasis in original). In No. 60, the pope affirmed the Catholic teaching that human life begins at conception.

However, the church teaching on the direct and voluntary taking of innocent human life does not settle the matter. In order to apply Canon 915, a bishop still has to determine that the Catholic public official has committed grave sin. Pursuant to Canon 1398, the clear case of the person who performs or procures an abortion results in an automatic penalty of excommunication.[58] Does public speech and government action favorable to the direct and voluntary taking of human life also constitute a clear case? The bishop's determination as to whether or not to bar the Catholic public official from Holy Communion would involve an application of the traditional principles of formal and material cooperation in evil. Formal cooperation in evil is always morally prohibited. In this regard, the application of Canon 915 to a Catholic public official finds confirmation in number 5 of the CDF principles, which states:

> Regarding the *grave sin* of abortion or euthanasia, when a person's *formal cooperation* becomes manifest (understood, in the case of a Catholic politician, as his consistently *campaigning and voting for permissive abortion and euthanasia laws*), his Pastor should meet with him, instructing him about the Church's teaching, informing him that he is not to present himself for Holy Communion until he brings to an end the objective situation of sin, and warning him that he will otherwise be denied the Eucharist. (emphasis added).[59]

Principle 5's identification of "campaigning and voting for permissive abortion and euthanasia laws" with formal cooperation in grave sin would seem to encompass even a vote to decriminalize abortion or euthanasia as well as voting in favor of public funding of these practices. For the bishop who agrees with this assessment, the application of Canon 915 to the Catholic public official constitutes a clear case. I shall say more about the principles of cooperation, the political autonomy enjoyed by Catholics, and individual conscience in the next section on hard cases. Suffice it to say at this point of the analysis that Principle 5 reflects the conclusion that consistent voting in favor of liberal abortion or euthanasia laws is a clear case.[60]

As to when grave sin is manifest ("*manifesto*"), the tradition draws a distinction between occult (private) and public (well-known) sin. Occult sin may be known to some, but it is not generally known throughout the community. Rumors and suspicion do not render occult sin public. In contrast, sin becomes public when

---

58. Canon 1392, § 2, *CIC-1983*, defines an accomplice to abortion as one without whose assistance the crime would not be committed, and states that such an accomplice incurs the automatic excommunication.

59. Congregation for the Doctrine of the Faith, *Vatican, U.S. Bishops: On Catholics in Political Life (Statement of Six Principles for the Application of Canon 915)*,134.

60. *See* Kevin T. McMahon, *Pro-Abortion Politicians and Voters and the Reception of Holy Communion*, 73 LINACRE QUARTERLY 153, 160-161 (2006).

there is widespread knowledge of it. The determination of what sin is public belongs to the competent ecclesiastical authority who must render any such decision with justice and charity always before his eyes. Church teaching holds that all persons are sinners in need of the redemptive love of Christ. The long-standing rule is that occult sinners who publicly approach the minister of Holy Communion should not be refused.[61] The rule regarding occult sinners rests on the need to spare the good reputation of the individual especially where refusal of Holy Communion by the minister would create suspicion and scandal.[62] In contrast, the tradition requires that those who persist in manifest grave sin may not receive Holy Communion. The refusal of Holy Communion can occur only in those rare cases when the proper ecclesiastical authority has recognized the widespread knowledge of the sin throughout the community.

3. "Obstinately Persists" The words "*obstinate perseverantes*" indicate that the legislator does not intend the stricture of Canon 915 to be applied indiscriminately or facilely. In order to determine whether a Catholic public official falls within the narrow parameters of the stricture, the bishop incurs the responsibility to examine carefully the whole of the voting record and public statements of the political official. To start, the determination that the grave sin is obstinate requires more than a superficial review. The bishop fulfills this responsibility by personally contacting the public official involved and attempting to persuade the official to correct his or her position. Canon 915 does not expressly require such a personal and individual approach. However, CDF Principle 5 calls upon the pastor of the Catholic political official to conduct just such a personal intervention and meeting.[63] Principle 6 states that only after such "precautionary measures" on the part of the pastor have been unsuccessful must the minister of Holy Communion refuse the sacrament to the person. Although Canon 915 does not mention a warning to the public official, the determination that one has obstinately persisted seems to require such a formal warning. A public official who speaks or votes publicly in favor of abortion or euthanasia could claim to be unaware of the possible canonical consequences of his or her actions. It could be argued that the official is not obstinately persisting until he or she has actual notice of the possible canonical consequences. In contrast, a Catholic who speaks or votes publicly in favor of abortion or euthanasia, and then refuses to correct this position after a warning by his or her pastor, would be "obstinate" within the meaning of Canon 915.

---

61. *See* Benedictus Pp. XIV, *Ex omnibus*, § 3f; Canon 912, *CIC-1983*.

62. *See* Canon 220, *CIC-1983*.

63. The use of the term *pastor* would not be limited to the person's bishop, but it would also include the parish priest as pastor of the parish to which the person belonged. *See* Canon 519, *CIC-1983*. However, the bishop as the chief pastor of the diocese has the final authority, and in most cases, it would seem that he would act as both the primary and ultimate judge in his diocese about whether or not to apply Canon 915.

Additionally, the bishop must take into account any specific circumstances that might excuse or mitigate the behavior of the public official. To mention one example, a politician who votes in favor of pro-abortion legislation or funding is not necessarily obstinately persisting in a pro-abortion position. Number 73 of *Evangelium Vitae* clarifies when a legislator might vote in favor of a specific pro-abortion bill. This is only permissible where a liberal abortion law is to be restricted by a more limited legislative provision. Thus, it would not be permissible for a legislator to vote in favor of a pro-abortion statute or funding unless the specific piece of legislation was restricting a more liberal pro-abortion law. Number 73 requires that a legislator who votes in favor of a more restrictive measure has the duty to make public his or her anti-abortion position on the issue ("whose absolute personal opposition to procured abortion was well known"). Advocates of the clear case approach to Canon 915 would conclude that if the examination establishes that a Catholic public official has an obstinate pro-abortion or pro-euthanasia position, it then becomes incumbent upon the bishop to exclude the official from Holy Communion.

B. The Justifications for the Application of Canon 915

The clear case approach to Canon 915 rests on at least four justifications. First, Canon 915 was designed to protect the Christian faithful from the public scandal caused when a pro-abortion or pro-euthanasia public official receives the Body and Blood of Christ. The second goal of Canon 915 is to safeguard the sanctity of the Eucharist from those who judge themselves justified in receiving the sacrament even while publicly and adamantly denying church teaching. Third, Canon 915 is intended to foster conversion for those who reject the church's teaching on the sanctity of life. In denying the reception of Holy Communion to pro-abortion and pro-euthanasia public officials, Canon 915 aims to correct an erroneous conscience and act as an incentive to the sinner. It corresponds to the principle that the *salus animarum* remains the supreme law of the church.[64] Finally, Canon 915 protects innocent human life from laws and policies which permit or encourage unjust killing. In light of these four goals, the bishop's duty to enforce Canon 915 is not abrogated by the possibility that its enforcement might be detrimental to other aspects of the good.[65]

C. Effects of Canon 915

As is obvious from the words of Canon 915, the refusal of Holy Communion due to obstinate and manifest grave sin is to be distinguished from excommunication and inderdict. Excommunication and interdict constitute canonical penalties

---

64. *See* Canon 1752, *CIC-1983*.

65. No. 74 of *Evangelium Vitae* recognizes that the pro-life stance on the part of Catholic public officials "may require the sacrifice of prestigious professional positions or the relinquishing of reasonable hopes of career advancement."

which are established in Book 4 of the 1983 Code of Canon Law. An excommunicated person is incapable of celebrating and receiving any of the sacraments and sacramentals of the church.[66] Additionally, an excommunicated person may not exercise any ecclesiastical office, ministry, or function, or posit an act of governance.[67] An interdict also prohibits one from celebrating and receiving the sacraments and sacramentals, but does not necessarily deprive one of the right to exercise ecclesiastical office.[68] In contrast, a person who has been refused Holy Communion for manifest grave sin under Canon 915 suffers only this particular ill effect. While it does not constitute a penal sanction in a technical or formal sense, it seems to me that the refusal of Holy Communion functions nonetheless as a kind of censure. At the least, it restricts the general right of the faithful to receive the Eucharist, which is recognized in Canon 912. Canon 18 therefore applies. It requires that: "Laws which prescribe a penalty, or restrict the free exercise of rights, or contain an exception to the law, are to be interpreted strictly." As it restricts the general right to receive the Eucharist, the strict interpretation of the relevant provision of Canon 915 requires that its application be limited only to clear and necessary cases.

In the alternative, a bishop might elect to conduct a penal trial and impose a *ferendae sententiae* penalty, excommunication, or interdict, rather than refuse Holy Communion to pro-abortion politicians. One might think that the trial with a pronounced penalty affords greater clarity than the alternative refusal of Holy Communion. The penalties are certainly more severe. As mentioned, the excommunicated person cannot receive any of the sacraments. Sacramental absolution cannot be given unless the excommunication has been lifted or there is danger of death. In contrast, the political official barred from reception of Holy Communion under the nonpenal provision of Canon 915 may continue to attend Mass, hear the Word of God, pray with the Catholic community, and receive the other sacraments. Although some might prefer a trial and *ferendae sententiae* censure, Canon 915 has vested the bishop with discretion to act pastorally or in a more formal juridic mode. In light of this canonical analysis, a strong argument can be made that the plain meaning of the words of Canon 915 along with the protocol for its application, the strong theological and canonical justifications that underpin the canon, and its limited effects render the application of Canon 915 a clear and central case.

---

66. *See* Canon 1331, § 1, 1 & 2°, *CIC-1983*.
67. *See* Canon 1331, § 1, 3°, *CIC-1983*.
68. *See* Canon 1332, *CIC-1983*.

7. THE INDETERMINACY CLAIM CONTINUED

Canon 915: "A Doubtful or Hard Case"

In the previous chapter, I explored the nature of the indeterminacy claim and offered an argument that the application of Canon 915 to Catholic public officials is a central case. Most of the bishops in the United States apparently thought that the application of Canon 915 constitutes a more difficult case. There are at least five objections that might be raised in relation to the application of Canon 915 as a clear case. The objections are based upon: (1) doubt about whether or not a Catholic public official, who favors permissive abortion or euthanasia laws, is in fact a "grave sinner"; (2) undue interference in the political process through an arbitrary application of law; (3) the social teaching of the church; (4) the sacramental nature of the Eucharist; and (5) other provisions of canon law, including the right to receive the sacraments and the diocesan bishop's authority. Each of these objections calls into question the clear case approach to Canon 915, and thus raises the indeterminacy claim. I shall present each of the five objections and then discuss them in terms of responses based upon what Joseph Raz describes as detached normative statements. My purpose here is not to evaluate whether or not the application of Canon 915 is a good church policy. Rather, I am attempting to clarify what might be the correct internal point of view of a bishop participant in relation to Canon 915.

To play on Raz's example, a rabbi, imam, Mormon bishop, or atheist could earn a doctorate in Catholic theology. The non-Catholic expert does not necessarily believe what Catholic theology and canon law espouse, but is able to function as a detached observer making normative statements about Catholic belief. Although I shall rely on Raz's example of the detached observer, a theological qualification is in order. Through the use of reason and study, a nonbeliever may well understand certain principles of natural law and theology. Canon law, however, would reflect the theological belief that grace enhances this natural understanding. Thus, canon law would consider the similarly intelligent and informed baptized Catholic, and even more so one who also holds sacramental office in the church, to have the assistance of grace in addition to natural ability to understand the inner meaning of some aspect of Catholic belief. In particular, the canon law would consider the Catholic bishop to be the recipient of special graces from his ordination and office that enable him to understand, interpret, and apply principles of Catholic teaching.

I. DOUBT REGARDING THE ATTRIBUTION OF "GRAVE SIN" TO THE PUBLIC OFFICIAL

The attribution of manifest grave sin to a Catholic public official who favors permissive abortion or euthanasia laws raises issues about the political autonomy enjoyed by Catholics, the principles of material and formal cooperation, and the primacy of individual conscience. Each of these issues could arguably bolster the indeterminacy claim with regard to Canon 915.

A. Political Autonomy

The Catholic tradition respects the proper autonomy of the Catholic laity in political affairs. The teaching acknowledges that Christian faith does not contain specific solutions to all political problems, and the Church can claim no expertise to determine all of the prudential choices faced by the governmental official regarding the political ordering of society through laws. As Pope John Paul II put it:

> Extremely sensitive situations arise when a specifically religious norm becomes or tends to become the law of the state without due consideration for the distinctions between the domains proper to religion and to political society. In practice the identification of religious law with civil law can stifle religious freedom, even going so far as to restrict or deny other inalienable human rights.[1]

The technical complexity of particular legislative and judicial situations, the different interpretations of basic principles of law, the variety of political and legal strategies for encoding the human good into the law, and the historical, sociological, and economic factors that influence the order of a society's law point to the autonomy of the political process and law. The Catholic tradition recognizes that the church possesses no authority to impose one solution given the legitimate plurality of political options. For example, a Catholic public official might believe that an act of abortion constitutes grave sin, but conclude that it ought not be punished by the state's criminal law. It is not the proper function of the state's criminal law to attempt to suppress all sin and vice. Arguably, all questions of punishment by the state are for the prudence of the civil magistrate. In light of the rightful political autonomy of the Catholic public official vested with governmental responsibility, the bishop could conclude that the application of Canon 915 is a hard case. In other words, for the bishop to exclude the Catholic public official from Holy Communion could be an undue interference in autonomy of the official's prudential judgment.

However, the bishop should take into account, the 2002 Doctrinal Note from CDF, *On Some Questions Regarding the Participation of Catholics in Political Life*, distinguished the legitimate plurality of prudential choices from choices that are

---

1. John Paul II, *Message for the 1991 World Day of Peace: "If you want peace, respect the conscience of every person,"* 4, 83 AAS 414–15 (1991).

not compatible with fundamental moral principles derived from the natural moral law.[2] Pope John Paul II was clear that Catholic lawmakers have a "grave and clear obligation to oppose" any law that threatens innocent human life.[3] Regarding the morality of permissive abortion or euthanasia laws, the Doctrinal Note states that "for every Catholic, it is impossible to promote such laws or to vote for them."[4] In evaluating Canon 915, the bishop should carefully balance the proper political autonomy of Catholics and the moral truth as taught by the church. In light of Catholic teaching, the rabbi who is an expert in Catholic theology might offer the following detached normative statement: It is not morally permissible for a public official in reaching prudential decisions to exercise political autonomy in a manner that is contrary to fundamental moral principles that protect innocent human life. Such a normative statement would not end the bishop's careful balancing of the factors in the decision-making process with regard to the application of Canon 915. The bishop must also consider whether the Catholic public official's action constitutes "grave sin" within the meaning of the canon.

B. Formal and Material Cooperation

Catholic moral theology and canon law have drawn a traditional distinction between formal and material cooperation in evil. According to the classic distinction articulated by Alphonsus Liguori, formal cooperation is never morally permissible, but material cooperation is sometimes permissible under certain circumstances. As previously mentioned, the CDF Principles identify campaigning or voting for a permissive abortion or euthanasia law to count as formal cooperation. Despite this identification, a bishop might still conclude that the application of Canon 915 is a hard case. Alphonsus Liguori described formal cooperation as that "which occurs in the bad will of the other."[5] Formal cooperation is a direct participation in the evil intent of the wrongdoer. The public official is not an abortionist. A bishop might question whether a public official who promotes or votes in favor of a particular piece of legislation has the requisite evil intent to come under the stricture or formal cooperation. For example, a vote to decriminalize abortion might simply reflect the legislator's prudential judgment

2. *See* Congregation for the Doctrine of the Faith, *Doctrinal Note on Some Questions Regarding the Participation of Catholics in Political Life*, 2, 3, and 5, November 24, 2002, *in* 32 ORIGINS 537, 539–41 (Jan. 30, 2003).

3. Ioannes Paulus Pp. II, Litterae Encyclicae, *Evangelium Vitae*, 73 (Die 25 mensis martii anno 1995), 57; 87 AAS 401, 486–87 (1995).

4. *Doctrinal Note on Some Questions Regarding the Participation of Catholics in Political Life*, 2, at 540.

5. Alphonsus Liguori articulated the classic statement about cooperation: "That [cooperation] is formal which occurs in the bad will of the other, and it cannot be without sin . . ." 2 THEOLOGIA MORALIS § 63 (L. Gaudé ed., Typographia Vaticana 1905–1912).

that the prohibition is impossible to enforce. The wrong of abortion is going to take place in spite of the prohibiting law, and thus the law is ineffectual and as a jurisprudential matter should be repealed. The bishop doubts that the Catholic legislator who votes to decriminalize is formally complicit in any act of abortion. In the bishops's view, the legislator is only voting to repeal an ineffective law, and the bishop does not believe that the legislator formally intends to cooperate in evil by this jurisprudential judgment. Alternatively, the Catholic public official might believe abortion to be a grave sin, but the official feels that it ought not to be punished in the criminal law. As previously discussed, the criminal law does not punish every type of sin. Again, the bishop doubts the public official's formal complicity in the bad will of the other.

Even if the bishop has doubt about formal cooperation, does the Catholic public officially materially cooperate in grave evil? In contrast to formal cooperation, Liguori held that material cooperation is permissible when: (1) the cooperator's act is good or indifferent in itself, (2) the cooperator has a reason for acting that is just, and (3) the cooperator's reason is proportionate to the gravity of the wrongdoing and to the closeness of the assistance.[6] The Catholic official who votes to decriminalize abortion may satisfy the first two conditions for permissible material cooperation. With regard to the first condition for permissible material cooperation, the official is arguably not endorsing abortion but recognizing it as an unfortunate social fact. As for the second condition, the reason for the vote to decriminalize abortion is to address the problem of an unenforceable and ineffective law.

The third condition for material cooperation could raise a problem for the bishop who thinks that the application of Canon 915 is a hard case. First, the third condition requires in relevant part that the cooperator's reason is proportionate to the wrongdoing. In John Paul II's view, abortion is always a grave wrong, and accordingly, the cooperator's reason necessarily fails the proportionality requirement. In the decriminalization example, while the closeness of the assistance would seem remote, as decriminalization does not change the social fact of abortion, the material cooperation would be morally impermissible because the proportionality requirement can never be satisfied. Second, the third condition's connection between the cooperation in evil and the closeness of assistance could also raise a problem. In contrast to the decriminalization example, the Catholic public official who votes in favor of funding for abortion or euthanasia violates not only the proportionality requirement but also the closeness requirement of the third condition. Without the government funding, certain acts of abortion or euthanasia would not take place. The gravity of the wrong remains unchanged, and now the closeness of the assistance is proximate. An imam with knowledge of Catholic teaching might observe that the grievous nature of the taking of

6. *See id.*

innocent human life never gives rise to a sufficiently proportionate reason for permissible material cooperation. Even in light of the normative statements offered by the rabbi and imam, the bishop must still consider the Catholic tradition on individual conscience.

C. Individual Conscience

One possible internal perspective of a bishop with regard to Canon 915 is to grant complete deference to the conscience of the Catholic political official. At the end of this section of the chapter, I suggest that absolute deference to individual conscience in the application of Canon 915 represents an antinomianism that renders it invalid as an internal perspective. In contrast, I am concerned here with the bishop who legitimately wants to take into account the conscience of a Catholic political official as one factor in the bishop's determination with regard to the application of Canon 915. Previously, I mentioned the Catholic public official who recognizes the legal fact of abortion as a recognized constitutional right even though the official believes that the judicial decision on which the right is based was wrongly decided. Presume that the public official has no direct power to revoke the constitutional right. At the same time, the official is charged with enforcing the law, voting to fund the provision of abortion through governmental programs, and/or administering some program which involves the provision of abortion. Realizing that the law is imperfect, such an official nonetheless understands the value of the rule of law and wants to live within its framework. On this basis, the public official concludes that one is legally obligated to uphold the law which recognizes abortion as a constitutional right until the law is changed. When the bishop and the Catholic public official discuss the situation, the bishop wants to respect the official's conscience.

This situation, however, raises similar issues to those already addressed in regard to political autonomy and material cooperation. The CDF Doctrinal Note indicates that a "well-formed Christian conscience" does not permit one to act in a way that assists in a gravely immoral act. In confirming the traditional teaching on conscience in *Veritatis Splendor*, Pope John Paul II observed that "conscience is not infallible; it can make mistakes."[7] "Correct conscience," the pope stated, "is a question of *objective truth*," rather than what a person "mistakenly, *subjectively* considers to be true." First, one's commitment to the rule of law does not release one from the obligation to form a correct conscience. If a state were to repeal its laws against homicide, the government official who abetted the ensuing homicidal regime could not be morally excused on the ground that the rule of law required cooperation. In the Catholic tradition, a correctly formed conscience

7. Ioannes Paulus Pp. II, Litterae Encyclicae, *Veritatis Splendor* (Die 6 mensis aug. anno 1993), 62; 85 AAS 1133–1228 (1993).

would oppose a grave moral wrong sanctioned by the state even when the grave wrong was in accord with the rule of law.

Second, Germain Grisez has indicated that continuous interaction with wrongdoing tends to dull the conscience to the gravity of evil.[8] The initial decision about cooperation in a given case might be well reasoned, but as the cooperation continues, the cooperator tends to become what he or she does. The more that one cooperates in evil, the more that one may discover a personally diminished capacity both in terms of one's ability to recognize the good and to resist evil. The Mormon with a doctorate in Catholic theology might feel compelled to remind the Catholic bishop that he incurs the responsibility to inform the Catholic public official of the church teaching that the conscience is unitary and indivisible. In the words of John Paul II: "there cannot be two parallel lives . . . on the one had, the so-called 'spiritual life,' with its values and demands; and on the other, the so-called 'secular life,' that is, life in a family, at work, in social responsibilities, in the responsibilities of public life and culture."[9] In accord with Catholic teaching, a detached normative statement would hold that the dignity of individual conscience does not abrogate one's responsibility to the common good in protecting innocent human life. Even if the bishop is persuaded by the normative statements of the rabbi on political autonomy, imam on cooperation in evil, and Mormon on individual conscience, the bishop might remain concerned about the effect of a doubtful law.

D. Doubtful Law

The lack of agreement among the U.S. bishops about the correct approach to Canon 915 may cause public doubt about the law. Such doubt further supports the indeterminacy claim. William Cardinal Keeler, another member of the bishops' task force, commented: "We are not yet united on how best to address these matters—locally or nationally, formally or informally, . . . There is no consensus on how the doctrinal note applies to particular issues."[10] The public lack of agreement among the U.S. bishops could convey the impression that canon law on the question of the refusal of Holy Communion as required by Canon 915 is in doubt. Given the present confusion, a Catholic political official could conclude

---

8. *See* GERMAIN GRISEZ, 3 DIFFICULT MORAL QUESTIONS 880 (Franciscan Press 1997).

9. Ioannes Paulus Pp. II, Adhoratio Apostolica, *Chistifideles laici* (Die 30 mensis decembris anno1988), 59; 42 AAS 81 (1989).

10. William Cardinal Keeler, *Summary of Consultations*, 34 ORIGINS 106 (July 1, 2004). Keeler's reference to "doctrinal note" refers to the *Doctrinal Note on Some Questions Regarding the Participation of Catholics in Political Life*, mentioned above and which was promulgated by the Congregation for the Doctrine of the Faith with the approval of Pope John Paul II on November 24, 2002. It is not clear whether Cardinal Keeler's statement was made with an awareness of the Six Principles communicated privately to the United States bishops by the Congregation for the Doctrine of the Faith.

that he or she is not bound by a law upon which the bishops themselves are unable to agree. This is especially the case in a diocese where the bishop has expressed public reluctance, or refusal, to apply Canon 915. The understandable confusion on the part of Catholic public officials and other laypersons does not, however, excuse the bishops from exercising the responsibility to interpret and apply canon law in a clear manner. The episcopal responsibility requires an appreciation of the rule of law in the life of the church. It is an elementary aspect of the rule of law that in order for a law to be effective, it must be promulgated, clear, and enforceable. A proponent of legal positivism might observe that if doubt about the law results, not from the law itself, but from the bishop's reluctance to interpret it correctly, then the reticence contravenes the rule of law in the church. However, any rabbi, imam, Mormon, or legal positivist could reasonably ask the bishop if doubtful law gives rise to the related issue that a specific enforcement of doubtful law might appear to be arbitrary.

II. UNDUE INTERFERENCE IN THE POLITICAL PROCESS THROUGH AN ARBITRARY APPLICATION OF LAW

The application of Canon 915 to Catholic public officials presents a sensitive case since it occurs in an ecclesial context in which the general disciplinary rules for worthy reception of Holy Communion have not been uniformly enforced. During the years prior to Vatican II, the standard practice was that any number of people at Sunday Mass did not approach the altar to receive Holy Communion. Some of these individuals had undoubtedly not observed the mandatory hours of preparatory fast; others may have been in so-called bad marriages; and still others carried some sense of serious sin. The ecclesiastical law that prevented reception of Holy Communion in such cases was clear and well known to Roman Catholics. In the United States, the situation changed in the years following Vatican II. Church discipline on the worthy reception of Holy Communion seemed to be rarely, if ever, mentioned or enforced. The general rule remains that in order to receive the Eucharist worthily one must observe the mandatory fast (at present one hour in the Latin Church), be properly disposed, and not be in the state of mortal sin.[11]

Our detached observers might offer two normative observations. First, when a bishop enforces Canon 915, it is well within his ecclesiastical responsibility, and the enforcement per se does not constitute interference in the political process. Rather, the enforcement is intended to bring order to the eucharistic assembly, and it is not intended as a breach of proper church-state relations.

---

11. To be properly disposed, the person should not be conscious of grave sin and must abstain from food and drink, except water and medicine, for at least one hour prior to reception of Holy Communion. *See* Canons 916 and 919, § 1, *CIC-1983*.

Second, given the general lack of notice and enforcement with regard to the requirements for the worthy reception of Holy Communion over the last several decades in the United States, the sudden application of Canon 915 to a Catholic political official might create the overall impression of an arbitrary application of the law. It was unfortunate that discussion about the application of Canon 915 coincided with the 2004 presidential election. In such circumstances, the application of Canon 915 could create the impression that a particular candidate or political party has been singled out in order to influence a specific political contest. In the 2004 presidential campaign, the Democratic nominee, Senator John Kerry, a Roman Catholic, had a well-established pro-choice stand. In fact, consistent with past practice, the National Democratic Party had a pro-choice plank in its platform, and in reality, it would have been difficult to secure the Democratic nomination for the presidency without publicly embracing the pro-choice position.

The refusal of Holy Communion to a particular candidate for office, especially one involved in a heated and close election campaign, might be viewed as an impermissible interference in politics on the part of church leaders who wish to influence the outcome of the election. The detached observer might note that canon law was never intended as a means to influence the outcome of any election to the government of the state. A correct enforcement of Canon 915 would, of course, not be limited to a particular political party or candidate. According to the detached observer, if Canon 915 is going to be applied to public officials, it needs to be applied to any candidate, regardless of party affiliation, who professes Catholic faith and at the same time obstinately persists in manifest grave sin. When Canon 915 has not been enforced for decades, its application to a political official coinciding with an electoral campaign obviously undermines confidence in canon law as an objective means of promoting peace, justice, and the common good. At the same time, the bishop is required to enforce the law without regard to political considerations even if it might be politically costly.

III. POLITICAL AND FINANCIAL THREATS TO THE CHURCH'S SOCIAL TEACHING AND CHARITABLE WORKS

An argument may be advanced that the refusal of Holy Communion to public officials could have an overall detrimental effect with regard to issues of social justice. This objection to the enforcement of Canon 915 goes something like the following. The positions of pro-choice public officials are often closer to the teaching of the Catholic Church on other issues of social justice than those of pro-life social conservatives. No matter what action the church takes, it is observed that the legal situation in the United States with regard to the legality of abortion on demand is not likely to change. While it would not alter the legality of abortion in the United States, the enforcement of Canon 915 might alienate socially progressive public officials from the church jeopardizing political and financial cooperation from valuable allies in advancing other important aspects of the Catholic social justice and charitable works.

The argument just described possesses a functional and pragmatic validity. However, from the perspective of Catholic moral theology, a question may be raised as to whether the objection constitutes a "proportionalist argument" which exhibits "an inadequate understanding of the object of moral action."[12] As described in the first part of this chapter, the relevant provision of Canon 915 serves to advance at least four goals related to individual and communal good. In light of the canon's goals, negative political and financial possibilities must be balanced against other aspects of the good such as the rule of law itself and the right order of the ecclesiastical community.

IV. SACRAMENTAL THEOLOGY

Some bishops declined to apply Canon 915 to public officials on the ground that such an action is inconsistent with the sacramental nature of the Eucharist. According to this internal perspective, the church's eucharistic theology conflicts with Canon 915 rendering its meaning indeterminate. Theologically, the Eucharist constitutes the "source and summit of Catholic faith."[13] When a Catholic in the state of grace receives Holy Communion, the church believes that he or she partakes of the Body and Blood of Christ, and becomes one with the Mystical Body of Christ.[14] Saint Augustine described the Eucharist as the *signum unitatis* (sign of unity) and *vinculum caritatis* (bond of charity).[15] The first aspect of the theological objection is that the application of Canon 915 to political officials disrupts the unity of the Eucharist. Bishop John Kinney, for example, argued that the application of Canon 915 "politicizes the Eucharist" and allows "Holy Communion to be used as a weapon in ongoing ideological battles."[16] As a detached normative statement, the theological objection rightly indicates that it would be wrong to introduce ideological considerations into the celebration of the Eucharist. The second aspect of the theological objection is that the application of Canon 915 offends the charity of the Eucharist. According to the Council of Trent, the Eucharist serves "as an antidote to free us from daily faults and preserve us from mortal sin."[17] This aspect of the theological objection rests on

12. *Veritatis splendor*, 75.

13. *Lumen Gentium*, 11; Canon 897, *CIC-1983*.

14. *See* CATECHISM OF THE CATHOLIC CHURCH 1391–1397 (2nd ed. Liberia Editrice Vaticana 1997).

15. *See* Augustine of Hippo, *In Ioannis Evangelium Tractatus XXVI*, 26, 13; 35 PL 1613.

16. Bishop John Kinney, *May 27, 2004 Statement*, *in* 34 ORIGINS 193 (Sept. 2, 2004).

17. Council of Trent, Session 13, Chap. 2 (Oct. 11, 1551), *in* 2 TANNER 693.

the view that it is inconsistent with divine charity to withhold the source of healing grace from one who humbly approached the altar in need of that grace. The third aspect of the theological objection is that the application of Canon 915 fosters moral perfectionism. This aspect of the objection suggests that it is hypocritical to bar a public grave sinner from the Eucharist as in reality all are sinners. The central mission of the church, the objection observes, is to proclaim redemption from sin through Word and Sacrament. Canonical discipline should be neither Donatist nor Jansenist in establishing standards of moral perfection for the worthy reception of Holy Communion.

Does the theological objection make the application of Canon 915 a doubtful case? A detached observer with expertise in the Catholic tradition, even an atheist, might respond that, in framing Canon 915, the legislator has fully considered the sacredness of the sacrament and its ecclesiological implications. Apart from the authority Canon 915 carries as a valid law, the detached atheist might add that solid theological reasons underpin this aspect of church discipline. First, as the sign of Catholic unity, the Eucharist means that all those who approach it remain in full communion with the teaching and governing authority of the church. The application of Canon 915 is not based on ideological or political grounds. Rather, the application is based upon verifiable outward conduct that contravenes the truth as defined by the church. Second, as the bond of charity, the Eucharist requires that one who is a member of the Body of Christ must be committed to protecting the sacredness of human life of the innocent and powerless. As the church understands it, there is perhaps no greater example of the poor and powerless in contemporary society than the unborn child. The application of Canon 915 is not intended to be mean spirited. In framing Canon 915, the legislator has concluded that pastoral charity sometimes requires firm action. Third, the legislator does not intend the application of Canon 915 to support a hypocritical moral perfectionism. As indicated in the first part of this chapter, Canon 915 applies to publicly manifest sin which continues even after pastoral admonition of the sinner. Precisely because such sin disrupts the unity and offends the charity of the Eucharist, the church has found it necessary to distinguish it from occult sin, which of its very nature is not known publicly. The canonical discipline remains that anyone with serious sin should not receive the Eucharist prior to sacramental confession.

Aware of the theological considerations and the history of the church's discipline, the detached atheist notes that the legislative authority has nonetheless chosen to promulgate the relevant provision of Canon 915. In affording an interpretation of Canon 915, the Congregation for the Doctrine of the Faith has affirmed its application to public officials who obstinately maintain positions in favor of abortion and/or euthanasia. It always remains possible for a bishop who objects to a particular canonical provision to voice his opposition to the

Holy See.[18] However, the rule of law requires that until the legislation or its official interpretation is changed by the proper authority, Canon 915 be correctly interpreted by the bishops. From the detached normative point of view, the atheist would correctly observe that the legislator believes Canon 915 to be in harmony with sacramental theology. If a bishop objects to the plain meaning of the canon, he should seek to change the canon through the process afforded in canon law.

V. OTHER PROVISIONS OF CANON LAW

Two additional canonical provisions might be considered to augment the hard case approach to the application of Canon 915. These are: (1) the right to receive the sacraments, and (2) the autonomy of the diocesan bishop.

A. The Right to Receive the Sacraments

Book 2 of the 1983 Code of Canon Law contains the *lex ecclesiae fundamentalis* (fundamental law of the church), which is a codification of certain fundamental rights enjoyed by all the members of the church. Canon 213 expressly recognizes the right (*ius*) of the faithful to receive the sacraments. Canon 912 reflects this fundamental right when it declares that: "Any baptized person who is not forbidden by law may and must be admitted to Holy Communion." Some bishops have implied that Canon 912 overrides the requirements of Canon 915.[19] A detached observer with some legal expertise in the interpretation of statutes might point out that such a conclusion demonstrates a lack of proper interpretation. None of the rights that are expressed in the *lex ecclesiae fundamentalis* are absolute in nature so that they simply abrogate another provision of the universal law of the church. The placement of Canon 915 in close proximity to the right stipulated in Canon 912 is evidence that the legislator intended the fundamental right to receive Holy Communion to be respected unless one of the conditions recognized in Canon 915 was present. If Canon 912 were interpreted to confer an absolute right to receive Holy Communion, it would negate all other conditions and restrictions on the reception of Holy Communion. Such a conclusion is not only contrary to the present Code of Canon Law, it also contradicts the sacramental tradition of the church, which has always recognized valid conditions and restrictions on the reception of the sacraments.

---

18. There are a variety of methods through which a bishop might voice his objection, such as through the nation conference of bishops, the papal nuncio, and/or directly to the appropriate dicastery of the Roman Curia.

19. *See* Archbishop William J. Levada, *Reflections on Catholics in Political Life and the Reception of Holy Communion*, 34 ORIGINS 104 (July 1, 2004); Bishop Denis Schnurr, *Catholics and Political Life*, 34 ORIGINS 187 (Sept. 2, 2004).

B. The Autonomy of Diocesan Bishop

Consistent with the theology of *communio* described in Chapter 1, each bishop is a member of the college of bishops, with the pope at its head. The diocesan bishop is not a mere administrative functionary who carries out Vatican policy. Rather, he is the head of his own church, which according to ancient theology contains everything within it that is necessary for salvation. It is clear from the brief statement issued by the bishops' task force that the U.S. bishops were concerned that their rightful autonomy in governing the diocese not be usurped by a general policy with regard to Canon 915. The bishop must, of course, consider the overall effect of the enforcement of Canon 915 within his specific diocese and in a given case.

A poignant example was obviously presented by the situation of Senator Kerry who resided in Boston and therefore had a canonical domicile within the Archdiocese of Boston. It seems evident that there was sufficient public information to cause the Archbishop of Boston to begin to ask whether Canon 915 applied. This was true not just in the Archdiocese of Boston, but in any diocese in which Kerry might approach the altar to receive Holy Communion. As far as I am aware, Cardinal Sean O'Malley of Boston did not exclude Senator Kerry from Holy Communion. In defense of O'Malley, a detached observer might suggest that it was not in the best interest of the church in Boston to take action against Senator Kerry or other politicians at this time. Boston was at the epicenter of the shock waves that hit the Catholic Church in the United States as a result of the clergy sexual abuse crisis. As a result, a detached observer could have legitimately determined that in those circumstances the enforcement of Canon 915 might have had a more detrimental than good effect. It would not be unreasonable to determine that the enforcement might disrupt the process of healing that the church in Boston needs. This prudent course of action, of course, would not permanently abrogate the need for enforcement of Canon 915. The autonomy of the diocesan bishop to consider the overall effect of enforcement of a positive law remains an aspect of the system of canon law. In order for the system of canon law to function properly, the bishop should not exercise his discretion in such a way that it damages the rule of law.

VI. ANTINOMIANISM AND LEGALISM

Up to this point in Chapters 6 and 7, I have examined the indeterminacy claim in light of the clear and hard case positions among the bishops responsible for the enforcement of Canon 915. The clear and hard case positions represent a possible internal perspective of the bishop participants. In this section of Chapter 7 I describe antinomian and legalistic perspectives and argue for their invalidity as approaches to Canon 915.

A. Antinomianism

A possible internal perspective of a bishop with regard to the application of Canon 915 would be to defer completely to the individual conscience of a Catholic public official. Vatican II affirmed the long-standing teaching of the Catholic tradition when it affirmed the dignity of individual conscience.[20] A member of the bishops' task force that considered the application of Canon 915, Archbishop William Levada, then of San Francisco, soon to succeed Cardinal Joseph Ratzinger as the Prefect for the CDF, stated: "The practice of the Church is to accept the conscientious self-appraisal of each person."[21] In Number 37 of the Encyclical *Ecclesia de Eucharistia*, John Paul II drew a distinction between the conscience and the outward conduct that falls within the parameters of the relevant provision of Canon 915:

> The judgment of one's state of grace obviously belongs only to the person involved, since it is a question of examining one's conscience. However, in cases of outward conduct which is seriously, clearly and steadfastly contrary to the moral norm, the Church, in her pastoral concern for the good order of the community and out of respect for the sacrament, cannot fail to feel directly involved. The *Code of Canon Law* refers to this situation of a manifest lack of proper moral disposition when it states that those who "obstinately persist in manifest grave sin" are not to be admitted to Eucharistic communion.[22]

If it were true that deference to a politician's conscience prohibited a bishop from refusing Holy Communion, the relevant provision of Canon 915 ("and others who obstinately persist in manifestly grave sin are not to be admitted to Holy Communion") would be rendered meaningless. In the absence of the penalties of excommunication or interdict, one could not prevent the grave and obstinate sinner from receiving the Eucharist. It is a fundamental principle of statutory interpretation that legislation is not intended to be meaningless. To the contrary, John Paul II's interpretation as contained in Number 37 of *Ecclesia de Eucharistia*, reveals that the supreme legislator in the Catholic Church intended the words of Canon 915 to enjoy full force. Number 37 interprets the relevant provision of Canon 915 to pertain to public and open conduct on the part of Catholic political officials who are not excommunicated or under interdict, a rightful deference to individual conscience notwithstanding. Complete deference to individual conscience would amount to an antinomian rejection of the law. Such antinomianism does not constitute a valid internal perspective for a bishop who incurs the responsibility to interpret and apply the law.

---

20. *See* Sacrosanctum Concilium Oecumenicum Vaticanum II. Declaratio De Libertate Religiosa, *Dignitatis Humane* (Die 7 mensis decembris anno 1965), 3, 2; 58 AAS 931 (1966).

21. Levada, *Reflections on Catholics in Political Life and the Reception of Holy Communion*, 104.

22. Ioannes Paulus Pp. II, Litterae Encyclicae, *Ecclesia de Eucharistia* (Die 17 mensis aprile anno 2003), 37; 95 AAS 433–75 (2003).

B. Legalism

As seen in previous chapters, antinomian and legalistic approaches to canon law often coincide. Abrogation of Canon 915 in deference to individual conscience could result in a legalistic approach to the church's traditional distinction between the internal and external fora. The internal forum pertains to matters of conscience, and it involves confidentiality in both sacramental and nonsacramental communications. In contrast, the external forum signifies all information which is public and verifiable. Public communications, votes, and other actions through which a political official advocates a pro-abortion and/or pro-euthanasia stance fall within the parameters of the external forum. A possible perspective of a bishop would be to approach the application of Canon 915 in a legalistic way suggesting it is wholly a matter of the internal forum. Such a perspective would argue that as a matter belonging to the internal forum the application of Canon 915 remains private and not subject to public enforcement. When something is revealed in the internal forum, it does not mean that this information has now been eradicated from the external forum. For example, one could imagine a situation in which a pro-choice politician made a sacramental confession regarding material cooperation in a statute that liberalized abortion. The confession would enjoy internal forum protection. However, this would not change the fact that the same politician had publicly spoken or acted in favor of abortion in the external forum.

The requirement of Canon 915 pertains to publicly manifest speech and action on the part of public officials who are baptized Catholics. It has nothing to do with the internal forum. Nor does it in anyway offend the confidentiality afforded the internal forum. In other words, the grave sin committed by a Catholic political official who publicly and obstinately continues to favor law, regulation, or funding in support of abortion or euthanasia remains a matter of the external forum, whether or not the official has resorted to the internal forum. Theologically, reception of the Eucharist is not a matter of purely personal choice based on subjective preference. Rather, the church believes that reception of the Eucharist is of its essence a communal act in which the believer is united to the Mystical Body of Christ. To sever the unity of this eucharistic theology from Canon 915 as a result of confusing the external and internal represents a legalistic approach to the issue. Legalism would also taint the decision of a bishop who fails to enter into dialogue with the Catholic public official and/or fails to take into account the specific circumstances of the case. Legalism remains contrary to the spirit of canon law and would not represent a valid internal perspective on the part of a bishop.

The clear and hard case approaches can each claim to be valid internal perspective to the application of Canon 915. Each of the approaches finds support in theological and canonical reason. Alternatively, bishops might approach the application of Canon 915 from antinomian and legalistic perspectives which I have argued remain inconsistent with the nature and function of canon law.

The arguments in favor of the hard case approach situate the application of Canon 915 within the penumbra of doubt suggesting that the meaning of the canon is indeterminate. As it places the application of Canon 915 within the penumbra of doubt, the hard case approach serves as an example of indeterminacy in canon law. The hard case approach should be evaluated with regard to its long term impact on the rule of law in the Church. Detached normative statements based on traditional Catholic teaching call into question the correctness of the hard case approach. To the extent that it causes injury to the rule of law, the hard case approach is contrary to the peace, order, and justice of the ecclesiastical community.

8. CONCLUDING OBSERVATIONS
Antinomianism, Legalism, and the Rule of Law

In this final chapter, I offer a conclusive synthesis of the study. The first part of the chapter identifies the natural and supernatural ends of canon law. The second part of the chapter summarizes the examples of clergy sexual abuse, the ownership of church property, and the application of Canon 915. Based upon the three examples, I present some general conclusions about antinomianism and legalism. The third part offers observations about canon law from the comparative perspective. In this third part, I return to the three basic questions posed in the Introduction about the nature of law, a legal system, and the rule of law. While primarily descriptive, the chapter also serves a prescriptive function. The comparison with Anglo-American legal theory not only clarifies the nature of canon law, but also suggests ways in which the system of canon law might more effectively fulfill the requirements of the rule of law. As canon law is the home system of the comparative study, the purpose of this book has not been to offer an exhaustive description or critique of Anglo-American legal theory. However, the comparison with the home system inevitably entails some level of descriptive and critical reciprocity. In these concluding observations, I shall try to avoid undue repetition, although some repetition is necessary for the synthetic summary.[1]

I. THE NATURAL AND SUPERNATURAL ENDS OF CANON LAW

Throughout this study, I have suggested that canon law advances natural and supernatural ends. On the natural level, canon law traces its origin to the interaction between individual and community. Fundamental justice requires that the community develop rules which are fair, understandable, and applied evenly. This basic justification of law intensifies as communities develop in sophistication. Canon law respects the dignity of the human person by protecting individual rights, while at the same time advancing the common good. It deals with the coordination of resources, interests, and rights in a just manner. It sets the conditions in which the human person may find a sense of participation, membership,

1. In this concluding chapter, when I simply summarize the material of the previous seven chapters, I shall keep footnotes to a minimum. I shall of course provide notes for any new material, direct quotations, and attributions.

and solidarity in the community.[2] By maintaining continuity with the past, the tradition of canon law offers security in the present and hope for the future.[3] Canon law represents an attempt to integrate these natural ends of the rule of law with supernatural ones. As a corpus of religious law, canon law may be understood as "an order derived from the theological notion of *communio*."[4] Canon law assists the Christian faithful to deepen their baptismal identity through participation in what transcends the self. It facilitates membership and participation in the church as the Mystical Body of Christ. Its supreme law is the salvation of souls.[5] It aims to set the conditions in the here and now, which point to the ultimate end of the human person, eternal happiness with God. Through fidelity to its inner meaning, canon law serves a symbolic function that communicates the supernatural destiny of the human person.

The measure of canon law is the extent to which it advances these natural and supernatural ends. Canon law is indispensable to achieving the natural ends, and it is helpful in facilitating the supernatural ends. Grace builds upon and perfects, rather than replaces, nature. When it fulfills its natural ends, the rule of law assists in setting those conditions in the church which favor the supernatural ends. I do not mean to conflate canon law with either its natural or supernatural ends. Canon law is a developed legal system, and it would be reductionistic to equate the legal system with its ends. Nor do I mean to suggest that canon law is merely a means to the natural and supernatural ends. As I shall suggest in the second part of this chapter, the authority of canon law to bind individuals depends in part on the believer's insight that the rule of law is a good in itself. My point here is that a consideration of the natural and supernatural ends demonstrates the importance of the rule of law and the danger raised by threats to it.

During the long course of its historical development, canon law has sometimes encountered resistance from antinomianism and legalism in fulfilling its natural and supernatural ends. As I discussed in Chapter 1, canon law confronts the antinomian objection that the early church was a spiritual rather than juridical reality. This objection fails to account for the numerous sacramental and juridical characteristics that are evident in sacred scripture and the historical development of the early church. The Christian experience from its origins was not

---

2. *See* Karol Wojtyla, *Participation or Alienation?*, *in* PERSON AND COMMUNITY, SELECTED ESSAYS 181–207 (Theresa Sandok, O.S.M. trans., Peter Lang 1993).

3. *See* AVERY DULLES, MODELS OF THE CHURCH, A CRITICAL ASSESSMENT OF THE CHURCH IN ALL ITS ASPECTS 39 (Doubleday 1974). *See also* JOSEPH RATZINGER, PRINCIPLES OF CATHOLIC THEOLOGY, BUILDING STONES FOR A FUNDAMENTAL THEOLOGY 86–87 (Ignatius Press 1987), which discusses the link between person, memory, community, and tradition.

4. EUGENIO CORECCO, THE THEOLOGY OF CANON LAW: A METHODOLOGICAL QUESTION 147 (Francesco Turvasi trans., Duquesne University Press 1992).

5. *See* Canon 1752, *CIC-1983*.

merely spiritual but necessarily entailed ecclesiological and juridical factors. Antinomianism undervalues the function of the natural ends in facilitating the supernatural ends of canon law. As mentioned in the Introduction, the various forms of legalism discount the supernatural ends that canon law is designed to facilitate. In its bureaucratic form, legalism insists that the letter of the law predominate over the ends. Another form of legalism involves the abuse of reason through a sophistry that obscures canon law's supernatural ends. A third form of legalism disrespects free will through an authoritarian imposition of canon law. While Saint Paul and the early Christians believed that the law has no power to save, they also understood the need for a basic order in the Christian community.

II. THE THREE EXAMPLES OF ANTINOMIANISM AND LEGALISM

In the previous chapters of this book, I have examined the sexual abuse crisis, the ownership of ecclesiastical property, and the application of Canon 915 to Catholic public officials as contemporary examples of antinomian and legalistic approaches to canon law. Although the examples are drawn from the experience of the Catholic Church in the United States, they offer insight into the long-standing theoretical and practical difficulties that these approaches pose to canon law.

A. Clergy Sexual Abuse

Chapters 2 and 3 explored the ways in which the antinomian and legalistic approaches of ecclesiastical authorities to the sexual abuse of minors in the United States resulted in injury to individuals and the common good. Antinomianism was evident in ignoring the canonical provisions designed to address a case of the sexual abuse of a minor by a priest. Although problems resulting from the statute of limitations and imputability may have impeded the prosecution of canonical action in certain cases, a priest who was guilty of serial child abuse likely could have been prosecuted. The prosecution might have prevented further abuse. At the least, it would have communicated that church authorities were intent to protect individuals and the common good. The image of the priest pedophile that was at the center of the 2002 crisis in the United States, and subsequently spread internationally, was constructed on the basis of the reality of priests who were serial abusers. The proper use of canon law would have conveyed to the public at large that there was no room in the Catholic priesthood for such criminals, and it may have tempered the social construction of reality that has become the sexual abuse crisis. I have not argued that the phenomena of clergy sexual abuse may be explained by antinomianism. Rather, my point is that antinomianism assists in explaining the failure of church authorities to rely on canon law in order to address the phenomena.

Not only did the failure to employ the canonical provisions in such cases damage the natural ends of canon law in protecting individuals and the common good, it also had theological consequences that injured the supernatural ends of canon law. It called into question the witness of clerical celibacy as a sacrifice in testimony to faith in Christ and love for his church. It disrupted the careful balance in the church's penal order between medicinal sanctions and the rare expiatory penalty such as permanent dismissal from the clerical state that reflects the relationship between canon law and the theology of forgiveness. It confused the ancient distinction between the internal and external fora, and the function of the distinction in facilitating the forgiveness of sin while maintaining individual dignity. It diminished the canonical recognition of the priesthood as a permanent state of life in the church that results from the reception of Holy Orders.

Given the nineteenth-century history of canon law in the United States, it was perhaps no surprise that the antinomianism of the sexual abuse crisis was met with legalism on the part of church authorities. When antinomian neglect of the proper role of law yields disorder, the response is sometimes a bureaucratic form of legalism. It focuses on rules rather than the justice that underlies the rules. The legalistic reaction of the U.S. bishops to the 2002 sexual abuse crisis raised doubt about the bishops' adherence to fundamental principles of natural justice such as innocent until proven guilty and the right to a fair procedure. The legalistic approach to canon law results in an environment of suspicion and doubt about fundamental justice in the public order of the church. For decades, the antinomian approach to cases of sexual abuse meant that canon law failed to protect the rights of the victim to be heard, receive justice for past injury, and prevent future harm. With canon law thus discredited, it became difficult to rely on it to protect the rights of an accused priest in the aftermath of the 2002 crisis. Legalism in response to antinomianism only further diminishes the function of canon law in fulfilling its natural and supernatural ends. Antinomianism and legalism with regard to cases of clergy sexual abuse of minors belied the unity of law and theology that is supposed to characterize the rule of law in the Catholic Church.

B. Church Property

As discussed in Chapters 4 and 5, the example of the ownership of church property also illustrates that antinomianism and legalism disrupt the unity of law and theology. Antinomianism diminishes the importance of canon law in safeguarding the ownership of property when it suggests that the church is only a spiritual reality. According to Thomas Aquinas, private property serves to avoid contentious disputes, affords an incentive to work, and ensures that goods receive proper care from their owners. In Thomistic theory, private property is a qualified and not absolute right. It is held in readiness for the community in a way that respects the requirements of distributive justice. Antinomianism fails to recognize that these natural justifications and qualifications of private property are just as applicable to the ecclesiastical community as to any other. Legalism tends to deny the theological elements that govern the church's ownership of property. Ecclesiastical property also serves supernatural ends, which canon law is designed to safeguard. The right of private property enhances the mission of the church to worship, teach, and engage in charitable services. Its supernatural dimension is further evident in light of the evangelical precepts of apostolic poverty and common ownership. While antinomianism reduces the church to a spiritual reality with no need for rules to protect the right to private property, legalism reduces the church to a merely temporal entity in which private property is acquired, owned, used, and sold with indifference to the supernatural community whose mission is the salvation of souls.

The controversy in the United States over the ownership of parish property exhibits antinomian and legalistic elements. During the nineteenth century, the U.S. bishops struggled for state recognition of the Catholic Church's right to hold its property in accord with the hierarchical structure of the church rather than in the then dominant congregational form. Eventually, the success of the bishops' efforts led to several different ways in which state law might respect the right of the church as a religious entity to hold and govern its property in accord with canon law. Given the arduous nineteenth-century struggle of the Catholic Church in the United States, it seems ironic that at the start of the twenty-first century, some ecclesiastical authorities seemed to suggest that parish property in the Catholic Church is held according to a congregational rather than hierarchical form of government. As mentioned in Chapter 5, the abrogation of the principle of hierarchy in favor of congregationalism disrupts the harmony between the *dominium* and *imperium* in the canonical design for the ownership of church property.

On the basis of Canons 1266 and 515 § 3 of the *CIC-1983*, the parish is a juridic person, and it may own its own property (*dominium*). These canons might be interpreted in isolation from other canonical provisions that recognize the function of hierarchical authority in regulating parish property (*imperium*). In particular, these two canons might be interpreted in isolation from other relevant canons that establish the hierarchical relation between the diocesan bishop and priest who serves as pastor of the parish. Moreover, this underinclusive interpretation of canon law overlooks the theological provisions about the parish as an integral part of a diocese. This kind of narrow interpretation combines elements of legalism and antinomianism. In neglecting the theological claim about the divine origin of the hierarchical form of church governance, the narrow reading represents legalism. At the same time, in failing to account for the legal structure by which canon law entrusts hierarchical authority with the regulation of ecclesiastical property, the narrow interpretation represents antinomianism. The interpretation's combination of legalism and antinomianism distorts the canonical vision for ecclesiastical property. By denying the principle of hierarchy, the interpretation transposes the absolute ownership of private property characteristic of pristine liberal political theory onto the canonical vision. This transposition displaces the unity of law and theology that recognizes a right to private property qualified by theological concerns about mission, distributive justice, the church's hierarchical nature, and the Gospel ideals of apostolic poverty and common ownership.

In addition to parish property, antinomianism and legalism influence the ownership of church property such as that associated with educational institutions, health care providers, and other charitable organizations. Canon law recognizes the importance of the civil law of the state in regulating church property. However, the incorporation of church property under the laws of the state was never intended to result in the secularization of the church property. Church property is "secularized" either when it is no longer directed by the juridic person that owns the property according to canon law, or when the property ceases to serve some purpose that furthers the mission of the church. During the second half of the twentieth century, church property in the United States was in fact secularized. Typically, the secularization occurred when control and sometimes title of property that was originally owned by a religious community or other church entity was transferred to a so-called "lay board of trustees." If transfer of title to church property occurs pursuant to the civil law, canon law requires that the juridic person selling the property follow the rules for the valid alienation of property. If the transfer of church property occurs in accord with the civil law without a valid alienation of the church property in canon law, the result is a *de facto* alienation of the property but an invalid *de iure* alienation. Ignoring the requirements of canon law for the valid alienation of church property reflects an antinomian approach to canon law.

The direction of church property that defiles the theological character and aims of the property is a form of legalism. In canon law, it is ultimately of little difference whether church property is under the direction of a diocese, a religious community, or laypersons. Laypersons who have received proper ecclesiastical approval have just as much right and responsibility as a diocese or religious community to own and direct property in order to exercise some apostolic function in the church. The transfer of a Catholic institution to the control of a board of directors, even one composed entirely of laypersons, does not necessarily mean that the institution has lost its Catholic mission or that its property no longer exists to serve that mission. In light of the fact that state law is willing to permit the church to hold and control its property in accord with its hierarchical form of governance, Catholic hierarchy, religious communities, and laypersons should rely upon the relevant provisions of state law in order to safeguard the theological character of ecclesiastical property. Merely following state law, while forsaking the canonical provisions for the regulation of church property, runs the risk that church property will cease to be used in a way that facilitates some aspect of the church's mission to engage in spiritual and corporal works of mercy. It further jeopardizes the symbolic function of church property as an institutional witness to the sacred in the secular order.

C. Canon 915

In Chapters 5 and 6, I examined antinomian and legalistic approaches to the application of Canon 915 to Catholic public officials. Relying on the legal theory of H. L. A. Hart, I presented arguments that support the clear case interpretation of Canon 915. The words of the applicable provision of Canon 915 seem clear in their plain meaning. In its historical development, the canon enjoys a long pedigree. The canon fulfills the requirements of the rule of recognition as it has been promulgated by the authority of the pope as part of the universal law of the Catholic Church. The lawmaker has promulgated Canon 915 for valid reasons relating to the order of the Eucharist, the avoidance of scandal, the protection of fundamental moral principles such as the sacredness of human life, and the salvation of souls. However, many bishops concluded that the interpretation of Canon 915 constitutes a more difficult case. Again, relying on Hart's theory, I offered analysis of the hard case approach. This internal point of view is based upon concerns about the political autonomy of a Catholic public official, respect for individual conscience, interference by the church in the political process, threats to other aspects of the church's moral and social teachings, and the right to receive the sacraments. Disagreement about the correct application of Canon 915 bolsters the indeterminacy claim about canon law. It suggests that the meaning of canon law is often unclear, open to various interpretations, and therefore highly subjective in nature. This kind of indeterminacy tends to have a negative impact on the rule of law.

The disagreement among the bishops also exhibits the characteristics of antinomianism and legalism in canon law. On the one hand, the clear case interpretation to the application of Canon 915 risks the pitfall of legalism. It would be sheer legalism to apply the canon without a full consideration of all the facts of the specific case. Such a legalistic application would not serve the legislative intent that underpins Canon 915. This kind of legalism risks fostering disrespect for the law. A lack of respect for the canonical provision would lead many to disregard it, and thus add to the impression of the indeterminate nature of canon law. On the other hand, the difficult case approach to Canon 915 leads to the antinomianism that sustains the indeterminacy charge. It would be sheer antinomianism to conclude that Canon 915 is abrogated by deference to the individual conscience of the person who approaches to receive the Eucharist. Likewise, the determination that Canon 915 never applies to Catholic public officials who persist in positions in opposition to the church's fundamental moral teaching reflects an antinomian approach to canon law. This approach completely ignores the legislative intent of the canon. Even more than legalism, antinomianism buttresses the argument in favor of the indeterminate nature of canon law.

It suggests that the meaning of the canon is so vague that its fair enforcement as part of a coherent policy is impossible.

D. General Conclusions about Antinomianism and Legalism

On the basis of the historical and contemporary manifestations of antinomianism and legalism, it is possible to draw several general conclusions. First, both antinomianism and legalism diminish the ability of canon law to fulfill its natural and supernatural ends. Antinomianism discounts the function of canon law in establishing the natural conditions that respect the dignity of persons through the protection of fundamental rights, that facilitate participation and solidarity in community, that enable the just coordination of resources, and that advance the common good. Legalism approaches canon law as a legal system separate from its inner theological meaning. It overlooks the distinctive religious character of the church as the community of faith formed around the Paschal Mystery of the Lord, which serves as a sign of God's presence in the world.

Second, although they are opposites, antinomianism and legalism often go together, and there is a rule of reciprocity according to which one tends to produce a reaction that leads to the other. The antinomian disregard for canon law yields disorder in ecclesiastical community which can open the way for an authoritarian and rigid legalism. Likewise, an overly strict regime of law can result in an antinomian response that denies the legitimacy of the law. For these same reasons, antinomian and legalistic approaches to canon law can coexist in the same situation in which each approach is a misguided attempt to counterbalance the other.

Third, it seems that the theological or spiritual essence of the church renders canon law vulnerable to antinomianism. The theological and pastoral elements of canon law do not inherently cause antinomianism. Neither theological nor pastoral concern per se denies the validity of canon law. To the contrary, as Klaus Mörsdorf and Eugenio Corecco have proposed, theology and its pastoral applications remain essential to canon law. However, an excessive or exclusive focus on theological and pastoral elements can lead to the disordered understanding which is antinomianism.

Fourth, when it is improperly understood, the exercise of authority in the church can lead to legalism. Because authority in the church is claimed to be derived from divine intention, the authority tends to elicit a high level of trust from the believer. This sacred trust may be subject to abuse by the office holder through a legalistic approach to canon law. The authoritarian form of legalism results when the office holder acts in a manner that is inconsistent with the example of Christ's humble service. The casuistical form of legalism reflects a skewed reasoning on the part of the office holder who interprets canon law in a way that distorts its inner meaning and purpose. The bureaucratic form of legalism occurs when the office holder overlooks the theological doctrines of the dignity of the individual person created in the image and likeness of God and of the community that embodies the presence of Christ within it.

Finally, a balanced approach to canon law requires an integration of faith and reason in ordering the church. The balanced approach realizes that while canon law has no power on its own to achieve salvation, canon law remains necessary to the order of the church. Canon law serves as a means for faith to flourish in the lives of persons and communities in the church. Antinomianism dismisses the canon law as a hindrance to the spiritual character of the church. It denies the role of reason in setting a just order for the community. Legalism emphasizes the role of law to such an extent that it denies the primacy of the spiritual and theological. It favors a form of reason divorced from faith. While antinomianism rejects canon law on the ground that it is incompatible with faith, legalism repudiates the attempt to integrate canon law and theology on the ground that it detracts from the efficacy of the law. As I believe the contemporary examples of the sexual abuse crisis, the ownership of church property, and the interpretation of Canon 915 make clear, antinomianism and legalism jeopardize the function of the rule of law in the Roman Catholic Church, resulting in great damage to individuals and the faith community.

III. THE RULE OF LAW: COMPARISON OF CANON LAW WITH ANGLO-AMERICAN LEGAL THEORY

At neuralgic points throughout this study, I have discussed aspects of Anglo-American legal theory in order to afford a comparative perspective on the function of canon law as the rule of law in the Catholic Church. Here, I return to three basic questions posed at the outset of this book from the perspective of Anglo-American legal theory. Does canon law count as law? Is canon law a system of law? Does canon law represent the rule of law? As evident from the discussion that follows, the basic questions are distinct but related. The comparative aspect of this study suggests that despite the dangers posed to it by antinomianism and legalism, canon law exhibits the essential characteristics of law, a developed legal system, and the rule of law.

A. Does Canon Law Count as Law?

According to Thomas Aquinas's well-known definition, law is "an ordinance of reason for the common good, promulgated by him who has care of the community"[6] The identification of reason, the common good, legislative power, and a receptive community are elements in the classical understanding of law discussed in Chapter 1. The classical understanding holds that law possesses the

6. ST, I-II, 90, 4.

authority to bind at least in part because it is grounded in divine and natural law. During the twentieth century, Anglo-American legal theorists, and the legal positivists in particular, directed attention to whether law's authority enjoys autonomy from moral rules. In light of this twentieth-century discussion, I ask: "Where does the authority of canon law come from?"

1. Canon Law and Coercive Power In modern democracies, the law's effectiveness derives at least in part from the fact that an individual who breaks a particular law is subject to punishment by the coercive power of the state. The state exercises the power to punish one found guilty of breaking the law by taking away the person's liberty, property, or even life itself. The coercive power of the state may only be exercised in accord with the requirements of procedural due process. F. A. Hayek posited a connection between the rule of law and the exercise of the state's coercive power. He suggested that law is to be "fixed and announced beforehand" by the governing authority in order for the individual "to foresee with fair certainty how the authority will use its coercive powers in given circumstances, and to plan one's individual affairs on the basis of this knowledge."[7] According to this theory, enforcement of the law through the state's coercive power is essential to the rule of law. If individuals may decide to break laws without consequence from the state, the overall peace, security, and common good of society cannot be guaranteed.

In contrast to the law of modern democracy, adherence to a great deal of canon law rests upon moral authority rather than any coercive power that church authorities might exercise. It is true that canon law has a limited tradition of penal sanctions. Some of the early church councils concluded canons with the threatened sanction: *Anathema sit*. The *CIC-1983* also contains provisions for penal sanctions such as excommunication.[8] Most of the canonical sanctions provided for in the *CIC-1983* are medicinal in nature. They are designed to bring about a change of heart in the offender and to be lifted once the offender has expressed true repentance. The penal sanctions in canon law are guided by the theology that any sin can be forgiven, and that the salvation of souls remains the supreme law of the church. However, the expiatory sanction of permanent removal from the clerical state of a priest who has been found guilty of sexually abusing a minor is a rare permanent penalty. Like any other human being, the guilty priest may be forgiven his sin, but the imposition of the sanction means that he may not exercise his office. The sanction is a legal recognition that an act of sexual abuse offends the dignity of the victim, constitutes a grave offense against the natural and divine prohibitions of such acts, and damages the common good. With the exception of the limited number of remedial and expiatory penal sanctions, compliance with canon law is largely voluntary, and coercive

---

7. Friedrich A. Hayek, The Road to Serfdom 54 (G. Routledge & Sons 1944).
8. *See* Canons 1311–1399, *CIC-1983*.

power does not count as a major factor in the law's authority. The minimalist provisions for sanctions and the general absence of coercive power in canon law raises a question about whether it counts as law from the perspective of the legal positivists. Given the concern of the early positivists about how law differs from other societal norms, one might ask whether canon law is different from any other normative rules of conduct defined by the church. In other words, is canon law really law or just another form of moral theology, and in the absence of sanctions, how does one tell the difference between the two?

2. Canon Law as Command John Austin distinguished law from other societal norms on the ground that law is the command of the sovereign. The law differs from other societal norms because the sovereign has elected to promulgate this particular norm as necessary to some aspect of the peace, security, and order of society. For example, the sovereign does not make all forms of lying illegal, but adopts a law that specifies perjury as a particular kind of lying which is illegal. Perjury threatens the correct operation of the legal system in its effort to ascertain the truth about a particular situation, and therefore it counts as a harmful form of lying in terms of the operation of the rule of law. Likewise, Catholic moral theology identifies all lying as morally defective, but the *CIC-1983* does not punish most forms of lying. Canon 1368 of the *CIC-1983* establishes perjury as a canonical offense for which a just penalty may be imposed. In promulgating Canon 1368, the pope has decided to make perjury a punishable offense in order to create an incentive to truth-telling in ecclesiastical tribunals. The canonical prohibition of perjury is an implicit recognition that perjury differs from other forms of lying in that it constitutes a particular and direct threat to the rule of law. This does not mean that the pope has exercised his governing authority in a way that suggests that other forms of lying do not violate the moral law or that perjury is necessarily the most morally serious form of lying. However, the governing authority of the church has recognized the necessity of the law against perjury as a way of safeguarding the natural and supernatural ends of the rule of law in the Catholic Church. Canon law's function as the rule of law in the church distinguishes it from other norms that claim moral authority.

As a religious system of law, canon law enjoys a theological dimension that is not present in secular systems of law. The member of the church who obeys some provision of canon law is recognizing the authority of the pope or bishop who promulgated the law. This authority arises not just from the reality of the church as a human community but also from the theological understanding of the origin of sacred power (*sacra potestas*). According to the theological understanding previously discussed, the pope and the bishop exercise governing authority as a result of the sacred power which is conferred by Christ. The theological understanding of the nature of *sacra potestas* contrasts with Hart's analogy in which he likened the command theory of law to the threat of a gunman.[9] The analogy between the gunman and the pope or bishop who promulgates a law seems less than appropriate. The argument from authority in the church reflects a fundamental trust in the good intention and fairness of the lawgiver. As the examples of antinomianism and legalism illustrate, there is no guarantee that every individual who exercises governing authority in the church will act in a manner that is worthy of the trust. Nonetheless, canon law attributes a grace to the office itself, and this grace remains always available to the individual office holder who disposes himself to accept and act in accord with it. The believer is disposed to obey the command of canon law in deference to the sacred office, which the believer accepts as established by divine intention.

3. The *Intellectus* of Canon Law Although it has a theological significance, obedience to the command of the lawgiver is not necessarily a complete, or even the best, explanation of canon law's authority. In the Thomistic definition, law is first described as an ordinance of reason. The reason (or what I have termed the *intellectus*) of canon law integrates natural, theological, and historical truths.[10] First, the *intellectus* of canon law reflects the universal and transcendent principles of natural law. Second, the *intellectus* expresses theological truths derived from the divine revelation of sacred scripture. Third, the *intellectus* also includes a historical consciousness that elicits respect for custom and tradition in shaping law according to present and future circumstances. The believer's insight about the *intellectus* of canon law is a critical element in explaining canon law's power to bind.

The *intellectus* of canon law rests on an anthropological foundation of one universal human nature which, having been redeemed by Christ, is dynamic rather than static, as it is actualized in a concrete and particular historical existence. The human person is endowed with intellect and free will. The intellect enables the human person to understand not only the purpose of a particular canonical norm but also how the particular norm fits into canon law as a legal system. Free will enables the human person to act in accord with the understanding of the particular and transcendent good identified by the intellect. The believer who voluntarily obeys canon law understands the authority of the law on the basis of divine law and natural law. One obeys the canon law derived from divine and

---

9. *See* Hart, The Concept of Law, 6–7.

10. Thomas employs the Latin word *ratio*, which I am translating with the word *reason*. In Chapter 1, I noted that Hans Urs von Balthasar attributes the word *intellectus* to Bonaventure when Bonaventure actually relies on the word *logica*. *See* Hans Urs von Balthasar, A Theological Anthropology 162–63 (Sheed & Ward 1967). Each of the three Latin words has a distinct definition. However, I am using them somewhat interchangeably to indicate that law is a product of practical reason. My point is that absent this internal *ratio*, *logica*, or *intellectus*, canon law would have no power to bind persons and communities in the church.

natural law because the failure to obey would damage one's participation in the ecclesial community as the Mystical Body of Christ and might interfere with the salvation of one's soul. From the perspective of faith, these are of course powerful motivations for obeying the canon law. To the extent that the believer understands that the canon law facilitates its supernatural and natural ends, the believer's understanding is the insight that counts as the explanation of canon law's authority. Insight about the *intellectus* of the law disposes the believer to exercise an act of the will in obedience to the law.

Canon law is not a mere copy of divine and natural law. While it reflects divine and natural law, canon law has its own positive character. As a human creation, positive law can never perfectly capture the law's inner meaning. However, the positive law is necessary for the sake of justice and the common good. For example, the requirement that a bishop voluntarily submit his resignation to the pope upon reaching the age of seventy-five, or that a novice in an institute of consecrated life complete a novitiate of at least one year's duration, might be described as "purely positive law." Neither of these provisions of canon law is strictly speaking required by divine or natural law. The promulgation of such positive law, however, creates a moral obligation that did not exist until the moment of the law's promulgation.[11] The particular provision of positive law becomes part of the rule of law. The bishop voluntarily submits his resignation as stipulated not only because it is the command of the pope, but also because the bishop understands the purpose of the retirement provision in maintaining sound government throughout the dioceses of the church. The bishop may not think that his continuation in office beyond the retirement age poses a particular threat to his diocese. Nor may he necessarily think that the retirement policy is the most desirable policy for the church. Nonetheless, the bishop understands the provision to advance a reasonable policy about retirement, and he accepts it as a rational policy choice made by the legislator. As a believer, the bishop recognizes the moral obligation to conform to the provision of positive law because it is part of the rule of law.

Likewise, the novice completes the novitiate not merely because it is the command of the constitutions of the religious community in accord with the *CIC-1983*, but because the novice understands the spiritual benefits that the novitiate year promises. The novice, with the concurrence of the religious superior, might conclude that in his or her particular case only eight months of novitiate is necessary, but the novice accepts the one-year canonical requirement as a an aspect of the rule of law for religious life in the church. In either the case of the bishop or of the novice, the believer's insight is that conformity with this particular provision of positive law is an aspect with conformity to the rule of law and the natural and

11. *See* John Finnis, *Propter Honoris Respectum: On the Incoherence of Legal Positivism*, 75 NOTRE DAME L. REV. 1597, 1607 (2000).

supernatural ends that it protects in the Catholic Church. The rule of law is itself a rational motive that affords the insight to the believer to obey the law. The function of canon law as the rule of law is a natural dimension of canon law's inner meaning from which canon law derives its authority. The believer understands that, absent the rule of law, there could be no lasting order, peace, and justice in the universal church. The rule of law serves both as an aspect of the *intellectus* from which canon law derives its authority and as a means to the natural and supernatural ends of canon law.

B. Does Canon Law Constitute a System of Law?

As previously mentioned, early legal positivists such as John Austin argued that law was distinguishable from other kinds of societal norms in that law was the command of the sovereign. H. L. A. Hart criticized Austin's command theory on the ground that it explains only the primary rules of law that either require or prohibit certain actions. Hart posited that the secondary rules of recognition, change, and adjudication were critical to any "system of law." Secondary rules "specify the ways in which the primary rules may be conclusively ascertained, introduced, eliminated, varied, and the fact of their violation conclusively determined."[12] Hart posited that the rules of recognition, change, and adjudication, taken together, "are enough to convert the regime of primary rules into what is indisputably a legal system."[13] As Hart considered these secondary rules to be characteristic of a "developed legal system," it follows that they are also foundational to the rule of law.[14] While the idea of a legal system and the rule of law are not synonymous, I am presuming that the effectiveness of the rule of law depends in part on the existence of a system of law. On the basis of this comparative study, I shall suggest that Hart's secondary rules may be identified in the system of canon law.

First, Hart argued that uncertainty over what norms carry binding force in a community requires a rule of recognition that specifies the properties by which a rule possesses legal validity in the legal system. For example, he described the rule of recognition in English law as "whatever the Queen in Parliament enacts is law."[15] As discussed in Chapter 1, the *CIC-1983* was promulgated by the pope, and it in turn acknowledges that the pope exercises legislative authority for the universal church and that the diocesan bishop exercises this authority for his diocese. However, canon law would not be accurately described as "a very simple system of law," in which system, what the pope or diocesan bishop enacts is law,

12. H. L. A. HART, THE CONCEPT OF LAW 94 (2d ed. Clarendon Press of Oxford University 1997).

13. *Id.*

14. *Id.* at 95.

15. *Id.* at 107.

and in which no legal limitations are imposed upon the legislative power.[16] Rather, the developed system of canon law has a sophisticated rule of recognition according to which a law's "pedigree" is more complex than merely acknowledging it as the command of one who exercises the power of governance. The legitimacy of canon law also entails multiple criteria such as its derivation from, or at least conformity to, sacred scripture and natural law, its integration of faith and reason, its continuity with tradition, its semantic stability, and its reception by the community. As I discussed above, canon law is not merely the command of the legislator. However, in terms of meeting the limited purpose of the rule of recognition which distinguishes law from other types of norms in the community, it is sufficient to determine that a particular provision has been enacted by the legislator.

Joseph Raz suggests that the rule of recognition is not so much a "power conferring" as a "duty imposing" rule.[17] This understanding of secondary rules fits well with the theological understanding of authority in canon law. The church views the institutionalization of authority in a way that is intended to transcend merely human social reality. In accord with this understanding, authority in the church is not simply the product of social necessity, but the result of the divine plan for salvation revealed by Jesus Christ. Canon law traces the source of the governing power to the original authority conferred on Peter and the other Apostles by Christ, which is shared by their successors, the pope and the bishops.[18] The authority is intended to be exercised in the example of the humble service of Christ who gave his life for the many.[19] The idea of the imposition of responsibility rather than the conferral of power fits canon law's theological claim about authority as humble service. The church does not bestow the governing authority on someone for the self-interested enjoyment of prerogatives but for the humble discharge of a sacred trust. Those vested with hierarchical authority in the church have the responsibility to serve in an intelligent manner that promotes the natural and supernatural ends of canon law. Antinomianism and legalism diminish the rule of recognition as a duty-imposing rule. The antinomian and legalistic approaches of church authorities to clerical sexual abuse, the ownership of church property, and the application of Canon 915 represent a refusal by these church authorities to fulfill the responsibilities imposed upon them by canon law.

Second, Hart further stipulated that in a legal system the static character of customary norms is addressed by a rule of change. In Chapter 1, I traced the origin of such a rule in canon law to the Council of Jerusalem, as recorded in

---

16. *Id.* at 100.

17. Joseph Raz, Practical Reasons and Norms 93 (Princeton University Press 1992).

18. *See* Canons 330, 331, 336, 337, and 375, *CIC-1983*.

19. *Cf.* Matthew 20:28; Mark 10:45; Luke 22:27; and John 13:12-17.

Acts of the Apostles, when Peter and the Apostles met with Paul and Barnabas to hold that the circumcision requirement of the Jewish Law did not bind gentile converts to Christianity.[20] The historical development of canon law from the early church to the medieval *Corpus Iuris Canonici* to the twentieth-century codifications suggests the continuity of this system of law through the rule of change. A modern example of this secondary characteristic of the rule of law is the process that led to the *CIC-1983*. Commencing at the end of Vatican II in 1965, the complex process involved a central commission composed of curial officials and other experts; the drafting of several schema; numerous consultations with diocesan bishops, religious superiors, and other experts throughout the world; and the final promulgation of the new Code by Pope John Paul II in 1983.

The process that led to the promulgation of the *CIC-1983* differed from the legislative process characteristic of the modern democracy. As previously discussed, canon law does not reflect an absolute separation of executive, legislative, and judicial powers. The process for the *CIC-1983* did not involve a separate legislative branch, let alone a bicameral legislature with a clearly defined process of how a bill becomes law. If the definition of the rule of law necessitates the separation of powers and the democratic legislative process, canon law does not meet the requirements for the rule of law. However, if a central goal of the democratic legislative process is to prevent the adoption of law by the imposition of the arbitrary will of an individual or group, this goal was achieved by the process that led to the *CIC-1983*. Although the promulgation of the *CIC-1983* was ultimately contingent on the pope's legislative power, the process depended on a large central commission with numerous subdivisions, consultation with all of the bishops throughout the world as well as with hundreds of diverse experts, the drafting of several major schema, and public debate about the merits of these drafts. Despite the fact that it was not the democratic legislative process, the complex process helped to ensure that canon law was modified in order to meet the needs of the contemporary church fulfilling the directive of Vatican II.

Canon law develops through changes to the positive character of the canons, and sometimes a change to the positive character of the canons reflects development in the church's doctrine. The inclusion of a list of fundamental rights at the beginning of Book II of the *CIC-1983* stemmed from a development which reflected a heightened focus on the church's teaching about the fundamental dignity of the human person.[21] Although the medieval canonists recognized the dignity of the individual and corresponding subjective rights, it was not until the *CIC-1983* that these rights were expressly recognized.[22] The millenary function

20. *See* Acts 15:6–29.

21. *See* Canons 208–223, *CIC-1983*.

22. *See* Brian Tierney, *The Origin of Natural Rights Language: Texts and Context*, in Rights, Laws, and Infallibility in Medieval Thought 626 and 638 (Variorum 1997), which discusses the subjective meaning of *ius* in medieval canon law. *Cf.* Walter Ullmann,

of a secondary rule of change is also evident in the historical development of canon law's theory of church property. The *CIC-1983* incorporates the ancient church's understanding which places an emphasis on the evangelical ideals of poverty and common ownership. The contemporary canons integrate this theological understanding with the medieval theory about the need for private property after the Fall and the recognition of a qualified right to private property. Additionally, the *CIC-1983* expresses respect for the modern theory of the secular state and defers to the state's role in protecting property rights. At the same time, current canon law establishes its own rules whereby the appropriate hierarchical authority in the church bears the responsibility to ensure that the acquisition, administration, use, and alienation of church property remain in accord with natural rights, theological values, and the mission of the church.

Finally, Hart claimed that a rule of adjudication is necessary to resolve disputes about interpretations of the rules. The *CIC-1983* requires each diocese to establish and maintain a diocesan tribunal and tribunal officials.[23] It also mandates the establishment of a tribunal of second instance, which hears an appeal from the decision of the diocesan tribunal.[24] It further establishes a system of judicial tribunals and administrative bodies at the level of the Holy See, while specific laws regulate jurisdiction and procedure in the exercise of the executive and judicial powers of government.[25]

The church tribunals differ from many kinds of tribunals that function in the modern secular democracies in that the decisions of the church tribunals do not enjoy precedential value. Rather, the judicial power in canon law is exercised primarily with a particular case in mind and not necessarily with an eye toward its implications for the development of the law.[26] Consequently, while canon

---

The Individual and Society in the Middle Ages 136–37 (Johns Hopkins Press 1966), which argues that the concept of the individual was of Enlightenment origin; and *see* John Finnis, Aquinas: Moral, Political, and Legal Theory 133–38 (Oxford University Press 1998); John Finnis, Natural Law and Natural Rights 206–07 (Clarendon Press of Oxford University 1986), which discuss the objective meaning of *ius* in Thomas Aquinas' thought. At Vatican II, the connection between human dignity, religious freedom, and the natural order was recognized in *Dignitatis Humanae.* The recognition laid the basis for the development by which a list of fundamental rights were incorporated into the *CIC-1983. See* Sacrosanctum Concilium Oecumenicum Vaticanum II, *Dignitatis Humanae* (Die 7 mensis decembris anno 1965), 58 AAS 929–46 (1966).

23. *See* Canons 1419–1437, *CIC-1983.*

24. *See* Canons 1338–1441, *CIC-1983.*

25. *See* Canons 1442–1445, 360–61, *CIC-1983*; and Ioannes Paulus Pp. II, Constitutio Apostolica De Curia Romana, Pastor Bonus (Die 28 mensis iunii anno 1988), 80 AAS 842–912 (1988).

26. *See* Canon 16, §3, *CIC-1983* (". . . an interpretation by way of a court judgment or of an administrative act in a particular case, does not have force of law. It binds only those persons and affects only those matters for which it was given.").

law has secondary rules which provide for tribunals, establish jurisdiction, and identify individuals who adjudicate disputes (judges and other tribunal officials), it does not have a recognized system through which judges in effect create law through the precedential values of their interpretations. Although lacking the power of precedent, the decisions of the canonical judges are not completely bereft of authority beyond the particular case at hand. The decisions of the Roman Rota, for example, have proved highly influential in shaping the canon law of marriage. Not only are the rotal decisions given careful consideration by other ecclesiastical judges in deciding like cases, but they are also carefully studied by canonists and theologians in articulating the church's doctrine and practice.

The authority of the rotal judge's reasoning sits well with Ronald Dworkin's view that judicial decision-making is a matter of interpretation in light of the soundest legal traditions within the complex environment of interrelated principles and ideals.[27] However, the rule of adjudication in canon law is not necessarily focused on judges or limited to the judicial power. Canon 16 of the *CIC-1983* provides that "laws are interpreted by the legislator and to that person to whom the legislator entrusts the power of interpretation." At the level of the church's universal law, the task of interpretation has been entrusted to the Pontifical Council for the Interpretation of Legislative Texts.[28] Canon law also draws a sharp distinction between judicial and administrative matters. The *CIC-1983* establishes procedural law for hierarchical recourse against the "single administrative act . . . posited in the external forum outside of a trial with the exception of those acts issued by the Roman Pontiff or an ecumenical council."[29] Recourse against the administrative act of the diocesan bishop may be brought to the competent Dicastery of the Roman Curia and from the Dicastery to the section of the Apostolic Signatura, which serves as the supreme administrative tribunal of the church. The kinds of administrative disputes are diverse in nature and concern matters such as the suppression of a parish, the removal of a pastor from office, the dismissal of a religious, the disputed election of a religious major superior, the dismissal of a professor from an ecclesiastical faculty, the suppression of a monastery or religious house, and the validity of action taken by the chapter in an institute of consecrated life.[30]

---

27. *See* Ronald Dworkin, Law's Empire 410–13 (Belknap Press of Harvard University 1986).

28. *See Pastor Bonus*, 154–58. *See also* Javier Otaduy, *Ecclesiastical Laws, in* Navarra-2004, 318–24.

29. Canon 1732, *CIC-1983*.

30. *See* Zenon Grocholewski, *La giustzia amministrativa presso la Segnatura Apostolica*, 4 Ius Ecclesiae 14–19 (1992).

C. Does Canon Law Fulfill the Requirements of the Rule of Law?

In the Introduction of this study, I described various aspects of the rule of law. First, the rule of law refers to rule by a system of law and not by the arbitrary and capricious will of an individual or group. Second, Anglo-American legal theory stipulates that the rule of law must include provisions for procedural justice. Third, certain theorists would argue that the rule of law entails an explanation of the law's authority that transcends procedural justice. As discussed above, canon law meets the requirements for a system of law which is the first aspect of the rule of law. I now examine the second and third aspects, and I also raise the issues of unjust law and indeterminacy as they relate to the concept of the rule of law.

1. Procedural Justice In Anglo-American legal theory, some form of procedural justice is essential to a legal system's adherence to the rule of law. Lon Fuller identified eight characteristics or demands of the rule of law. Law must be: (1) general and not *ad hoc*, (2) publicized, (3) prospective and not retroactive, (4) clear, (5) logical, (6) capable of obedience in practice, (7) stable and not subject to too frequent change, and (8) administered in a way that is congruent with the rule as announced.[31] Recognizing the "utopian aspiration" that a legal system embodies all eight of the desiderata perfectly, Fuller nonetheless admonishes: "A total failure in any one of these eight directions does not simply result in a bad system of law; it results in something that is not properly called a legal system at all."[32] In light of the specific examples that I have discussed in this book, the nexus between procedural justice and the rule of law raises questions about canon law as the rule of law.

What do the decades of antinomian refusal on the part of the U.S. bishops to utilize the penal process in clergy sexual abuse cases suggest about the viability of the rule of law? In response to the 2002 sexual abuse crisis, what does the legalistic response of the bishops indicate about procedural justice? In the wake of the crisis, Avery Cardinal Dulles, S.J., faulted the bishops' response on several procedural grounds. First, in utilizing the definition of sexual abuse which they adopted in 2002 to settle cases that were most often decades old, the bishops violated the principle against the retroactive application of law. Additionally, the bishops' response ignored the canonical period of prescription (statute of limitation) in which an action against an accused priest might be brought. Further, Dulles argued that the bishops' response to the 2002 crisis abrogated the presumption of innocence.[33] Adherence to these procedural requirements of the rule of law might not have enjoyed popular support in the heat of the crisis, but would have served the interests of fairness in the long term. Antinomian and legalistic

---

31. *See* Lon L. Fuller, The Morality of Law 39 (Yale University Press 1967).

32. *Id.*

33. *See* Avery Dulles, *Rights of Accused Priests, Toward a Revision of the Dallas Charter and the "Essential Norms,"* 188 America 19, 21 (June 21–28, 2004).

responses to the ownership of church property and the application of Canon 915 raise similar kinds of questions about the rule of law in the life of the church. Does the *de facto* alienation of church property without observing the procedural requirements stipulated in canon law support the rule of law? Likewise, does the bishops' refusal to agree on a correct interpretation of Canon 915 indicate a lack of respect for the procedures suggested by the Holy See as an aspect of the rule of law in the church? The injury to individuals, communities, and the church as a whole presented by these examples illustrate the responsibility of those with governing power in the church to honor the requirements of procedural justice.

Fuller contends that his eight procedural requirements constitute the natural internal morality of law.[34] He conceives the internal morality of the law to be a type of natural law, stating that it is "a procedural as distinguished from substantive natural law."[35] For Fuller, the procedural form of the law ensures the moral substance of the law. Hart disagrees, suggesting that what Fuller identifies as the internal morality of the law are not moral principles, but notions of purpose and efficiency. Faithful to his own positivist theory, Hart argues that the procedure by which law is made is "independent of law's substantive aims just as the principles of carpentry are independent of whether the carpenter is making hospital beds or torturer's racks."[36] As Hart observes, law might fulfill the eight procedural requirements, but remain "unfortunately compatible with very great iniquity."[37] Whether one views Fuller's requirements as part of the natural law or maxims of legal efficacy, it seems clear that the eight procedural requirements remain indispensable to the rule of law.

Hart does recognize a certain "minimum" content of "natural procedural justice."[38] He concedes that a legal system consists of general rules which require that "like cases be treated alike."[39] For Hart, such procedural justice is "justice in the administration of the law, and not justice of the law."[40] A legal system might satisfy "the minimum requirements . . . with the most pedantic impartiality" and yield "laws which were hideously oppressive."[41] While Fuller is concerned with too little procedural legality, Hart seems to acknowledge that a rigid, narrow, and exclusive adherence to the procedural law of a legal system would be

34. *See* Fuller, The Morality of Law, 96–106.

35. *Id.* at 96–97.

36. H. L. A. Hart, *Book Review of The Morality and the Law by Lon L. Fuller*, 78 Harv. L. Rev. 1281, 1284 (1965).

37. Hart, The Concept of Law, 202.

38. H. L. A. Hart, *Positivism and the Separation of Law and Morals*, 71 Harv. L. Rev. 593, 623–24 (1958).

39. *Id.* at 624.

40. *Id.*

41. *Id.*

too much legality.[42] I have already defined such pedantic scrupulosity as a form of legalism. Judith Shklar critiques this kind of "extreme legalism" as a reduction of the morality of the law to mere rule following.[43] Assuming that procedural justice cannot ultimately ensure the fundamental fairness of the rule of law, the question arises about the substantive authority of the law.

2. Substantive Justice According to Jürgen Habermas, neither coercion, nor command, nor procedural justice suffices to guarantee the rule of law.[44] In a democratic society, Habermas observes that the "legitimacy" and "binding force" of the rule of law depends on its power to communicate that it derives from the legitimate political process.[45] He contends that the rule of law requires "rational motives for obeying the law," which make it "possible for everyone to obey the legal norm on the basis of insight."[46] The Catholic Church is not a democracy, but the motives for obeying canon law are natural and supernatural. On a natural level, one perceives the importance of the rule of law for the good of individuals and the community. A member of the Catholic Church has the right to anticipate a fundamental and just order in the ecclesiastical community. On the supernatural level, grace enhances this natural insight. One freely chooses to be a member of the church as a result of faith and the desire for eternal salvation. This kind of ultimate insight suggests that canon law's power to bind stems not simply from its reality as an order of reason but also as an order of faith. The natural and supernatural *intellectus* or substantive inner meaning of canon law transcends coercion, command, and process. As the earlier examples of the bishop and novice illustrate, the rule of law itself is a substantive rational motive that affords insight to persons to obey canon law.

Insight about the rule of law stems from a communal context. The rule of law is justified on the basis of the anthropological reality that the human person is a social being whose interactions with other persons, communities, and society necessitate a system of ordered justice. The rule of law presumes a society of persons who value a set of norms that are designed to achieve fundamental fairness. The Thomistic description requires that law be given to a receptive community in order to advance the common good. On the natural level, the rule of law aims to facilitate those conditions in which persons experience optimal opportunities

---

42. *See* Leslie Green, *Positivism and Inseparability of Law and Morals,* 83 N. Y. U. L. Rev. 1035, 1057 (2008).

43. *See* Judith N. Shklar, Legalism: Law, Morals, and Political Trials 122 (Harvard University Press 1964). *But see* Neil MacCormick, *The Ethics of Legalism,* 2 Ratio Juris 184, 188–89 (1989), which advocates a restatement of Fuller's description of the rule of law as "ethical legalism".

44. *See* Jürgen Habermas, Beyond Facts and Norms 189 (William Rehg trans., MIT Press 1996).

45. Jürgen Habermas, *Three Normative Models of Democracy, in* 1 Constellation 8 (1994).

46. Habermas, Beyond Facts and Norms 121.

for participation, solidarity, and membership in the community. On the supernatural level, the rule of law assists in setting the conditions in which the Christian community is "the communion of the Catholic Church on this earth who are joined with Christ in its visible structure by the bonds of the profession of faith, the sacraments, and ecclesiastical government."[47] The believer's insight about the function of the rule of law in facilitating these natural and supernatural ends is nourished within the local, particular, and universal communities of the church.

The theological understanding of office and *sacra potestas* in canon law reinforces the authority of the rule of law. As discussed in Chapter 1, the division of the legislative, executive, and judicial powers of government in canon law exhibits a qualitative difference from the separation doctrine in liberal political theory. The political theory rests on a suspicion of the governing authority. In Raz's understanding, the rule of law requires: independent, transparent and fair hearings; review of governing officials; and limitations on the governing power.[48] The hermeneutic of suspicion attempts to check the concentration of too much government power in one individual or group, the abuse of power for personal gain, and undue limitations on individual liberties. In contrast, the unitary power of governance, vested in the bishop for his diocese and the Roman Pontiff for the universal church, displays trust that the governing power will be exercised in accord with the natural and supernatural ends of canon law.

The hermeneutic of trust, however, does not mean that the governing power in canon law is without limitation. To an extent defined by law, the acts of governance placed by the diocesan bishop are subject to review by Roman Curia on behalf of the Roman Pontiff. The exercise of the bishop's legislative power is not subject to judicial review, but it may not be contrary to the universal law of the church. Hierarchical recourse against the bishop's executive act may be brought to the appropriate Dicastery of the Roman Curia and eventually to the Apostolic Signatura. Appeal from the judicial power that is exercised by the diocesan tribunal may be brought to the Roman Rota and then to the Apostolic Signatura. Recourse directly to the person of the Roman Pontiff is also possible. The bishop, who abuses the governing power or culpably neglects some duty of his office, is liable to penal sanctions as specified in canon law; and in a power that is rarely utilized out of respect for the *communio* of the church, the Roman Pontiff may remove a diocesan bishop from office.[49] While he is bound by natural and divine law, the governing power of the Roman Pontiff is not subject to review.[50] The Pontiff's governing power derives from his primacy as the Successor to

47. Canon 205, *CIC-1983*.

48. *See* Joseph Raz, The Authority of Law, Essays on Law and Morality 216–17 (Clarendon Press of Oxford University 2002).

49. *See* Canon 1389, §§ 1 and 2, *CIC-1983*.

50. *See* Canons 332, §1 and 333, § 3, *CIC-1983*.

Saint Peter, Bishop of Rome, and Vicar of Christ, who is entrusted with a ministry of unity among all the particular churches that comprise the universal church.[51] The theological understanding of the grace of the bishop's office suggests that insight would be offered to the office holder about the function of the rule of law in the life of the church. Although his governing power is not subject to review, the theological understanding is that the grace of office offers the pope superabundant insight about respect for the rule of law. Whether for those who exercise governing power or those who wish to direct their own conscientious actions in accord with it, the theological understanding buttresses the authority of canon law to bind.

3. Unjust Law The moral obligation to obey specific canons that flows from the rule of law raises the question of unjust law. As mentioned in the Introduction, Hart focused on law from an intersystemic expository viewpoint and did not seem particularly concerned about unjust law, while Fuller thought that fidelity to his eight procedural desideratum protected against unjust law. The natural law theorist, John Finnis, asks how injustice in law affects the obligation to obey the law. Given that the legal system of canon law is by and large just, does a particular injustice in canon law impose any obligation on the believer to obey the canonical provision that results in the injustice? Noting that Thomas Aquinas never adopted the slogan that "unjust law is no law," Finnis argues that there may be a "collateral obligation" to obey a specific unjust law in deference to the rule of law.[52] However, Finnis argues that unjust law does not create a moral obligation in precisely the same way that just law does. According to Finnis, "the ruler and his rules" have authority "only because of what is needed if the common good is to be secure and advanced."[53] According to Finnis, "stipulations made for partisan advantage, or (without emergency justification) in excess of legally defined authority, or imposing inequitable burdens on their subjects, or the directing of doing things that should never be done, simply fail, of themselves, to create any moral obligation whatever."[54] In Chapter 1, I discussed the role of canonical equity as a response to various types of injustice in law. The fact that the legislator has incorporated provisions for responding to unjust law through

---

51. *See* Canon 331, *CIC-1983*. Pope John Paul II convened a Synod of Bishops, who met in Rome May 21–24, 2001, in order to discuss the relationship between the Petrine office and the College of Bishops. In Number 44 of *Novo Millennio Ineunte*, the Pontiff stated: "The new century will have to see us more than ever intent on valuing and developing the forums and structures which, in accordance with the Second Vatican Council's major directives, serve to ensure and safeguard communion. How can we forget in the first place those specific services to communion which are the Petrine ministry and, closely related to it, episcopal collegiality?" Ioannes Paulus Pp. II, Litterae Apostiolica, *Novo Millenio Ineunte* (Die 6 mensis ianuarii anno 2001), 44, 93 AAS 266–309 (2001).

52. *See* Finnis, Natural Law and Natural Rights, 364–65.

53. *Id.* at 359.

54. *Id.* at 360.

canonical equity adds to canon law's inner meaning. The incorporation communicates the legislator's intent to respect the dignity of individuals and the common good by protecting against unjust law. The provisions for canonical equity enhance the authority of canon law by deepening the rational motives and insight of the believer who chooses to obey.

4. Indeterminacy of Law Finally, the *intellectus* of canon law may afford a moral foundation that mitigates the force of the indeterminacy claim. As discussed in Chapter 6, the indeterminacy claim stresses the vague meaning of law over its precision and clarity. It holds that law does not provide correct answers to legal questions. It doubts whether the application of abstract rules to specific legal cases yields consistent results.[55] The indeterminacy claim calls into question the very idea of the rule of law. It leads to the conclusion that there are not persuasive reasons which enable like cases to be decided alike. The disagreement among the U.S. bishops about the application of Canon 915 bolsters the indeterminacy claim by suggesting that there is not a correct approach to the law's meaning and application. However, as I suggested in Chapter 6, antinomian and legalistic approaches to canon law, rather than sound canonical and theological reasons, may be more responsible for the confusion over Canon 915 than the law's indeterminacy.

The rise of the indeterminacy claim in Anglo-American legal theory coincides with the positivist approach to law, which calls for the separation of law from moral value. The separation ostensibly avoids the so-called "naturalistic fallacy" in which moral values are derived from facts.[56] Legal positivism takes an intersystemic viewpoint which is not an attempt to eliminate moral consideration from human deliberation. As throughout this comparative study, my point here is not to offer a general criticism of legal positivism. Rather, this dominant aspect of Anglo-American legal theory functions as a counter example with regard to canon law and indeterminacy. The separation of law from moral value tends to support the perception of law's indeterminacy. If positive law is not grounded in immutable moral principles, doubt may be raised about the authority of the law. One might conclude that answers to legal questions are based on the relative circumstances of political, economic, and social facts rather than moral principles. The perception that legal decisions stem from political, economic, and social power rather than moral principle is not likely to afford respect for law so that persons are disposed to obey it. From the natural law perspective, the split

55. Ronald Dworkin's rejection of the indeterminacy claim in favor of the position that there are right answers to legal questions is based in no small part on his argument that, from the perspective of reason, some answers to legal questions are more correct than others. *See* Ronald Dworkin, *A Reply by Ronald Dworkin, in* RONALD DWORKIN AND CONTEMPORARY JURISPRUDENCE 275–78 (M. Chen ed., Duckworth 1984).

56. *See* HILARY PUTNAM, THE COLLAPSE OF THE FACT/VALUE DICHOTOMY AND OTHER ESSAYS 28–40 (Harvard University Press 2002).

between law and moral value produces a lack of coherence—a coherence the law depends upon for its authority to bind. Finnis argues that legal positivism is "incoherent" because it "has nothing to say to officials or private citizens who want to judge whether, when, and why the authority and obligatoriness claimed and enforced by those who are acting as officials of a legal system, and by their directives, are indeed authoritative reasons for their own conscientious action."[57] As it is firmly grounded in natural and supernatural truths, canon law does not suffer from this incoherence. Rather than bolster the indeterminacy claim, the coherence of canon law offers insight to the believer about deference to the law's authority.

In sum, the descriptive aspect of this comparative study suggests that canon law meets the requirements for law, a system of law, and the rule of law. As it contains only a minimum of penal sanctions, canon law's authority is not primarily derived from coercive power. In accord with the early legal positivists' understanding, canon law reflects the will of the sovereign governing power vested in the pope and the bishops. The theological understanding of sacred power enhances the duty of obedience the believer owes to canon law. However, the command theory is neither the sole nor best explanation of canon law's authority. Canon law's authority ultimately rests on the insight of the believer who voluntarily obeys canon law because it functions as the rule of law that advances natural and supernatural ends. At the same time, the study's prescriptive function suggests that challenges also remain. Canon law fulfills Hart's requirements of a developed system of law as it exhibits not just primary rules but also the secondary rules of recognition, change, and adjudication. The examples of clergy sexual abuse, the ownership of church property, and the application of Canon 915 indicate that antinomian and legalism sometimes diminish the adherence of ecclesiastical officials in abiding by the secondary rules. On the basis of the three examples, the secondary rules for procedural justice seem particularly susceptible to antinomian and legalistic maladies. When the rule of law is weakened, serious injury results to individuals and the common good. Antinomianism and legalism may thus obscure the individual and communal perceptions of the *intellectus* of canon law, and threaten the insight that affords the basis for canon law's authority. Despite the issues raised by antinomianism and legalism, the *intellectus* of canon law remains grounded in natural and supernatural truth which affords a metaphysical basis for the rule of law.

IV. CONCLUSION

Canon law attempts to fulfill its natural requirements even as it integrates these with the supernatural requirements of faith. Stephan Kuttner observed that the

---

57. *See* Finnis, *Propter Honoris Respectum: On the Incoherence of Legal Positivism*, 1611.

medieval canonists developed a legal methodology that brings into harmony "all the tensions and dissonances, all the apparent incompatibilities of the spiritual and the temporal, the supernatural and the natural."[58] Although canon law is neither sacred scripture nor a constitution, the medieval legacy serves as a reminder that canon law fulfills a vital function in the church. Antinomianism so privileges the spiritual that it discounts the importance of the rule of law. Legalism forsakes the theological, and places the law above the supernatural destiny of the human person. A balanced approach to canon law recognizes its auxiliary but vital function as a bridge between theology and practical action. Despite the probability that antinomianism and legalism are likely to pose continuing problems, canon law remains a system of religious law that serves as the rule of law in facilitating its natural and supernatural ends.

58. Stephan Kuttner, Harmony from Dissonance: An Interpretation of Medieval Canon Law 50 (The Archabbey Press 1960).

BIBLIOGRAPHY

1. SACRED SCRIPTURE

HOLY BIBLE, REVISED STANDARD VERSION, CATHOLIC EDITION, prepared by the Catholic Biblical Association of Great Britain (Oxford University Press 1966).
NOVUM TESTAMENTUM GRAECE ET LATINE. NOVAM VULGATUM BIBLIORUM SACRORUM EDITIONEM SECUTI APPARATIBUS TITULISQUE ADDITIS EDIDERUNT KURT ALAND ET BARBARA ALAND UNA CUM INSTITUTO STUDIORUM TEXTUS NOVI TESTAMENTI MONASTERIENSI (WESTPHALIA) (Deutsche Bibelgesellschaft 1984).

2. CHURCH DOCUMENTS

A. Collections

DECRETUM D. GREGORII PAPAE IX, COMPILATIO, *in* 2 CORPUS IURIS CANONICI (A. Frieburg ed., Editio lipsiensis seconda, Akademische Druck-u. Verlagsanstalt 1959).
DECRETUM MAGISTRI GRATIANI (CONCORDIA DISCORDANTIUM CANONUM), *in* 1 CORPUS IURIS CANONICI (A. Frieburg, ed., Editio lipsiensis seconda, Akademische Druck-u.Verlagsanstalt 1959).
DENZINGER, HENRICUS J., ENCHIRIDION SYMBOLORUM, DEFINITIONUM ET DECLARATIONUM DE REBUS FIDEI ET MORUM (Herder 1932). English translation from ENCHIRIDION SYMBOLORUM (13th ed.) by Roy J. Deferrari, THE SOURCES OF CATHOLIC DOGMA (Loreto Publications 2001).
GASPARRI, PETRUS CARD., IUSTINIANUS CARD. SERÉDI EDS., CODICIS IURIS CANONICI FONTES (Typis Polyglottis Vaticanis 1923–1939).
MIGNE, J. P., PATROLOGIAE CURSUS COMPLETUS, SERIES GRAECA (1857–1866).
MIGNE, J. P., PATROLOGIAE CURSUS COMPLETUS, SERIES LATINA (1844–1855).
TANNER, NORMAN P., S.J., DECREES OF THE ECUMENICAL COUNCILS (Sheed & Ward and Georgetown University Press 1990).

B. Patristic Sources

Ambrose, *Expositionis in Evangelium secundum Lucam Libri X*, 7, 124.15 PL 1819.
Ambrose, *In Psalmum CXVIII Expositio*, 8, 22.15 PL 1372.
Augustine of Hippo, *De Baptismo Contra Donatistas*, IV, 23, 30.43 PL 170, 174.
Augustine of Hippo, *De Moribus Ecclesiae Catholicae, et De Moribus Manichaeorum Libri II*,I, 35.32 PL 1342–44.
Augustine of Hippo, *Epistola 105*, 2, 3f. 33 PL 396–97.
Augustine of Hippo, *Epistola 247*, 33 PL 1062–64.
Augustine of Hippo, *Enarrationes in Psalmos*, 38, 12.38 PL 327.
Augustine of Hippo, *In Ioannis Evangelium Tractatus XXVI*, 26, 13.35 PL 1612–13.
Augustine of Hippo, *In Ioannis Evangelium Tractatus CXXIV*, 6, 25–26.35 PL 1436–37.
Augustine of Hippo, *Sermo 227, In die Paschae, IV, Ad Infantes, de Sacramentis*, 38 PL 1099–1101.

Burchard, Bishop of Worms, Decretorum, 140 PL 539–1058.
Cassian, John, *De Coenobiorum Institutis*, 2, 5.49 PL 84–86.
Chrysostom, John, *Homiliae in Epistolam primam ad Timotheum*, 12, 4.62 (11) PG 562–63.
Cyprian of Carthage, *Epistolae 5, 6, 7, 10–19*, 4 PL 235–46, 259–81.
Cyprian of Carthage, *Epistolae 59–61*, 4 PL 369–74.
Irenaeus, *Adversus Haereses Libri Quinque*, 4, 30, 1. 7 PG 1065.
Ivo, Bishop of Chartes, *Epistola XXXV*, 162 PL 46–47.
Possidius, *Vita S. Augustini Episcopi*, 19.32 PL 50.

C. Magisterial (Chronologically Ordered)

Concilium Oecumenicum Chalcedonensis, Canon 9, 1 Tanner 91, & *Canon* 17, 1 Tanner 17.
Council of Trent (April 8, 1546), no. 783. Denzinger, The Sources of Catholic Dogma, 244.
Council of Trent, Session 13, Chap. 2 (October 11, 1551), 2 Tanner 693.
Rituale Romanum, tit. IV, c.1, *De sanctissimo Eucharistiae*, n. 8, (1614), in 7 Codicis Iuris Canonici Fontes 143, n. 4598.
Benedictus Pp. XIV, Ex omnibus (Die 16 mensis octobris anno 1756), § 3f, in 2 Codicis Iuris Canonici Fontes n. 441.
Concilia Provincialia Baltimori habita ab anno 1829 usque ad annum 1849 (Joannem Murphy et Socium 1851).
Coll. Propaganda Fide, n. 1116 (Die 1 m. aug. a. 1855), *in* 8 Codicis Iuris Canonici Fontes 546, n. 6426.
Acta et Decreta Concilii Plenarii Baltimorensis Tertii (Joannis Murphy et Sociorum 1886).
Leo Pp. XIII, Litterae Encyclicae, *Rerum Novarum* (Dei 15 mensis maii anno 1891), 10–17, *in* 11 Leonis XIII P.M. Acta 97–144 (Editrice Vaticana 1892).
Pius Pp. X, Motu Proprio, *Arduum sane munus* (Die 18 mensis decembris anno 1903), 37 ASS 549–51 (1903–1904).
Pius Pp. X, Constitutio Apostolica de Romana Curia, *Sapienti Consilio* (Die 29 mensis iunii anno 1908), 1 AAS 7–35 (1909).
Codex Iuris Canonici Pii X Pontificis Maximi iussu digestus Benedicti Papae XV auctoritatepromulgatus (Die 27 mensis maii aanno 1917), 9 (II) AAS 3–521 (1917).
Pontificia Commissio ad Codicis Canones Authentice Interpretandos: Acta Officiorum (Die 22 mensis maii anno 1923), 16 AAS 251 (1924).
Pius Pp. XI, Litterae Encyclicae, *Quas primas* (Die 11 mensis decembris anno 1925), 17 AAS 599–610 (1925).
Pius Pp. XI, Litterae Encyclicae, *Quadragesimo anno* (Die 15 mensis maii anno 1931), 23 AAS 177–228 (1931).
Pius Pp. XI, Constitutio Apostolica, *Ad incrementum decoris* (Die 15 mensis augusti anno 1934), 26 AAS 517–20 (1934).
Sacra Congregatio De Disciplina Sacramentorum, Instructio, *Provida Mater* (Die 1 mensis iulliianno 1932), 28 AAS 313–72 (1936).
Pius Pp. XII, *Allocutio adstantibus Praelatis Auditoribus ceterisque Officialibus et Administris Tribunalis Sacrae Romanae Rotae necnon eiusdem Tribunalis Advocatis et Procuratoribus* (Dei 1 mensis oct. anno 1942), 34 AAS 338–43 (1942).
Pius Pp. XII, *Litterae Encyclicae, Mystici Corporis Christi* (Die 29 mensis iunii anno 1943), 35 AAS 191–248 (1943).
Pius Pp. XII, Constitutio Apostolica, *Provida Mater Ecclesia* (Die 2 mensis febraurii anno 1947), 39 AAS 114–24 (1947).

Ioannes Pp. XXIII, *Sollemnis Allocutio ad Em. mos Patres Cardinales in Urbe praesenteshabita in coenobio Monachorum Benedictinorum ad S. Pauli extra Moenia, post Missarum solemnia, quibus Beatissimus Pater in Patriarchiali Basilica Ostiensiinterfuerat* (Die 25 mensis ianuarii anno 1959), 51 AAS 65–69 (1959).

Suprema Sacra Congregatio Sancti Officii, Instructio de Modo Procedendi in Causis Sollicitationis, *Crimen sollicitationis* (Die 16 mensis martii anno 1962). This documentwas never officially published by the Holy See. A copy of the original Latin version isavailable at http://www.cbsnews.com/htdocs/pdfcrimenlatinfull.pdf.

Paulus Pp. VI, *Ad E. mos Patres Cardinales et ad Consultores Pontificii Consilii Codici Iurs Canonici recognoscendo* (Die 20 mensis novembris anno 1965), 57 AAS 985–89 (1965).

Nota Explicativa Praevia, Ex Actis Ss. Oecumenici Concilii Vaticani II, Facta ab Exc. mo. Secretario Generali Ss. Concilii in Congregatione Generali (Die 16 mensis novembrisanno 1964), 57 AAS 72–75 (1965).

Sacrosanctum Concilium Oecumenicum Vaticanum II, Constitutio Dogmatica de Ecclesia, *Lumen Gentium* (Die 21 mensis novembris anno 1964), 57 AAS 5–89 (1965).

Sacrosanctum Concilium Oecumenicum Vaticanum II, Decretum De Pastorali Episcoporum Munere in Ecclesia, *Christus Dominus* (Die 28 mensis octobris anno 1965), 58 AAS 673–96 (1966).

Sacrosanctum Concilium Oecumenicum Vaticanum II, Constitutio Dogmatica de Divina Revelatione, *Dei Verbum* (Die 18 mensis novembris anno 1965), 58 AAS 817–35 (1966).

Sacrosanctum Concilium Oecumenicum Vaticanum II, Declaratio De Libertate Religiosa, *Dignitatis Humanae* (Die 7 mensis decembris anno 1965), 58 AAS 929–46 (1966).

Sacrosanctum Concilium Oecumenicum Vaticanum II, Decretum De Activitate Missionali Ecclesiae, *Ad Gentes* (Die 7 mensis decembris anno 1965), 58 AAS 947–90 (1966).

Sacrosanctum Concilium Oecumenicum Vaticanum II, Decretum De Presbyterorum Ministerioet Vita, *Presbyterorum Ordinis* (Die 7 mensis decembris anno 1965), 58 AAS 991–1024 (1966).

Sacrosanctum Concilium Oecumenicum Vaticanum II, Constitutio pastoralis de ecclesia inmundo huius temporis, *Gaudium et Spes* (Die 7 mensis decembris anno 1965), 58 AAS1025–1120 (1966).

Paulus Pp. VI, Constitutio Apostolica de Romana Curia, *Regimini Ecclesiae Universae* (Die 15 mensis augusti anno 1967), 59 AAS 885–928 (1967).

Pontificia Commissio Codici Iuris Canonici Recognoscendo, *Acta Commissionis: 1. Principiaquae Codicis Iuris Canonici recognitionem dirigant, 1 Communicationes* 77–88 (1969).

Paulus Pp. VI, *Ad Praelotos Auditores et Officiales Tribunales Sacrae Romanae Rotae* (Die 29 mensis ianuarii anno 1970), 62 AAS 111–18 (1970).

Paulus Pp. VI, Epistola Apostolica, *Octogesima adveniens* (Die 14 mensis maii anno 1971), 63 AAS 401–41 (1971).

Paulus Pp. VI, *Allocutiones: Ad Praelatos et Officiales Tribunalis Sacrae Romanae Rotae a Beatissimo Patre novo litibus iudicandis ineunte anno coram admissos, "Aequitas Canonica"* (Die 8 m. februarii a. 1973), 65 AAS 95–103 (1973).

Pontificia Commissio Codici Iuris Canonici Recognoscendo, *Schema canonum de modoprocedendi pro tutela iurium seu de processibus*, 8 Communicationes 183–200 (1976).

Pontificia Commissio Codici Iuris Canonici Recognoscendo, *Schema Codicis Iuris Canonici* (Libreria Editrice Vaticana 1980).

Pontificia Commissio Codici Iuris Canonici Recognoscendo, *Relatio complectens synthesim animadversionum ab Em. mis atque Exc. mis Patribus Commissionis ad ultimum schema Codicis Iuris Canonici Exhibitarum, cum responsionibus a Secretaria et Consultoribusdatis* (Typis Polyglottis Vaticanis 1981).

Ioannnes Paulus Pp. II, *Ad eos qui plenario coetui Pontificiae Commissionis Codici IurisCanonici recognoscendo interfuere admissos* (Die 29 mensis octobris anno 1981), 73 AAS 720–24 (1981).

Codex Iuris Canonici auctoritate Ioannis Pauli Pp. II promulgatus (Die 25 mensis ianuarii anno 1983), 75 (II) AAS 1–317 (1983).

Ioannes Paulus Pp. II, Constitutio Apostolica, *Sacrae Disciplinae Leges* (Die 25 mensis ianuarii anno 1983), 75 (II) AAS vii–xiv (1983).

Ioannes Paulus Pp. II, *Il Diritto inserisce il Concilio nella nostra vita*, 15 Communicationes 128–29 (1983).

National Conference of Catholic Bishops, *Canonical Delicts Involving Sexual Misconduct and Dismissal from the Clerical State* (United States Catholic Conference 1983).

Pontificia Commissio Codici Iuris Canonici Authentice Interpretando, *Responsiones adproposita dubia*, 16 Communicationes 52–90 (1984).

Ioannes Paulus Pp. II, Litterae Encyclicae, *Sollicitudo Rei Socialis* (Die 30 mensis decembrisanno 1987), 80 AAS 513–86 (1988).

Ioannes Paulus Pp. II, Allocutiones, *Ad Romanae Rotae Auditores simul cum officialibus et advocatis coram admissos, anno forensi ineunte* (Die 25 mensis ianuarii anno 1988), 80 AAS 1178–81 (1988).

Ioannes Paulus Pp. II, Constitutio Apostolica De Curia Romana, *Pastor Bonus* (Die 28 mensis iunii anno1988), 80 AAS 842–912 (1988).

Ioannes Paulus Pp. II, Adhoratio Apostolica, *Chistifideles laici* (Die 30 mensis decembris anno 1988), 42 AAS 81 (1989).

Codex Canonum Orientalium auctoritate Ioannis Pauli Pp. II promulgatus (Die 18 mensis octobris anno 1990), 82 AAS 1033–1363 (1990).

Ioannes Paulus Pp. II, Litterae Encyclicae de perenni vi mandati missionalis, *Redemptoris Missio* (Die 8 mensis decembris anno 1990), 83 AAS 249–340 (1991).

Ioannes Paulus Pp. II, Litterae Encyclicae, *Centesimus Annus* (Die 15 mensis maii anno 1991), 83 AAS 793–887 (1991).

Pope John Paul II, *Message for the 1991 World Day of Peace: "If you want peace, respect the conscience of every person."* 83 AAS 414–15 (1991).

Regolamento Generale della Curia Romana (Die 4 mensis februarii anno 1992), 82 AAS 202–67 (1992).

Congregatio pro Doctrina Fidei, *Litterae ad Catholicae Ecclesiae Episcopos de aliquibus aspectibus Ecclesiae prout est Communio* .(Die 28 mensis maii anno 1992), 85 AAS 838–50 (1993).

John Paul II, *Clergy Sexual Misconduct, Vatican–U.S. Bishops' Committee to Study Applying Canonical Norms*, 23 Origins 102–03 (July 1, 1993).

Ioannes Paulus Pp. II, Litterae Encyclicae, *Veritatis Splendor* (Die 6 mensis augusti anno 1993), 85 AAS 1133–1228 (1993).

Congregatio Pro Doctrina Fidei, *Epistola ad Catholicae Ecclesiae Episcopos De Receptione Communionis Eucharisticae a Fidelibus Qui Post Divortium Novas Inierunt Nuptias* (Die 14 mensis septembris anno 1994), 86 AAS 974–79 (1994).

Ioannes Paulus Pp. II, Litterae Encyclicae, *Evangelium vitae* (Die 25 mensis martii anno 1995), 87 AAS 401–522 (1995).

Ioannes Paulus Pp. II, Constitutio Apostolica, *Universi Dominici Gregis* (Die 22 mensis februarii anno 1996), 88 AAS 305–42 (1996).

CATECHISM OF THE CATHOLIC CHURCH (2nd ed. Liberia Editrice Vaticana 1997).
Ioannes Paulus Pp. II, Motu Proprio, *Ad tuendam fidem* (Die 1 mensis iulii anno 1998), 90 AAS 457–61 (1998).
Pontifical Council for Legislative Texts, Declaration II, *Concerning the Admission to Holy Communion of the Faithful Who Are Divorced and Remarried,* June 24, 2000, 30 ORIGINS 174–75 (Aug. 17, 2000).
Ioannes Paulus Pp. II, Litterae Apostolicae, *Novo Millenio Ineunte* (Die 6 mensis ianuarii anno 2001), 93 AAS 266–309 (2001).
Congregatio pro Doctrina Fidei, *De delictis gravioribus eidem Congregationi pro Doctrina Fidei reservatis* (Die 18 mensis maii anno 2001), 93 AAS 785, 786–87 (2001).
Essential Norms for Diocesan/Eparchial Policies Dealing with Allegations of Sexual Abuse of Minors by Priests, Deacons, or Other Church Personnel: Pending "Recognitio," 32 ORIGINS 107–08 (June 27, 2002).
Charter for the Protection of Children and Young People, 32 ORIGINS 102–06 (June 27, 2002).
Letter of the Cardinal Prefect of the Congregation for Bishops, 32 ORIGINS 341 and 343 (Oct. 31, 2002).
Congregation for the Doctrine of the Faith, *Doctrinal Note on Some Questions Regarding the Participation of Catholics in Political Life,* November 24, 2002, 32 ORIGINS 37, 539–41 (Jan. 30, 2003).
Ioannes Paulus Pp. II, Litterae Encyclicae, *Ecclesia de Eucharistia* (Die 17 mensis aprilis anno 2003), 95 AAS 433–75 (2003).
Most Reverend Raymond L. Burke, *Pastoral Letter to Christ's Faithful of the Diocese of La Crosse, On the Dignity of Human Life and Civic Responsibility* (Diocese of La Crosse 2003).
RITUALE ROMANUM, EDITIO PRINCEPS (Malino Sodi & Juan Javier Flores Arcas eds., Liberia Editrice Vaticana 2004).
Congregatio de Culto Divino et Disciplina Sacramentorum, Instructio, *Redemptionis sacramentum, De quibusdam observandis et vitandis circa Sanctissimam Eucharistiam* (Die 25 mensis martii anno 2004), 96 AAS 549–601 (2004).
Congregation for the Doctrine of the Faith, *Vatican, U.S. Bishops: On Catholics in Political Life (Statement of Six Principles for the Application of Canon 915),* 29 ORIGINS 133–34 (July 29, 2004).
Dario Cardinal Castrillon, *Letter to United States Bishops Concerning the Assets of Merged Parishes,* 6 ORIGINS 190 (Aug. 31, 2006).
Benedictus Pp. XVI, Litterae Apostolicae Motu Proprio Datae, *De Aliquibus Mutationibus in Normis De Electione Romani Pontificis* (Die 11 mensis iunii anno 2007), 99 AAS 776–81 (2007).
Benedictus Pp. XVI, Motu Proprio, *Summorum Pontificum* (Die 7 mensis iulii anno 2007), 99 AAS795–99 (2007).
Congregatio De Institutione Catholica (*De Seminariis Atque Studiorum Institutis*) (Die 15 mensis decembris anno 2008), Prot No. 1009/2002.

3. BOOKS

ACKROYD, PETER, THE LIFE OF THOMAS MORE (Nan A. Talese 1998).
ALBERIGO, GIUSEPPE & JOSEPH A. KOMANCHAK, HISTORY OF VATICAN II (Orbis Books 1995).
AMARI, EMERICO, CRITICA DI UNA SCIENCIA DELLE LEGISLATIONI COMPARATE (Tip. de R. I. de' Sordo-Muti 1857).

Amiot, François, Les Idées Maîtresses de Saint-Paul (Les Éditions du Cerf 1959).
Aquinas, Thomas, Sancti Thomae Aquinatis: Opera Omnia, Leo XII, P.M. (Ex Typographia Polyglota S. C. De Propaganda Fide, 1882). English translation by the Fathers of the English Dominican Province (Christian Classics 1981).
Aristotle, The Politics, *in* The Complete Works of Aristotle: The Revised Oxford Translation (Jonathan Barnes ed., Princeton University Press 1984).
Austin, John, The Province of Jurisprudence Determined (W. E. Rumble ed., Cambridge University Press 1995).
Bacon, Francis, De dignitate et augmentis scientiarum, *in* 2 The Works of Francis Bacon (James Spedding, Robert L. Ellis, & Douglas D. Heath eds., Herd and Houghton 1869).
Balthasar, Hans Urs von, The Christian State of Life (Sister Mary Frances McCarthy trans., Ignatius Press 1983).
Balthasar, Hans Urs von, A Theological Anthropology (Sheed & Ward 1967).
Barrett, C. K., A Critical and Exegetical Commentary on the Acts of the Apostles,International Critical Commentary (T & T Clark 1994).
Barrett, John D. M., A Comparative Study of the Councils of Baltimore and the Codeof Canon Law (The Catholic University of America 1932).
Bellomo, Malino, The Common Legal Past of Europe (Lydia G. Cochrane trans.,Catholic University Press 1995).
Berman, Harold, Law and Revolution: The Formation of the Western Legal Tradition (Harvard University Press 1983).
Berman, Harold, Law and Revolution II: The Impact of the Protestant Reformation on the Western Legal Tradition (Bleknap Press of Harvard University 2003).
Bix, Brian H., A Dictionary of Legal Theory (Oxford University Press 2004).
Bix, Brian, Jurisprudence: Theory and Content (3rd ed. Carolina Academic Press 2004).
Boff, Leonardo, Church: Charism and Power (John W. Diercksmeier, trans., Crossroad 1986).
Bonaventure, Doctoris Seraphici S. Bonaventurae opera omnia, edita studio et cura pp. Collegii a S. Bonaventura (Ex Typographia Collegii S. Bonaventurae 1882–1889).
Bonhoeffer, Dietrich, Letter and Papers from Prison (Eberhard Bethge ed.Touchstone of Simon & Schuster 1997).
Boston Globe Investigative Staff, Betrayal, The Crisis in the Catholic Church (Little Brown Back Bay Books 2003).
Bouyer, Louis, L'Église de Dieu (Cerf 1970).
Brooke, Rosalind B., Early Franciscan Government, Elias to Bonaventure (Cambridge University Press 1959).
Brown, Peter, Augustine of Hippo (University of California Press 1969).
Brown, Raymond E., Priest and Bishop, Biblical reflections (Paulist 1970).
Bruce, F. F., The Book of the Acts, Revised Edition (Eerdmans Publishing 1988).
Bruce, F. F., Commentary on the Book of Acts, *in* The New International Commentary of the New Testament (F. F. Bruce ed., Eerdmans Publishing 1975).
Brundage, James A., Medieval Canon Law (The Medieval World) (Longman 1995).
Brundage, James A., The Medieval Origins of the Legal profession, Canonists, Civilians, and Courts (University of Chicago Press 2008).

BUCKLAND, W. W., A TEXT-BOOK OF ROMAN LAW FROM AUGUSTUS TO JUSTINIAN (Peter Steinrev., 3rd ed. University of Cambridge Press 1966).

BURR, DAVID, OLIVI AND FRANCISCAN POVERTY: THE ORIGINS OF THE USUS PAUPER CONTROVERSY (University of Pennsylvania Press 1989).

BURR, DAVID, THE SPIRITUAL FRANCISCANS, FROM PROTEST TO PERSECUTION IN THE CENTURYAFTER SAINT FRANCIS (Pennsylvania State University Press 2001).

CAFARDI, NICHOLAS P., BEFORE DALLAS, THE U.S. BISHOPS' RESPONSE TO CLERGY SEXUALABUSEOF CHILDREN (Paulist Press 2008).

CAPPELLO, FELIX M., S.J., DE CURIA ROMANA IUXTA REFORMATIONEM A PIO X (FridericusPustet 1911).

CHADWICK, HENRY, THE EARLY CHURCH (Penguin Books 1967).

CHODOROW, STANLEY, CHRISTIAN POLITICAL THEORY AND CHURCH POLITICS IN THE MID-TWELFTH CENTURY: THE ECCLESIOLOGY OF GRATIAN'S DECRETUM (University of California Press 1972).

CICOGNANI, AMLETO GIOVANI, CANON LAW (2nd ed. rev. Newman Bookshop 1934).

COCCOPALMERIO, FRANCESCO, DE PAROECIA. Roma: Editrice Pontificia (Università Gregoriana, 1991).

COCHINI, CHRISTIAN, S.J. THE APOSTOLIC ORIGINS OF PRIESTLY CELIBACY (Ignatius Press 1990).

CONGAR, YVES, I BELIEVE IN THE HOLY SPIRIT (David Smith trans., Seabury Press 1983).

CORECCO, EUGENIO, THE THEOLOGY OF CANON LAW: A METHODOLOGICAL QUESTION (Francesco Turvasi trans., Duquense University Press 1992).

CORECCO, EUGENIO, CANON LAW AND COMMUNIO, WRITINGS ON THE CONSTITUTIONAL LAW OF THE CHURCH (Graziano Borgonovo and Arturo Cattaneo, eds., Liberia Editice Vaticana 1999).

CORPUS IURIS CIVILIS (Paul Krueger, Theodor Mommsen, Rodolf Schoell, & Wilhelm Kroll eds., 1954–1959).

CORTESE, ENNINO, IL DIRITTO NELLA STORIA MEDIEVALE, 1: L'ALTO MEDIOEVO, 2: IL BASSO MEDIOEVO (Il Cingo Galileo Galilei 1995).

CURRY, THOMAS J., FAREWELL TO CHRISTENDOM: THE FUTURE OF CHURCH AND STATE IN AMERICA (Oxford University Press 2001).

CUSS, DOMINIQUE, IMPERIAL CULT AND HONORARY TERMS IN THE NEW TESTAMENT (University Press 1974).

DAWSON, JOHN P., THE ORACLES OF LAW (University of Michigan Press 1968).

DE LUBAC, HENRI., THE MOTHERHOOD OF THE CHURCH (Sergia Englund trans., Ignatius Press 1982).

DENZINGER, HEINRICH, THE SOURCES OF CATHOLIC DOGMA, translated by Roy J. Deferrari from ENCHIRIDION SYMBOLORUM (13th ed. Loreto Publications 2001).

DERRETT, J. DUNCAN M., LAW IN THE NEW TESTAMENT (Darton, Longmann, & Todd 1970).

DIGNAN, PATRICK J., A HISTORY OF THE LEGAL IN-CORPORATION OF CATHOLIC CHURCH PROPERTY IN THE UNITED STATES (1784–1932) (Catholic University of America 1933).

DOYLE, THOMAS P., A. W. R. SIPE, & PATRICK J. WALL, SEX, PRIESTS, AND SECRET CODES (Volt Press .2006).

DUCHESNE, LOUIS, EARLY HISTORY OF THE CHRISTIAN CHURCH FROM ITS FOUNDING TO THE END OF THE FIFTH CENTURY (John Murray 1947).

DULLES, AVERY, MODELS OF THE CHURCH, A CRITICAL ASSESSMENT OF THE CHURCH IN ALL ITS ASPECTS (Doubleday 1974).

DWORKIN, RONALD, LAW'S EMPIRE (Belknap Press of Harvard University 2001).

Dworkin, Ronald, Taking Rights Seriously (Harvard University Press 1978).

Endicott, Timothy A. O., Vagueness in Law (Oxford University Press 2000).

Erdö, Peter, Storia della scienza del diritto canonico: Una introduzione (Editrice Pontificia Università Gregoriana 2000).

Fenet, P. Antoine, Recueil complet de travaux préparatoires du Code civil (Dépot, rue Saint-André-des-Arcs 1827).

Ferme, Brian E., Introduzione alla storia del diritto canonico (Pontificia Università Lateranense 1998).

Findlay, Stephen W., Canonical Norms Governing the Deposition and Degradation of Clerics: A Historical Synopsis and Commentary (The Catholic University of America 1941).

Finkelhor, David, Child Sexual Abuse: New Theory and Research (Free Press 1984).

Finnis, John, Aquinas: Moral, Political, and Legal Theory (Oxford University Press 1998).

Finnis, John, Natural Law and Natural Rights (Clarendon Press of Oxford University 1980).

Foakes-Jackson, F. J., The Acts of the Apostles (Hodder and Stoughton 1960).

Friedrich, Carl J., Transcendent Justice: The Religious Dimension of Constitutionalism (Duke University Press 1964).

Fuller, Lon L., The Morality of Law (Yale University Press 1967).

Gaudé, L., Theologia Moralis (Typographia Vaticana 1905–1912).

Gaudemet, Jean, L'Eglise dans L'Empire Romain: IVe–Ve Siècles (Sirey 1990).

Gaudemet, Jean, Sources du droit de l'église en occident du IIe au VIIe siècle (Les Editions du Cerf 1985).

Gaudemet, Jean, Sources du droit de l'église en occident du VIIIe au XXe siècle: Repères canoniques, sources occidentales (Les Editions du Cerf 1993).

Ghirlanda, Gianfranco, S.J., Il diritto nella Chiesa mistero di comunione (EditricePaoline e Roma: Editrice Pontificia Università Gregoriana 1990).

Glendon, Mary Ann, Abortion and Divorce in Western Law, American Failures, European Challenges (Harvard University Press 1987).

A Greek-English Lexicon of the New Testament and Other Early Christian Literature (Frederick W. Danker ed., 3rd ed. University of Chicago Press 2000).

Grisez, Germain, Difficult Moral Questions: The way of the Lord Jesus (FranciscanPress 1999).

Grosheide, F. W., Commentary on the First Epistle to the Corinthians, *in* The New International Commentary of the New Testament (Ned B. Stonehouse & F. F.Bruce eds., Eerdmans Publishing 1974).

Grotius, Hugo., De iure belli ac pacis libri tres, in quibus ius naturae gentium, item iuris publici praecipua explicantur (H. Milford ed., Clarendon Press, 1925).

Guilday, Peter, A History of the Councils of Baltimore, 1791–1884 (Arno Press 1969).

Habermas, Jürgen, Beyond Facts and Norms (William Rehg trans., MIT Press 1996).

Haenchen, Ernst, The Acts of the Apostles: A Commentary (Westminster Press 1971).

Hamburger, Philip, Separation of Church and State (Harvard University Press 2002).

Harnack, Adolf von, The Constitution and Law of the Church in the First Two Centuries (Williams & Norgate 1910).

Hart, H. L. A., The Concept of Law (Joseph Raz & Penelope Bullock eds., 2nd ed. Clarendon Press of Oxford University 1994).

Hart, H. L. A., Essays in Jurisprudence and Philosophy (Oxford University Clarendon Press 1983).
Hayek, Friedrich A., The Road to Serfdom (G. Routledge & Sons 1944).
Heid, Stefan, Celibacy in the Early Church: The Beginnings of a Discipline of Obligatory Continence for Clerics in East and West (Ignatius Press 2000).
Helmholtz, R. H., The Spirit of Classical Canon Law (University of Georgia Press 1996).
Hertling, Ludwig F. von , Communio: Church and Papacy in Early Christianity (Jared Wicks, S.J. ed., Loyola University Press 1972).
Hobbes, Thomas, De Cive, *in* De Cive: The English Version (Howard Warrender ed., Clarendon Press of Oxford University 1983).
Hobbes, Thomas, Leviathan (J. C. A. Gaskin ed., Oxford University Press 1998).
Holdsworth, Sir William, History of the English Law (Methuen 1938).
Holifield, E. Brooks, God's Ambassadors: A History of the Christian Clergy in America (Wm. B. Eerdmans Publishing Co. 2007).
Hume, David, A Treatise on Human Nature (David Fate Norton & Mary Jane Norton eds., Oxford University Press 2001).
Interpreter's Bible (The) (George A. Buttricks ed., Abingdon-Cokesbury 1952).
Jedin, Hubert & John Dolan, History of the Church (Burns & Oates 1980).
Jenkins, Philip, The New Anti-Catholicism: The Last Acceptable Prejudice (Oxford University Press 2003).
Jenkins, Philip, Pedophiles and Priests: Anatomy of a Contemporary Crisis (Oxford University Press 1996).
Jeremias, Joachim, New Testament Theology: The Proclamation of Jesus (John Bowden trans., Scribner 1971).
John Jay College, 2004 Annual Report on the Implementation of the Charter for the Protection of Children and Young People (United States Conference of Catholic Bishops 2005).
John Jay College, The Nature and Scope of Sexual Abuse of Minors by Catholic Priests and Deacons in the United States (United States Conference of Catholic Bishops 2004).
Jolowicz, Herbert F. & Barry Nicholas., Historical Introduction to the Study of Roman Law (Cambridge University Press 1977).
Jolowicz, Herbert F., Roman Foundations of Modern Law (Oxford University Press 1957).
Jonsen, Albert R. & Stephen Toulmin, The Abuse of Casuistry: A History of Moral Reasoning (University of California Press 1989).
Justinian, Codex., *in* The Civil Law including the Twelve Tablets, the Institutes of Gaius, the Rules of Ulpian, the Opinions of Paulus, the Enactments of Justinian, and the Constitutions of Leo (S. P. Scott ed., Central Trust Co. 1932).
Justinian, Novellae, *in* The Civil Law including the Twelve Tablets, the Institutes of Gaius, the Rules of Ulpian, the Opinions of Paulus, the Enactments of Justinian, and the Constitutions of Leo (S. P. Scott ed., Central Trust Co. .1932).
Kahn-Freund, Otto, Comparative Law as an Academic Subject (Clarendon Press of Oxford University 1965).
Kairys, David, The Politics of Law (Pantheon Books 1982).
Kelsen, Hans, Introduction to the Problems of Legal Theory (B. L.Paulson & S. L. Paulson trans., Clarendon Press of Oxford University 1992).

Kemp, Eric Waldram, An Introduction to Canon Law in the Church of England (Hodder and Stoughton 1967).

Kennedy, Duncan, A Critique of Adjudication {*fin de siècle*} (Harvard University Press 1997).

King, Martin Luther, Jr, I Had a Dream: Writings and Speeches that Changed the World (James Melvin ed., Harper Collins 1992).

Kirk, Kenneth E., Conscience and Its Problems: An Introduction to Casuistry (Westminster John Knox Press 1999).

Knowles, David, O.S.B, The Evolution of Medieval Thought (Helicon Press 1962).

Knox, John, Chapters in the Life of Paul (Douglas R. A. Hare ed., Mercer University Press 1987).

Knox, Wilfred A., Saint Paul and the Church of Jerusalem (University Press 1935).

Kuttner, Stephan, Harmony from Dissonance: An Interpretation of Medieval Canon Law (Archabbey Press 1960).

Kuttner, Stephan, Studies in the History of Medieval Canon Law (Variorum 1990).

Laurent, Charles, The Busy Pastor's Guide to a Resume of Canon Law and Moral Theology (O. Dolphin 1924).

Lawrence, C. H., The Friars, The Impact of the Early Mendicant Movement on Western Society (Longman 1994).

Lebreton, Jules & Jaques Zeiller, The History of the Primitive Church (Trans. from the French, 2nd ed. Macmillan 1949).

Leibniz, Gottfried Wilhelm, Nova methodus discendae docendaeque iuris prudentiae, *in* 3 Gottfried Wilhelm Leibniz, opera omnia, nunc prima collecta, in classes distributa, praefationibus et indicibus exornata, studio Ludovici Dutens (Apud Fratres de Tournes 1768).

Levi, Leone, International Law, with Materials for a Code of International Law (Appleton Co. 1888).

Lewis & Short, A Latin Dictionary (Oxford University Press 1987).

Liddell Henry G. & Robert Scott, A Greek-English Lexicon (Oxford University Press 1968).

Linacre Institute, After Asceticism: Sex, Prayer and Deviant Priests (Author House 2006).

Locke, John, Second Essay Concerning Civil Government, *in* Locke, Two Treatises of Government (Peter Laslet ed., Cambridge University Press 1988).

Loisy, Alfred, The Gospel and the Church (Christopher Home trans., Charles Scribner's Sons 1904).

Luther, Martin., The Christian in Society II, *in* 45 Luther's Works (Walther I. Brandt & Helmut T. Lehmann eds., Muhlenberg Press 1962).

Luther, Martin, Three Treatises, Originally Published in the American Edition of Luther's Works. (Helmut T. Lehmann ed., Fortress Press 1966).

Maclaren, Drostan, Private Property and Natural Law, Aquinas Papers No. 8 (Blackfriars 1948).

Mahoney, John, The Making of Moral Theology (Clarendon Press of Oxford University 1987).

Maida, Adam J. & Nicolas P. Cafardi, Church Property, Church Finances, and Church-Related Corporations (Catholic Health Association of the United States 1984).

MAITLAND, FREDERICK W., ROMAN CANON LAW IN THE CHURCH OF ENGLAND (Burt Franklin 1968).

MARIUS, RICHARD, THOMAS MORE (Vintage Books 1985).

MARTINEZ-TORRON, JAVIER, DERECHO ANGLOAMERICANO Y DERECHO CANÓNICO, LAS RAICES CANÓNICAS DE LA *COMMON LAW* (FACULTAD DE DERECHO UNIVERSIDAD COMPULTENSE 1991).

MCGRATH, JOHN J., CATHOLIC INSTITUTIONS IN THE UNITED STATES: CANONICAL AND CIVIL LAW STATUS (Catholic University Press 1968).

MCGREEVY, JOHN T., CATHOLICISM AND AMERICAN FREEDOM (Norton 2003).

MCKENNA, KEVIN E., DEFENDING RIGHTS IN THE CHURCH (Paulist Press 2007).

MEIER, JOHN P., A MARGINAL JEW, VOL. III, COMPANIONS AND COMPETITORS (Bantam Doubleday 2001).

Meier, John P., A Marginal Jew: Rethinking the Historical Jesus, Vol. IV, Law and Love (Yale University Press 2009).

MOORMAN, JOHN, A HISTORY OF THE FRANCISCAN ORDER (Clarendon Press of Oxford University 1968).

MOOTS, PHILIP R. & EDWARD MCGLYNN GAFFNEY, JR, CHURCH AND CAMPUS: LEGAL ISSUES IN RELIGIOUSLY AFFILIATED HIGHER EDUCATION (University of Notre Dame Press 1979).

MORE, THOMAS, UTOPIA (Cambridge University Press 1940).

MORE, THOMAS, 8 THE YALE EDITION OF THE COMPLETE WORKS OF THOMAS MORE (Yale University Press 1961).

MUNCK, JOHANNES, THE ACTS OF THE APOSTLES, *in* THE ANCHOR BIBLE (William F. Albright & David N. Freedman eds., Doubleday 1967).

NEW JEROME BIBLICAL COMMENTARY (THE) (Raymond E. Brown, S.S., Joseph A.Fitzmyer, S.J, & Roland E. Murphy, O. Carm. eds., Prentice Hall 1990).

NEWMAN, JOHN HENRY CARDINAL, AN ESSAY ON THE DEVELOPMENT OF DOCTRINE (6th ed. University of Notre Dame Press 2005).

NEWMAN, RABBI J., SEMIKHAH: A STUDY OF ITS ORIGINS, HISTORY, AND FUNCTION IN RABBINIC LITERATURE (Manchester University Press 1950).

NICHOLAS, BARRY, AN INTRODUCTION TO ROMAN LAW (3rd ed. Clarendon Press of Oxford University 1962).

OJETTI, BENEDICT, S.J., DE ROMANA CURIA (Apud Universitatem Gregorianam 1910).

ÖRSY, LADISLAS, THEOLOGY AND CANON LAW (Liturgical Press 1992).

PELIKAN, JAROSLAV, INTERPRETING THE BIBLE AND THE CONSTITUTION (Yale University Press 2004).

PLATO, LAWS, *in* II THE WORKS OF PLATO (Benjamin Jowett trans., Random House 1937).

POSCHMAN, BERNHARD, PENANCE AND THE ANOINTING OF THE SICK (Francis Courtney trans., Herder and Herder 1964).

POSNER, RICHARD A., OVERCOMING LAW (Harvard University Press 1995).

POWERS, JOSEPH M., S.J., EUCHARISTIC THEOLOGY (Herder 1967).

PRYOR, DOUGLAS W., UNSPEAKABLE ACTS: WHY MEN SEXUALLY ABUSE CHILDREN (New York University Press 1996).

PUTNAM, HILLARY, THE COLLAPSE OF THE FACT/VALUE DICHOTOMY AND OTHER ESSAYS (Harvard University Press 2002).

RASHDALL, HASTINGS, THE UNIVERSITIES OF EUROPE IN THE MIDDLE AGES (Oxford University Press 1936).

RATZINGER, JOSEPH, Milestones, MEMOIRS: 1927–1977 (Rasmo Leiva-Merikakis trans., Ignatius Press 1998).

Ratzinger, Joseph, Principles of Catholic Theology, Building Stones for a Fundamental Theology (Ignatius Press 1987).

Ratzinger, Joseph, The Theology of History in St. Bonaventure (Zachary Hayes trans., Franciscan Herald Press 1971).

Rawls, John, A Theory of Justice (Harvard University Belknap Press 1971).

Raz, Joseph, The Authority of Law: Essays on Law and Morality (Clarendon Press of Oxford University 2002).

Raz, Joseph, The Concept of a Legal System: An Introduction to the Theory of Legal System (Clarendon Press of Oxford University 1980).

Raz, Joseph, Practical reason and Norms (2nd ed. Princeton University Press 1990).

Reeves, Marjorie, The Influence of Prophecy in the Later Middle Ages: A Study of Joachimism (Clarendon Press of Oxford University 1969).

Report of the Attorney General on the Sexual Abuse of Children in the Archdiocese of Boston, Office of the Attorney General Commonwealth of Massachusetts, July 23, 2003.

Rodes, Robert E., Jr., Ecclesiastical Administration in Medieval England: The Anglo-Saxons to the Reformation (Notre Dame University Press 1977).

Rodopoulos, Panteleimon, An Overview of Orthodox Canon Law (W. J. Lillie trans., Orthodox Research Institute 2007).

Roper, William, The Life of Sir Thomas More, *in* Two Early Tudor Lives (Richard S. Sylvester & Davis P. Harding eds., Yale University Press 1962).

Schnackenburg, Rudolf, The Gospel of Matthew (Robert R. Burr trans., Eerdmans 2002).

Sheehan, Michael M., C.S.B., Marriage, Family, and Law in Medieval Europe, Collected Studies (James K. Farge ed., Toronto: University of Toronto Press 1996).

Shklar, Judith N., Legalism: Law, Morals, and Political Trials (Harvard University Press 1964).

Sohm, Rudolf, Outlines of Church History (May Sinclair trans., Macmillan 1895).

Stickler, Alfons Cardinal, The Case for Clerical Celibacy, Its Historical Development and Theological Foundations (Ignatius Press 1995).

Sullivan, Francis J., S.J., From Apostles to Bishops, The Development of the Episcopacy in the Early Church (Newman Press 2001).

Tamanaha, Brian Z., On the Rule of Law: History, Politics, Theory (Cambridge University Press 2004).

Terry, Karen & Margaret Leland Smith, 2006 Supplementary Report to the Natureand Scope of Sexual Abuse of Minors by Catholic Priests and Deacons in the United States, available at http://www.nccbuscc.org/ocyp/JohnJayReport.pdf.

Tierney, Brian, Rights, Laws and Infallibility in Medieval Thought (Variorum 1997).

Trisco, Robert F., Bishops and Their Priests in the United States (Garland Publishing 1988).

Twain, Mark, Letters from the Earth (Bernard DeVoto ed., Harper Perennial Classics 1974).

Weil, Simon, The Need for Roots: Prelude to a Declaration of Duties Towards Mankind (Arthur Wills trans., Routledge Classics 2002).

Wiljens, Myriam, Theology and Canon Law: The Theories of Klaus Mörsdorf and Eugenio Corecco (University Press of America 1992).

Williams, Robert A., Jr., The American Indian in Western Legal Thought: The Discourses of Conquest (Oxford University Press 1990).

WINROTH, ANDERS, THE MAKING OF GRATIAN'S DECRETUM (Cambridge University Press 2000).
WOESTMAN, WILLIAM H.O.M.I., ECCLESIASTICAL SANCTIONS AND THE PENAL PROCESS, A COMMENTARY ON THE CODE OF CANON LAW (Saint Paul University 2003).
VAN DE WIEL, CONSTANT, HISTORY OF CANON LAW (Peters Press 1991).
VASOLI, ROBERT H., WHAT GOD HAS JOINED TOGETHER: THE ANNULMENT CRISIS IN AMERICAN CATHOLICISM (Oxford University Press 1998).
ZWEIGERT, KONRAD & HEIN KÖTZ, INTRODUCTION TO COMPARATIVE LAW (Tony Weir trans., 2nd ed. rev. Clarendon Press of Oxford University 1992).

4. ARTICLES

Ademi, Gurri, *Legal Imitations: Michael Oakshott and the Rule of Law*, 1993 WISCONSIN L.REV. 839–96 (1993).
Alesandro, John A., *General Introduction, in* CLSA-1985 at 1–22.
Araujo, Robert John, S.J., *The International Personality and Sovereignty of the Holy See*, 50 CATH. U. L. Rev. 291–360 (2001).
Arias, Juan, *Sanctions in the Church, in* OTTAWA-1993 at 817–867.
Bainbridge, Stephen M. & Aaron H. Cole, *The Bishop's Alter Ego: Enterprise Liability andthe Catholic Priest Sex Abuse Scandal*, 46 JOURNAL OF CATHOLIC LEGAL STUDIES 65–106 (2007).
Baura, Eduardo, *Dispensations, in* 1 NAVARRA-2004, 644–51.
Beal, John P., *Doing What One Can: Canon Law and Clerical Sexual Misconduct*, 52 JURIST 642–83 (1992).
Beal, John P., *Hiding in the Thickets of Law, Canonical Reflections on Some Disturbing Aspects of the Dallas Charter*, 187 AMERICA15–19 (Oct. 7, 2002).
Beal, John P., *The 1962 Instruction 'Crimen Sollicitationis': Caught Red-Handed or Handed a Red-Herring*, 41 STUDIA CANONICA 199–236 (2007).
Bernadin, Joseph Cardinal, *Statement Announcing Policy on Clerical Sexual Misconduct with Minors*, 22 ORIGINS282–83 (Oct. 1, 1992).
Bertrams, Wilhelm, S.J., *De analogia quoad structuram hierarchicam inter Ecclesiam universalem ac Ecclesiam particularem*, 56 PERIODICA267–308 (1967).
Burke, Raymond L., *Prophecy for Justice: Catholic Politicians and Bishops*, 190 AMERICA11–15 (June 21–28, 2004).
Brown, Neville, *A Century of Comparative Law in England: 1869–1969*, 19 AM. J. COMP. L. 232–52 (1971).
Bruce, F. F., *The Curse of the Law, in* Paul and Paulinism: Essays in honour of C. K. BARRETT 27–36 (Alden Press 1982).
Cicero, ad Att., VI, 1, 15. *Letters to Atticus*, Vol. II, *in* THE LOEB CLASSICAL LIBRARY121 (D. R. Shackleton Bailey ed. and trans., Harvard University Press 1999).
Coccopalmerio, Francesco, *Il concetto di parrocchia nel Vaticano II*, 106 LA SCUOLA CATTOLICA 123–42 (1978).
Conn, James, S.J., *L'Applicatione della 'Ex Corde Ecclesiae' negli Stati Uniti: Analisi e Valutazione delle 'Ordinationes,' in* PAROLA DI DIO E MISSIONE DELLA CHIESAS193–214(A cura di Davide Cito e Ferando Puig, Giuffrè 2009).
Coriden, James A. & Frederick R. McManus, *The Present State of Roman Catholic Canon Law Regarding Colleges and Sponsoring Religious Bodies, in* CHURCH AND CAMPUS:

Legal Issues in Religiously Affiliated Higher Education 141–53 (University of Notre Dame Press 1979).

Coughlin, John J., O.F.M., *Canonical Equity*, 30 Studia Canonica 403–35 (1996).

Coughlin, John J., O.F.M., *The Clergy Sexual Abuse Crisis and the Spirit of Canon Law*, 44 Boston College L. Rev. 977–97 (2003).

Coughlin, John J., O.F.M., *Restoring the Faith: Responding to Clergy Sexual Abuse through Justice, Redemption, and Reconciliation*, Jurist, Legal Intelligence, Nov. 11, 2002, *available at* http//jurist.law. pitt.edu/forum/forumnew70php.

Curran, Robert Emmett, S.J., *The McGlynn Affair and the Shaping of the New Conservative Catholicism, in* The American Catholic Religious Life: Selected Historical Essays 183–201 (Joseph M. White ed., 1988).

De Paolis, Velasio, *Animadversiones ad << schema documenti quo disciplina sanctionum seu peonarum in Ecclesia Latina dennuo ordinatur>>*, 63 Periodica 489–507 (1974).

De Paolis, Velasio, *Il Libro VI del Codice di Diritto Canonico: Diritto Penale, Disciplina Penitenziale o Cammino Penitenziale?*, 90 Periodica 85–106 (2001).

Donahue, Charles, *Comparative Law Before the "Code Napoléon," in* The Oxford Handbook of Comparative Law 3–32 (Mathias Reiman & Reinhard Zimmermann eds., Oxford University Press 2006).

Dulles, Avery, S.J., *Rights of Accused Priests, Toward a Revision of the Dallas Charter and the"Essential Norms,"* 188 America 19–23 (June 21–28, 2004).

Dworkin, Ronald., *Pragmatism, Right Answers, and True Banality, in* Pragmatism in Law and Society 359–88 (Michael Brint & William Weaver eds., Westview Press 1991).

Dworkin, Ronald, *A Reply by Ronald Dworkin, in* Ronald Dworkin and Contemporary Jurisprudence 275–78 (M. Chen ed., Duckworth, 1984).

Epstein, Richard A., *Property Rights Claims of Indigenous Populations: The View from the Common Law*, 31 U. Tol. L. Rev. 1–15 (1999).

Ferme, Brian E., *'Graviora delicta': The Apostolic Letter M.P. sacramentorum sanctitatis tutela, in* Il Processo Penale Canonico 365–82 (Zbigniew Suchecki ed., Laternan University Press 2003).

Final Report: Bishops and Catholic Politicians, 36 Origins 97–100 (June 29, 2006).

Finkelhor, David, Gerard Hotaling, I. A. Lewis, & Christine Smith, 14 Child Abuse and Neglect 19–18 (1990).

Finnis, John, *Propter Honoris Respectum: On the Incoherence of Legal Positivism*, 75 Notre Dame L. Rev. 1597–1611 (2000).

Flanagan, N. M., 7 New Catholic Encyclopedia, s. v. "Jerusalem, Council of." 889–90.

Fuenmayor, Amadeo de, *The Canonical Status of Physical Persons, in* 1 Navarra-2004, 735–36.

Fuller, Lon L., *Positivism and Fidelity to Law—A Reply to Professor Hart*, 71 Harv. L. Rev. 630–72 (1958).

Ganz, David, *The Ideology of Sharing: Apostolic Community and Ecclesiastical Property in the Early Middle Ages, in* Property and Power in the Early Middle Ages 17–30 (Wendy Davies & Paul Fouracre eds., Cambridge University Press 1995).

Garnett, Nicole Stelle, *The Neglected Political Economy of Eminent Domain*, 105 Mich. L. Rev. 101-150.

Garrity, R., Spiritual and Canonical Values in Mandatory Priestly Celibacy, 27 Studia Canonica 217–60 (1993).

Gasparri, Petrus Card, *Praefatio,* Codex Iuris Canonici Pii X Pontificis Maximi iussu digestus Benedicti Papae XV auctoritate promulgatus (Die 27 m. maii a. 1917), 9(II) AAS xix–xxxviii (1917).
Gaudemet, Jean, *La doctrine des sources du droit dans le Décret de Gratien,* 1 Revue de droit canonique 6–31 (1951).
Gauthier, Albert-M. O.P., *On the Use of Roman Law in Canon Law, in* Unico Eccle siaeservitio: Canonical Studies Presented to Germain Lesage, O.M.I., on the Occasion of His 75th Birthday and of the 50th Anniversary of His PresbyteralOrdination 53–67 (Faculty of Canon Law, St. Paul University 1991).
Greeley, Andrew, *Canon Law and Society, in* The Future of Canon Law, 48 Concilium 130–42 (N. Edelby, T. Urresti, & P. Huizing, eds., Paulist Press 1969).
Green, Leslie, *Positivism and Inseparability of Law and Morals,* 83 N. Y. U. L. Rev. 1035–58 (2008).
Green, Thomas J., *The Future of Penal Law in the Church,* 35 Jurist 212–75 (1975).
Green, Thomas J., *The Pastoral Governance Role of the Diocesan Bishop: Foundations, Scope, and Limitations,* 49 Jurist 472–506 (1989).
Green, Thomas J., *Theology and Canon Law: The Theories of Klaus Morsdorf and Eugenio Corecco,* 54 Theological Studies 203 (1993).
Gregory, Bishop Wilton, *Presidential Address Opening Dallas Meeting,* 32 Origins 97 and 99–102 (July 27, 2002).
Grocholewski, Zenon, *Atti e ricorsi amministrativi,* 57 Apollinaris 259–79 (1984).
Habermas, Jürgen, *Three Normative Models of Democracy,* 1 Constellation 1–10 (1994).
Hart, H. L. A., *Positivism and the Separation of Law and Morals,* 71 Harv. L. Rev. 593–629 (1958).
Helmholz, R. H., *Discipline of the Clergy: Medieval and Modern,* 6 Ecc. L. J. 189–98 (2002).
Helmholz, R. H., *Thomas More and the Canon Law, in* Medieval Church Law and the Origins of the Western Legal Tradition: A Tribute to Kenneth Pennington 375–88 (Wolfgang P. Müller & Mary E. Sommar eds., Catholic University Press 2006).
Herranz, Archbishop Julián, Zenit, Nov. 4, 2002, available at http://www.zenit.org.
Hervada, Javier., *Commentary on Book II,* in Ottawa-1993, 185–86.
Hill, R., *Ordination of Married Protestant Ministers,* 51 Canon Law Society of America Proceedings 95–100 (1989).
Hug, Walter, *The History of Comparative Law,* 45 Harv. L. Rev. 1027–70 (1932).
Ingels, Gregory, *Dismissal from the Clerical State: An Examination of the Penal Process,* 33 Studia Canonica (1999), 169–212.
Jones, Lisa & David Finkelhor, *Explanations for the Decline in Child Abuse Cases,* OJJDP Bulletin, Office of Juvenile Justice and Delinquency Program, Office of Justice Program, United States Department of Justice (2004).
Kantorowicz, Hermann, *The Quaestiones Disputatae of the Glossators,* 16 Tijdschrift voor Rechtsgeschiedenis/Revue d'histoire du droit 1–67 (1939).
Kasper, Walter, *The Theological Foundations of Human Rights,* 50 Jurist 148–66 (1990).
Kauper, Paul G. & Stephen C. Ellis, *Religious Corporations and the Law,* 71 Mich. L. Rev. 1499–1521 (1973).
Keeler, William Cardinal, *Summary of Consultations,* 34 Origins 106 (July 1, 2004).
Kennedy, Robert T., *Book V, The Temporal Goods of the Church, in* CLSA 2000, 1451–1525.

Kennedy, Robert T., *McGrath, Maida, Michiels: Introduction to a Study of the Canonical and Civil Law Status of Church Related Institutions in the United States*, 50 JURIST 351–401 (1990).

Kinney, Bishop John., *May 27, 2004 Statement, in* 34 ORIGINS 192–93 (2004).

Kuttner, Stephan, *The Father of the Science of Canon Law*, 1 JURIST 2–19 (1941).

Lambert, Edouard, *Conception général et définition de la science du droit comparé*, Congrès international de droit comparé, tenu à Paris du 31 juillet au 4 août 1900, *reprinted in* RECHTSVERGLEICHUNG 30–51 (Konrad Zweigert & Hans-Jürgen Puttfraken eds.,Wissenschaftliche Buchgesellschaft 1978).

Le Bras, Gabriel, *Canon Law, in* THE LEGACY OF THE MIDDLE AGES 325–26 (C. G. Crump & E.F. Jacob eds., Oxford University Press 1926).

Lefebvre, Charles, *"Équité," in* 5 DICTIONNAIRE DE DROIT CANONIQUE, col. 394 (Sous la direction de R. Naz, Letouzey et Ane 1953).

Lefebvre, Charles, *Equity in Canon Law, in* EQUITY IN THE WORLD'S LEGAL SYSTEMS: A COMPARATIVE STUDY 93–109 (Ralph A. Newman ed., Établissements Émile Bruylant 1973).

Leiter, Brian, *Legal Realism and Hard Positivism, in* HART'S POSTSCRIPT: ESSAYS ON THE POSTSCRIPT TO THE CONCEPT OF LAW 355–70 (Jules Coleman ed., Oxford University Press 2001).

Levada, Archbishop William J., *Reflections on Catholics in Political Life and the Reception of Holy Communion*, 34 ORIGINS 104 (July 1, 2004).

Lombardi, Federico, S.J., *Vatican Statement on the NY TIMES Story on Abusive Wisconsin Priest*, 39 ORIGINS 693–94 (Apr. 8, 2010).

Maida, Adam J., *Canonical and Legal Fallacies of the McGrath Thesis on the Reorganization of Church Entities*, 19 THE CATHOLIC LAWYER 275–86 (1973).

MacCormick, Neil, *The Ethics of Legalism*, 2 RATIO JURIS 184–93 (1989).

McCann, Dennis P., *The Common Good in Catholic Social Teaching, in* IN SEARCH OF THE COMMON GOOD 121–46 (Patrick D. Miller & Dennis P. McCann eds., T & T Clark 2005).

McMahon, Kevin T., *Pro-Abortion Politicians and Voters and the Reception of Holy Communion*, 73 LINACRE QUARTERLY 153-163(2006).

Morrisey, Francis G., *Book V., The Temporal Goods of the Church, in* CLSGB&Ireland, 707–47.

Morrisey, Francis G., *The Pastoral and Juridical Dimensions of Dismissal from the ClericalState and of Other Penalties for Sexual Misconduct*, 53 CLSA PROCEEDINGS 221–39(1991).

Neuhaus, Richard John, *Bishops at a Turning Point*, 146 FIRST THINGS 76–81 (Oct. 2004).

Note, *Judicial Intervention in Disputes over Church Property*, 75 HARV. L. REV. 1142–54(1962).

Note, *The Myth of Johnson v. M'Intosh*, 52 UCLA L. REV. 289–329 (2004).

O'Brien, Raymond C., *Pedophilia: The Legal Predicament of the Clergy*, 4 J. CONTEMP. HEALTH L. & POL'Y 91, 151–52 (1988).

O'Malley, John W., S.J., *The Scandal: A Historian's Perspective*, 186 AMERICA 14–17 (May 27,2002).

Onclin, Willy, *The Church Society and the Organization of Its Powers*, 27 JURIST 13–14 (1967).

Onclin, Willy, *L'organisation des pouvoirs dans L'Église, in* ACTES DU CONGRÈS DE DROIT CANONIQUE: CINQUANTENAIRE DE LA FACULTÉ DE DROIT CANONIQUE, Paris, 22–26 avril 1947 at 369–75 (Letouzey et Ané 1957).

Örsy, Ladislas, S.J., *Book I, General Norms, in* CLSA-1984, 42–43.

Otaduy, Javier, *Ecclesiastical Laws, in* 1 NAVARRA-2004, 221–436.

Overview of the Synod's Propositions, 35 ORIGINS 348 (Nov. 3, 2005).

Pepper, Stephen L., *The Lawyer's Amoral Ethical Role: A Defense, A Problem, and Some Possibilities*, AMERICAN BAR FOUNDATION RESEARCH JOURNAL 613–35 (1986).

Porter, Jean, *The Common Good in Thomas Aquinas, in* IN SEARCH OF THE COMMON GOOD106–20 (Patrick D. Miller & Dennis P. McCann eds., T & T Clark 2005).

Pound, Roscoe, *The Influence of French Law in America*, 3 ILL. L. Rev. 354–63 (1909).

Pound, Roscoe, *The Place of Comparative Law in the American Law School Curriculum*, 8 TUL. L. Rev. 161–70 (1943).

Provost, James H., Book II, *The People of God, in* CLSA-1984, 117–37.

Radin, Margaret Jane, *Property and Personhood*, 34 STANFORD L. Rev. 957–1013 (1982).

Ratzinger, Joseph, *The Pastoral Implications of Episcopal Collegiality*, THE CHURCH AND MANKIND, 1 CONCILIUM 39–67 (Paulist Press 1969).

Re, Edward D., *Comparative Law Courses in the Law School Curriculum*, 1 AM. J. COMP. L. 233–42 (1952).

Renken, John A., *Parishes and Pastors, in* CLSA-2000, 673–724.

Rietmeijer, Jan, *The Competence of the Bishop in Matters of Dispensation, in* THE FUTURE OF CANON LAW, 48 CONCILIUM 101–14 (Paulist Press 1969).

Rocca, Maria J., *Privileges, in 1* NAVARRA-2004, 619–43.

Schnurr, Bishop Denis, *Catholics and Political Life*, 34 ORIGINS 187 (Sept. 2, 2004).

Setién, José, *Tensions in the Church, in* THE FUTURE OF CANON LAW, 48 CONCILIUM 66–80 (Paulist Press 1969).

Sherman, Charles P, *A Brief History of Medieval Roman Canon Law*, 39 CANADIAN LAW TIMES638–52 (1919).

Singer, Joseph, *The Player and the Cards: Nihilism and Legal Theory*, 94 YALE L. J. 1–70 (1984).

Soper, E. Philip, *Legal Theory and the Obligation of a Judge: The Hart/Dworkin Dispute*, 75 MICH. L. Rev. 473–519 (1977).

Strauss, Peter L., *An Introduction to Administrative Justice in the United States, in* ADMINISTRATIVE LAW: THE PROBLEM OF JUSTICE, ANGLO AMERICAN AND NORDIC SYSTEMS 491–829 (Giuffrè 1991).

Tejero, Eloy, *The Sanctifying Office in the Church*, in 3/1 NAVARRA-2004, 382–89.

United States Bishops' Meeting, *Twenty-Eight Suggestions on Sexual Abuse Policies*, 24 ORIGINS 443–44 (Dec. 8, 1994).

Urrutia, Francisco J., S.J., *Administrative Power in the Church According to the Code of Canon Law*, 20 STUDIA CANONICA, 253–73 (1986).

Urrutia, Francisco J., S.J., *La potestà amministrativa secondo il diritto canonico, in* DE IUSTITIA ADMINISTRATIVA IN ECCLESIA 73–100 (Pio Fedele mod., Officium Libri Catholici 1984).

Van Hoecke, Mark, *Deep Level Comparative Law, in* EPISTEMOLOGY AND METHODOLOGY OF COMPARATIVE LAW165–95 (Mark Van Hoecke ed., Hart Publishing 2004).

Vlazny, John, Archbishop of Portland, Oregon, *Archdiocese Files for Bankruptcy Protection*, 34 ORIGINS 113–15 (July 15, 2004).

Weigel, George, *Scandal Time, Once More*, TODAY'S CATHOLIC, Apr. 11, 2010, at 15.

Weisberg, D. Kelly, *The "Discovery" of Sexual Abuse: Experts' Role in Legal Policy Formulation*, 18 U. C. DAVIS L. REV. 1–10 (1984).

Winniger, Paul, *A Pastoral Canon Law, in* The Future of Canon Law, 48 CONCILIUM 51–65 (Paulist Press 1969).

Wojtyla, Karol, *Participation or Alienation?*, *in* PERSON AND COMMUNITY, SELECTED ESSAYS 197–207 (Theresa Sandok O.S.M. trans., Peter Lang 1993).
Woodward, Kenneth L., *A Political Sacrament*, op. ed. N.Y. TIMES, May 28, 2004, A21.
Zirk-Sadowski, Marek, *Legal Epistemology and the Transformation of Legal Cultures*, *in* EPISTEMOLOGY AND METHODOLOGY OF COMPARATIVE LAW 21–34 (Mark Van Hoeckeed., Hart Publishing 2004).

INDEX

D

E

F

G

P

R

S

www.ingramcontent.com/pod-product-compliance
Lightning Source LLC
Chambersburg PA
CBHW020211310126
39041CB00002B/92
* 9 7 8 0 1 9 5 3 7 2 9 7 7 *